CAUTIOUS
REVOLUTION

Recent Titles in
Contributions in Political Science

CAUTIOUS REVOLUTION

THE EUROPEAN COMMUNITY ARRIVES

CLIFFORD HACKETT

CONTRIBUTIONS IN POLITICAL SCIENCE
NUMBER 261

GREENWOOD PRESS
NEW YORK • WESTPORT, CONNECTICUT • LONDON

Library of Congress Cataloging-in-Publication Data

Hackett, Clifford P.
  Cautious revolution : the European Community arrives / Clifford
Hackett.
      p.   cm.— (Contributions in political science, ISSN 0147-1066 ; no. 261)
  Includes bibliographical references.
  ISBN 0-313-27416-9 (lib. bdg. : alk. paper)
  1. European Economic Community. I. Title. II. Series.
HC241.2.H24   1990
337.1'42—dc20   90-34318

British Library Cataloguing in Publication Data is available.

A paperback edition of *Cautious Revolution: The European Community Arrives*
is available from Praeger Publishers; ISBN: 0-275-93605-8.

Library of Congress Catalog Card Number: 90-34318
ISBN: 0-313-27416-9
ISSN: 0147-1066

First published in 1990

Greenwood Press, 88 Post Road West, Westport, CT 06881
An imprint of Greenwood Publishing Group, Inc.

Printed in the United States of America

The paper used in this book complies with the
Permanent Paper Standard issued by the National
Information Standards Organization (Z39.48-1984).

10 9 8 7 6 5 4 3 2 1

To Bea
Who unites the best in America and Europe

Contents

Figure and Tables

Preface

This book began as an attempt to preserve the conclusions of a seminar held in Washington, D.C., in 1985/86, sponsored by the Council on Foreign Relations, for which I was the rapporteur. The seminar was organized to acquaint (or in some cases, to reacquaint) the participants with the growth of the European Community in the 1970s and early 1980s when little attention was being paid by the press or the academic community in this country to the progress Europe was making toward the integration which began after World War II and to which the United States gave such important support. The seminar organizers believed that this progress needed a written description, some further details, and some policy recommendations.

What has resulted from these efforts is a book different from both the seminar and its organizers' original expectations, one that may be useful in the university classroom and as a European Community "primer." The book stresses the historical background of the Community and its institutions. It also emphasizes the broad social, cultural, and historical background of Western Europe as the backdrop into which readers, particularly those new to European studies, may place the Community. Finally, the book brings the Community to the eve of the 1992 single market for a more promising vista than that available in mid-decade.

A united Europe is assumed to be in the best interest of Europeans, who have suffered so much from civil war in this century, and of Americans who are aligned by history, culture, and viewpoint with Europe. The observant European can also learn from American history how much patience and effort unity demands. Beyond these assumptions, there is little guidance for either American or European policy makers except for suggesting some ways Washington can pay better attention to European Community (EC) developments.

This book is not a complete description of the European Community. There are too many programs, projects, documents, and problems to attempt an exhaustive account. Some important subjects—the environment, consumer protection, and fisheries, to name a few—are not covered at all. Other areas, like education, the governments of the 12 member states, and regional problems and policies are discussed only partially or in passing. Just as there is no way to describe the history, institutions, and programs of the U.S. government in one small volume, there is no way to cover comparable aspects of the European Community—even after only four decades—in one work.

This book's title deserves some explanation. The revolution which began with the Schuman Declaration in 1950 is proceeding with a caution appropriate to the long and scarred European history of grand ideas brought to earth by reality. The subtitle was originally "The Growth of a United Europe" but was changed in early 1990 to avoid any suggestion that the events in eastern Europe were leading to a single political or economic entity called Europe. That is not the case, in my view, although the European Community will, I believe, develop generous and comprehensive programs to help the eastern part of the continent. This help will not come, I believe, in the form of Community membership for a long time, if ever, to those countries formerly tied closely to the Soviet Union. In the last decade of the twentieth century, western Europeans are slowly losing their nationalism, that is, their genius, while eastern Europeans are slowly regaining theirs, that is, their hope.

Acknowledgments

Many individuals and institutions helped the author write this book. In the Commission, Gabrielle Jaegert-Cimorelli in the Centre d'information of DG X was most helpful; in the Parliament, Roland Bieber and Brunni Kees were always available for assistance beyond the call of normal duties. The EC Statistical Office was especially patient in supplying documents, guidance, and special help; the EC Delegation in Washington, especially its library staff, was called upon frequently. The OECD publications office in the same city provided help on many occasions, while the Morgan County Library in West Virginia and the American and George Washington University libraries provided many books and reference assistance. The Library of Congress, especially its Congressional Research Service, was very helpful on trade matters, while Donna Vogt was particularly accommodating on agricultural questions.

J. Robert Schaetzel, former U. S. Ambassador to the European Community, inspired the seminar which led to this book; Alton Frye, Linda Harsh, and David Kellogg of the Council on Foreign Relations offered good advice and help in getting this work published.

CAUTIOUS REVOLUTION

1

Introduction:
The Idea of a Community

Nothing is possible without men; nothing is lasting without institutions.
—Jean Monnet, *Memoirs*

Many ideas about possible postwar political structures circulated in Europe during and after the Second World War. They ranged from dismemberment of Germany, to its complete union with France; from a "United States of Europe" by which Churchill meant a loose association of democracies, to de Gaulle's "Europe of States" by which he meant a French-dominated union of sovereign powers. Others, including perhaps Monnet himself, used the expression "the United States of Europe" in more explicit reference to the model given by the American form of constitutional growth. When the outline of Monnet's plan for a coal and steel community was announced in 1950, the continent had passed through five years of political ferment, seeking a different approach to the European political system which had produced two world wars in 25 years.

There was, in this period, a general if ill-defined rejection of nationalism and a belief that organizations standing above the nation-state were essential for peace. Already, the Marshall Plan had encouraged, even forced, western European countries to think together about recovery programs. Through the Organization for European Economic Cooperation—later to become the broader Organization for Economic Cooperation and Development (OECD)—the Marshall Plan initiated

European economic cooperation, removed some trade restrictions, and solved some currency problems.

There were also more ominous events: the Soviet attempt to isolate Berlin led to a confrontation with the United States. Although armed conflict was avoided, the airlift to the former German capital demonstrated the Western will to resist provocative Soviet moves. The cold war had begun while the problems of the last "hot war" were still unsolved. This new situation in Europe paved the way for European Community institutions.

At the global level, the United Nations became the successor to the League of Nations. But for the European continent, there was no prototype of a new organizing principle. Yet it was here that the century's two world wars had started. A new concept—an idea of Europe—was present but still undefined, unfocused, and in danger of being pushed aside in favor of the urgent problems of recovering from the disastrous war.

While few made specific reference to the age of Charlemagne or to the later medieval images of one Europe, there seemed to develop, in this five-year span, a yearning for values more basic than the nation. There was also the fear of another outburst of the violence that nationalism and the nation-states had spawned. "Whatever the degree of emphasis, the heart of the message as it emerged was everywhere the same: Europe is older than the nations that have evolved from it and have brought about its collapse by destroying the common heritage."[1] No one who thought seriously about this matter believed that a true political union in Europe could be accomplished easily, or rapidly, or in explicit imitation of any other government. A peaceful union of this kind, on this scale, was unknown in history.

The institutions of the European Community do not exist today as the result of any grand design. Despite his immediate and deeply held commitment to organizing postwar Europe differently, even Jean Monnet did not have an overall plan. He had wanted an Anglo-French union in 1940. Ten years later Konrad Adenauer had an idea for a Franco-German union which Monnet supported but thought impossible to achieve. As head of the French government's planning office, Monnet solved the key problem dividing France and Germany: control of the coal-rich Saar basin which Germany wanted back and the still mighty industrial Ruhr area of Germany which was under international authority. Both areas were deeply involved in Nazi Germany's war efforts and both constituted obstacles to any attempt at Franco-German amity. Europe's immediate need was answered with the European Coal and Steel Community (ECSC), the first network binding the original six member countries; behind this solution was a long-range political vision of nations, peoples, and men treating one another as equals, without desire or dread of domination by others. Monnet's vision of political union did not proceed smoothly although its initial success was impressive. His work, especially in the first years designing and leading the Coal and Steel Community, set the pattern for the Community's institutional structure today. How the ECSC evolved is the subject of this chapter.

It was around the long-range political goal embedded in the Coal and Steel Community that a creative conspiracy was assembled by Monnet and a few friends. But they also began with an immediate political problem which threatened to paralyze France, their native country. A smaller and humbled Germany was to once again become a modern industrial power which could not exist without requisite raw materials. Yet politically, France could not allow the unrestricted rebuilding of basic German industries. Out of the dilemma came the idea, which Monnet and others had considred in various forms over the years, for a common market for coal and steel to unite the disparate French and German interests. If successful, the plan would bind the two countries together in such an intimate union that the tendency toward national domination would be forever contained.

CREATING A COMMON MARKET

Coal and steel are not usually considered the materials of political union, yet their essential roles in building the machines of war made these raw materials a logical place for Monnet to start. If countries could bind their basic industries together across national boundaries into a common market, war would become more difficult and political union more likely. At the same time, deciding who would control the industrial strength of the Saar and Ruhr could be postponed or at least eased.

The idea for the coal and steel community crystallized around mid-April 1950 when Monnet met several times with Etienne Hirsch, an old friend, and Paul Reuter, a law professor whom Monnet had recently met. Monnet recalls, in his *Memoirs,*[2] that the 1950 coal and steel plan had roots in his 1943 discussions when Free French forces were centered in Algiers. Seven years later, the urgency to end Franco-German disputes over the Saar and Ruhr facilitated those earlier ideas.

Perhaps another influence was a statement made the year before by Konrad Adenauer shortly after he became the West German chancellor. Speaking against the continuation of the International Ruhr Authority which the Allies were pressing, Adenauer said, "I should agree to an authority that supervised the mining and industrial areas of Germany, France, Belgium and Luxembourg."[3] He had also made clear in an interview with an American journalist in 1950, that his proposed union of France and Germany was intended to be a foundation for the building of Europe.[4]

Knowing of Adenauer's implicit support and aware that Robert Schuman, the French foreign minister, was similarly inclined, Monnet, Hirsch, and Reuter worked on an April weekend at Monnet's office and then at his home, outlining a plan which Schuman would take to London the next month for a key foreign ministers' meeting on Germany.

The coal and steel industries were the immediate concerns of these three collaborators but the goals were clearly historical; they were not economic or even political except in the largest sense. A provocative sentence from one of the trio's earlier drafts said that the purpose was "to make a breach in the ramparts of national sovereignty which will be narrow enough to secure consent but deep enough to open the way toward the unity that is essential to peace."[5] Forty years later, the fight over the internal market proposes a similar breach for the same purpose.

A Productive Triangle

The triangular basin constituting the geographic center of the coal and steel plan is about as large as the states of Delaware and Maryland combined. It includes the Ruhr and Saar rivers, their valleys, south-eastern Belgium, and the Grand Duchy of Luxembourg. Forming a right-angled triangle, this ancient and mineral-rich land is about 140 by 190 by 235 miles. Its longest dimension runs approximately north-south in a line from Dortmund, Germany, to Strasbourg, France. In this area of about 13,000 square miles lie the gritty landscape and the grim cities which make household hardware, structural steel, cars and trucks, and the implements of war for much of Western Europe. In 1950 it also represented a grave political problem for France and for all of Europe as well.

The problem was how France could maintain good relations with Germany while limiting that country's ability to dominate this industrial triangle. This was no abstract concern; the French government had stumbled for decades over control of the basic resources in this area. Now, once again, the issue for France—one of the four occupying powers in Germany—was how this valued land could be used to strengthen France and to restrain Germany. By 1949, western Germany began again to show dynamic growth. But since French steel production depended on Ruhr coal, it was a matter of months before the shaky French economy could be stifled by the declining export of German coal which would now be needed at home.

France tried, with grudging support from Britain and the United States, to restrict German steel production under the International Ruhr Authority. Adenauer's insistence on equality for Germany produced his idea about an authority over the entire area's basic industries. But a reawakening German economy also produced the tension with which a reluctant France now faced equally unattractive alternatives: a bitter and ultimately futile attempt to restrain German growth or a hazardous course of political passivity while two French generations still remembered wars with a more powerful Germany.

Monnet seized this moment when Germany wanted joint action with France yet could not itself act first and when France needed an act to restrain Germany effectively while appearing to be both decisive and constructive. He would give France the instrument to behave responsibly. France alone had both the motive to carry out Adenauer's suggestion and the opportunity which came in the May meeting in London. If France insisted on restraining German industrial production, its Western allies could not abandon it. But the conference would certainly end in failure if France forced this conclusion. Thus Monnet's plan for a common market and common development of both countries' basic resources was precisely timed and carefully shaped for use by perhaps the only man in either country who could use it.

That man was French Foreign Minister Robert Schuman, himself a product of the mixed heritages of the coal and steel triangle. Schuman was born in Luxembourg in 1886. He would be 65 years old the next year, an age most men retire. Schuman's accomplishments, however, lay before him. He was, he often said, a man of the frontier, having a French father and a Luxembourg mother who had fled to Luxembourg when Lorraine was occupied by the Germans in the Franco-Prussian war. Schuman himself served as a German civil officer during World War I. He then became involved in French political life between the wars. The Franco-German frontier shifted around him several times during his long life and the movements marked him indelibly. He was imprisoned by the Nazis, resumed his political life in 1945, and became a minister, foreign minister, and prime minister, all by 1950. He was committed to a reconciliation with Germany and now, as foreign minister again, he had an opportunity as well as a strong personal motive to commit France to that reconciliation. Looking back, only France could have taken a successful initiative at the London conference but it was not obvious in April 1950 that it would in fact occur. And it would not have occurred without the courage of Schuman and his special insights into solving the historical and geographical problem which had condemned France and Germany to coexist along the Rhine River and its tributaries.

The Monnet initiative posed immediate political hazards, and not only to Schuman. George Bidault, the prime minister, was suspicious of any plan which released Germany from the restraints of military occupation. He had been given the same draft of the Monnet plan which Schuman received. But Schuman seized an initiative which may have caused Bidault to hesitate. As Monnet notes in his *Memoirs*, there was thus a Schuman, not a Bidault Plan. There is no doubt, however, that George Bidault was the more representative Frenchman in his deep skepticism of Germany.[6]

American Support

The plan Schuman eagerly accepted was sent immediately to Konrad Adenauer on the weekend before the London meeting. He also embraced it. The French initiative, supported also by Dean Acheson, the American secretary of state, dominated the London talks. After the meeting ended, however, Britain refused to join the Schuman Plan while Italy and the Benelux countries, the latter already in a customs union, were ready to participate. In less than two months, the Monnet idea went from scraps of drafting paper to a June conference in Paris on implementing the plan. It was, as Monnet described it, a "bold, constructive act."

In April 1951, the treaty on a coal and steel community was signed in Paris after a nine-month conference at which Monnet led the French delegation but exercised, to the amazement of both French and other colleagues, a truly supranational role. It took another year from the signing of the Treaty of Paris until it went into effect. A preparatory period followed as ECSC institutions set up offices in Luxembourg. Monnet was named the first president of the High Authority. A united Europe seemed underway.

The heart of the plan Monnet and his friends drafted for Schuman was the High Authority which would exercise administrative powers over the coal and steel community. Within a few months of the start of the High Authority in the summer of 1952, a genuine free market in coal and steel was in operation. Forerunner to today's Commission of the European Communities,[7] the High Authority was a genuine innovation in international politics. It represented a transfer of sovereignty and not merely an intergovernmental organization. The High Authority was not simply the sum of national authorities since it could conceivably take actions which some or all of the national governments opposed.

The other organs in the Schuman Plan were a Common Assembly which would supervise the High Authority; a Council of Ministers to represent the member governments; and a Court of Justice to settle legal disputes. These four elements, in somewhat different relationships to each other and with some significant changes in function, today form the principal institutions of the European Community. The key relationship, however, in 1952 and nearly forty years later, is that between the High Authority—now called the Commission—and the Council of Ministers. The High Authority embodies the aspirations to rise above national sovereignty; the Council represents the political roots of that sovereignty.

Immersed in the system of nation-states, most Europeans found it difficult to imagine a different kind of world. Monnet had overcome that difficulty although he was himself, as he proudly acknowledged, clearly the product of a country he loved dearly and which exemplified all of the passions and limitations of nationalism.

Looking back from 1975 as he was writing his memoirs, Monnet reflected upon the conclusion of the tense debate in the conference on the relation of the Council and the High Authority: "From that moment on, indeed, the system had acquired its definitive form: a supranational authority, a council of national Ministers, parliamentary and judicial control." Monnet's brief description was accurate but premature. As we shall see in the next chapter, the evolution of these key institutions is still incomplete.

But the European Coal and Steel Community was a success from the moment it was conceived as a solution to two problems: ending the Franco-German disputes over the resources of the Saar and Ruhr regions, and starting a pattern of cooperation to produce "the unity that is essential to peace," in Monnet's words.[8]

The move toward a united Europe suffered a major defeat two years later when a companion treaty to the coal and steel pact was rejected. The French National Assembly turned down the European Defense Community (EDC) after the five other proposed members had ratified it. The victory of the coal and steel treaty and the defeat of the EDC had this in common: the two treaties were attacked from both right and left by forces of French nationalism. The first treaty succeeded because it was a limited answer to immediate problems; the second failed because it was too sweeping a solution to an equally immediate and equally profound problem—the rearming of Germany.

Opposition by de Gaulle

A clear glimpse of the difference between the two issues can be seen in the attitude of Charles de Gaulle, who opposed both treaties. He dismissed the Schuman Plan as a "mish-mash of coal and steel" and an essentially technical agreement. The EDC was, however, in his words, "a crafty scheme for a so-called 'European' army" to be run by the Americans.[9] The wonder of modern Europe was not that a European army almost succeeded in 1954 but rather that today's European institutions lead directly back to the patience, modesty, and determination of Adenauer, Monnet, and Schuman in using coal and steel as the raw materials of supranational politics.

The plan for combining institutions of the ECSC and EDC was now dead. The experience remains a good example of a phenomenon now familiar in European institutions: dramatic proposals often fail while modest ones often succeed. The failure of the EDC had a decisive effect on the direction of integration; if it had succeeded, defense and foreign policy would have been closely tied to economic cooperation. The joint institutions planned for the two communities would have then applied to a European political community, an idea stillborn with the defeat of the EDC.

Instead, the modest Coal and Steel Community became the nucleus of Europe. Would defense and political responsibilities have been too much and have come too soon? (The North Atlantic Treaty Organization had already been founded in 1949 with wider membership than the ECSC and the proposed EDC). Would two defense organizations have helped or hindered a new Europe? Would the United States, already impatient with the slow progress toward European integration, have been satisfied or even further frustrated had Europe created its own army as well as its own political authority, and the two simultaneously?

Such idle questions can illuminate some of the dark areas still not addressed in the European Community's structure today, where the search for political authority continues and where the predominant U.S. role in European defense still defines NATO and, negatively, delineates the weakness of a united Europe. From today's perspective, the defeat of the defense community represented a defeat also of the federalist plan for European integration. Movement over the next 35 years would be marked by smaller steps in fields other than defense. The dream of supranationality was rudely interrupted in Paris in the summer of 1954 in the institution appropriately called the national assembly.

A Decision to Relaunch

The defeat of the EDC was severe and unanticipated; the European movement now desperately needed success. The foreign ministers of the six agreed to meet in Messina, Italy, in June 1955 with a shared but unfocused conviction that if political and military integration was blocked then expanded economic cooperation must follow. Some doubted this conviction, however. In France, principled objection to integration would unite war veterans and economic nationalists. In Germany, Ludwig Erhard fervently believed in free trade. Not only was he suspicious of a six-country economic alliance; he also believed that atomic energy—the putative dramatic industrial tool of the future—might better be pursued by direct ties with the United States and Britain, rather than with Germany's weaker European partners.

Monnet met several times with Paul Henri Spaak, the Belgian foreign minister, in the Ardennes in the snowy winter of 1954/55 to discuss "relaunching" European integration. Monnet was leaving his post as head of ECSC's High Authority to concentrate the attention of a small group of private citizens on this rebirth. The two men discussed how public and private venture could redirect trade and the new industrial future into support for a European economic community. Their guidelines became the agenda for the foreign ministers' meeting in June. Spaak's intelligence and enthusiasm dominated both the Messina meetings and its results. He was named chairman of a committee to study how the economic and atomic communities should be organized.

The Spaak Report, completed after many months of work directed by the energetic Belgian, became the basis of the treaties which created the European Atomic Energy Community (Euratom) and the European Economic Community (EEC). Called the Rome Treaties, they adopted the same structure which had operated successfully for the Coal and Steel Community from 1952: an executive, now renamed the Commission; an assembly, today called the European Parliament;[10] a Council of Ministers; and a Court of Justice. An advisory body to the Council and to the Commission, composed of representatives of industry, labor, and consumers was to be called the Economic and Social Committee and corresponded to the Consultative Committee of the ECSC.

TWO NEW COMMUNITIES

Two sets of institutions were created by the Rome Treaties, one for the Economic Community and an identical set for Euratom. Atomic energy was the only area chosen by the Spaak committee for sector integration. The atomic future seemed so bright in 1957 that some believed France's principal goal in the Rome Treaties was to lead the new energy industry in Europe. France also saw the Euratom treaty as a means of gaining a central role in nuclear research and development since it could aspire to military as well as civilian dominance in this field within the Community. Germany, its principal industrial rival, was already limited to peaceful nuclear development by the Western European Union Treaty and the new treaty now channeled that research through a six-nation organization. Euratom never became the centerpiece of European integration because the treaty failed to give budgetary support to Community nuclear development. Once Germany was permanently restrained from possessing nuclear weapons, France preferred national to European control of atomic matters. Euratom's star never rose as high as it was in the imagination of its creators.

The Rome Treaties, signed in Rome on March 25, 1957, went into effect on January 1, 1958. Although the sentimental birthday of the European Community remains May 9 (the date Schuman announced the French initiative on the Coal and Steel Community), the real birthday of the Community's structure and accomplishments is the first day of 1958, when in different cities and with still separate institutions, the work began.[11]

The assemblies and courts of the ECSC, EEC, and Euratom were immediately merged, effective January 1, 1958. It was only in 1967 that the three commissions and the three councils of ministers were similarly combined by treaty.[12]

AN OVERVIEW

This book describes Monnet's vision of Europe which today still has considerable support as an alternative to the twentieth-century nation-state. It also acknowledges that European nationalism is more durable than many thought in 1950. By looking at Western Europe as a cultural, social, and geographical unit, this book presents the basis for the slow construction of Monnet's vision in the specific form it took in the European Community. To that extent it both describes and shares his viewpoint.

Starting with chapter 3, this book deals with the development, institutions, and programs of the Community. The final chapter treats the relation of that development to American concerns, from the aftermath of World War II to today's less idealistic understanding of what the European Community means for the United States in terms of trade, global rivalry and cooperation, and defense questions.

An American writing about the European Community must avoid two extremes: skepticism that anything truly new can appear on the old continent and enthusiasm for a form of political organization which seems to owe something important to the history and traditions of his own country.

Still another requirement is economy. The diversity and depth of European history preclude any detailed treatment of earlier attempts to organize Europe into a single unit, yet without some background it is not possible to understand fully why Europeans, and their friends, became committed at the end of the Second World War to a new political order. For this reason, the next chapter looks at the peoples of Western Europe, the lands they occupy, and their twentieth-century political and cultural heritage. This broad and brief account is intended primarily for novices of post-World War II European history. Economy also limits discussion of the cold war, which was the immediate world into which the European Community was born, developments in Eastern Europe (except peripherally), and important areas like the Middle East and Africa except as examples of the Community's global role.

This book then begins its account of the Community in the crucial postwar years before 1950 when decisive directions came for a different kind of Europe. During this period, recovery was starting but there were still bitter residues of the conflict in both the victors and the defeated. It was during and especially at the end of that war when the institutions of the present Community had their beginning in the minds of a few far-sighted people.

Transnational Parties

The chapter on institutions is presented in some detail so that those who have not followed closely the course of recent European integration can be brought up to date while those in the newer generations may discover some of the remarkable things which have happened in Europe during the past 30 years. Among the institutions, the Parliament is given lengthy attention because of its potential to represent a true European body politic. This aspiration is still long from realization but the transnational party structure, the importance of political rather than national groupings, and the European principle of parliamentary control are all reasons justifying this emphasis.

One of the most remarkable of these events was the emergence of Jean Monnet, an unassuming but dedicated purveyor of radical ideas. He believed that the western European countries had to yield some sovereignty to a federation with important economic and political powers. As a Frenchman without apparent ideology, employed as a high-level planxer by his government, Monnet was in the perfect disguise as he pursued his audacious plans.

Another radical idea of Monnet, crystallized in his mind as early as 1943/44, was the conviction that Germany must be detached from its industrial center in the Ruhr which, in turn, had to be placed under a European authority for the benefit of all, including a demilitarized Germany.

Both of these ideas of Monnet have important American aspects. The United States went through a period after the American Revolution when its individual states resisted giving up sovereignty to a central government. The European Community today may be in the same kind of transition but with a much longer history of separate existence for its constituent parts. If Americans consider how they would greet the idea today of explicitly granting part of our economic and political sovereignty to the United Nations, we can get some idea of how radical a course the Europeans entered upon in 1950 and why there are still strong doubters.

Monnet's ideas about what to do with Germany after World War II also had American counterparts. The world has lived so long with a German army within NATO that one tends to forget the serious debate among the wartime Allies, and also within the Roosevelt administration during that war, on whether Germany should ever have another army, whether it should be broken up into several smaller states, or whether it should be turned into a farm economy by completely removing its industrial structure and forbidding its reestablishment as part of the peace settlement.[13]

Monnet's plan was radical, direct, and simple: to detach German political control from German industrial power. The Coal and Steel Community was the answer to this, the most vexing question the United States faced in early post-World War II Europe. For while the United States had to support France, one of its wartime allies and now fellow occupation power in Germany, in placing some kind of restraint on German power, it also wanted to support Konrad Adenauer, Germany's leader, who insisted on equality of treatment for his nascent democracy.

Monnet's plan satisfied both France and Germany and was also sensitive to the American viewpoint. Americans could be happy with the result even if it differed from earlier ideas about postwar Germany.

This book was written primarily for Americans so its account of European integration relates to many points in our history and to our own institutions and practices. A balance has been sought between more extreme forms of historical reductionism by which all European efforts to unite are seen in relation to the American experience, and the more popular view today that there are few antecedents from the American side of the Atlantic which are useful to Europeans as they try to unite.

Supporting European Union

Beyond the historical parallels, there is another sense in which this book relates to this country. From the time of our entrance into World War II, we were involved with the question of what form postwar Europe would take. During and after that war, our country had a generally coherent policy of encouraging some form of European union. Many in our country were convinced that the two world wars of this century, into which we were reluctantly drawn, were products of virulent nationalism which had to be restrained unless a third, and perhaps final, world war were to take place. Yet events immediately after the war turned the common attention of the United States and Western Europe toward the Soviet Union and its hegemony over much of Eastern Europe. Unification efforts proceeded but only in that part of the Continent which was outside Soviet control and only behind the military shield provided by the North Atlantic Treaty Organization (NATO) which we erected with Western Europe against the threats from the east.

Besides serving as model and beyond the historical fact of American support for a uniting Europe after 1945, the United States has a third and more direct relation to the European Community. We already feel the effects of the Community's agricultural, trade, and monetary policies. As the development of a Community foreign policy proceeds, it will become increasingly, and perhaps painfully, evident that Europe will not always follow our desires and directions in political and security matters. Dealing with a uniting Europe will continue to make demands on us well beyond those of dealing with its individual member countries. A united Europe has costs as well as long-term benefits for the United States.

The middle chapters deal with specific problems involving the trade, agriculture, and monetary policies of the Community. In these areas 30 years of labor by its institutions have produced a number of programs which greatly affect how Western Europeans live, work, farm, and trade. In a few more years, there will be even greater effects on how they study, travel, and consume. These policies also directly affect other countries, including our own.

Because this book is not purely historical in outlook, there is an attempt to relate these developments in the Community to contemporary issues. Europeans, at least since the early 1960s, have been born into a credible integrated Community. Unlike their parents, they have not witnessed its transformation from a far different, and much narrower, world. Parents in Europe find (and public opinion polls confirm) a complacency regarding Europe in their children which the older generation finds puzzling and disturbing, remembering their own involvement in the debates on European integration which were then matters of urgency and controversy. The Community is past dismantling but it seems to have lost its ability to inspire.

A Vague Globalism

Renewed nationalism has not been reborn in the "successor" generation in Europe either, no matter how prevalent it may have been in the generation of their parents. Young Europeans seem to think of themselves as citizens of the world when they consider environmental or nuclear questions; they see themselves as Europeans largely in vague terms. They seem to regard themselves as somewhat casual residents of the Community country in which they reside. The nationalism of their parents and grandparents has evaporated but so has any fervor for a united Europe. Monnet would undoubtedly consider this development an opportunity; he thrived on problems, and the unfocused globalism of the young European who is indifferent to the European Community is a major political problem for Europe today.[14]

The chapter on high technology and the industrial future relates directly to this younger European generation. The sluggish European economies seem to be partly due to the Community's inability to respond appropriately to the new competitiveness of the global economy. Japan, the newly industrialized countries of the Pacific, and the United States all seem to exceed Community members in developing, assembling, and marketing the newer technologies. This chapter looks both backward to the causes of the slow European response and ahead to possible remedies.

Community policies and programs are so blended into the lives of Europeans that it is often difficult to sort out national from Community influences. The major exception is in foreign (including defense) policy where Community coordination is quite limited. The chapter on political cooperation, the Community name for this coordination, looks at the process and its successes and limitations. The final chapter deals with the American interest today in the entire range of Community efforts toward a coordinated economic and political life and to its present reform goals. Thirty-five years ago we seemed to understand clearly as a country the American interests in both winning the war and helping form the peace. Today we are less confident of our friends in Europe and of our judgments (we too have gone through some trials in the intervening years). This chapter deals directly with our policy options on Community development after reconsidering our basic policy inclination toward a united Europe.

American Federalism

For Americans, an attempt to build a union from the many separate elements of Europe has an appeal based on their own history. The circumstances were much different in the confederation of American states which led to the Constitution in 1787. European scholars are especially adept at pointing out those differences when they examine the parallels with the European Community.[15] But an Italian historian writing on American federalism and its relevance to today's Europe takes a longer view of the nation-state and federalism:

The era of the nation-state has been a relatively short phase in a bi-millennial European history of encounters and fusions, no less than of clashes and separations. One needs a visionary, perhaps, . . . to see the history of American federalism, both normative and institutional, as nothing less than a first chapter in the larger book of transnationalism in the West. In this vision, the formation of a new, continental, multi-state nation at the end of the 18th century can be appraised as both a relatively late chapter in the world-wide birth and growth of the modern nation-states, the chapter of a book in which France, England, Spain and other countries have a much earlier place, and also as a very early chapter in another book still being written in which other multi-state, continental entities such as the European Community will also have, one can expect, a relevant place.[16]

The birth and growth of the European Community in less than a half-century is the most exciting story of our generation. But how important are these events in the course of history? If the momentous events of the entire twentieth century had to be recorded on a single page of the *New York Times,* I would put the uniting of Europe at the top of the front page. Only the end of colonialism, the concomitant rise of the new global powers, and the mastery of the atom are its rivals for long-term significance. These latter stories could be written today; the first, the subject of this book, is still open.

With all of its problems, there is a buoyancy about this idea of making something bigger and better from the old pieces of Europe. It is an idea which should appeal to the American love of the new and untested. It is still characteristic for Americans to believe that things can get done even when seemingly impossible. Building Europe against many obstacles and many doubters from many disparate bits and pieces is an American-size task.

Monnet once tried to explain the need for something beyond intergovernmental cooperation to manage a European Community. He naturally met resistance in every national capital, starting with his own. After patiently explaining to a fellow French official how a coal and steel community would have to make decisions for the common good of all its members even by overriding, at times, a single country's objections, Monnet was asked to stop the heretical explanation. Those who knew Monnet are confident that he did not stop but probably tried another approach. In another story Monnet was once talking with a close collaborator, Francois Fontaine. The latter noted, "We shall face great difficulties and we shall use them to make further progress." Monnet responded, "You've understood what Europe's all about."[17] This book tries to indicate what Monnet was all about by looking at some of his accomplishments.

A NOTE ON TERMS, SOURCES, AND REFERENCES

Throughout this book, the terms "European Community" and "Community" are used to indicate the entire institutional and programmatic structure based on the Treaty of Paris of 1951, which established the European Coal and Steel Community, and on the Treaties of Rome of 1957, which established the European Atomic Energy Community (Euratom) and the European Economic Community (also often called the Common Market, a term which is occasionally used to refer to the entire Community). "European Community" is the preferred term here since it is the only one which takes account of the potential of political, as well as the reality of economic integration.[18]

Chapter endnotes contain some important details as well as references to other works on the Community. Appendix C contains a description of the Community budget process. Appendix A lists the members of the 1989-94 Commission, the Community's executive body, their fields of responsibility, and each of the subdivisions of the directorates-general which they supervise. The Community's summits are listed in Appendix B.

A bibliography lists most books referred to in the text and some other basic works about the Community, including EC publications of general interest and those relating to the major chapter divisions. There has been relatively little work in recent years on the whole Community and its broader aspirations, especially in the United States. The 1992 internal market program has provoked some American interest. The bibliography of recent works in English includes both a few American works on the legal and economic aspects of Community growth and several European books on institutional development, although even there much of the work being done today is sponsored by the Community institutions themselves.

The *Memoirs* of Jean Monnet, a principal architect of the Community, are frequently cited. Unless otherwise noted, the quotations are from the American edition (New York: Doubleday, 1978), cited simply as *Memoirs*.

Eurostat, the shortened name of the Statistical Office of the European Communities, is used throughout to indicate that Community source. This office is located in Luxembourg, which is also the home of the Office for Official Publications of the European Communities (called EC Publications Office in the text).

Statistics are a special problem in dealing with the EC. There is no common statistical base with the United States, and many extrapolations are required for comparisons. Translating ECU into dollars, or the reverse, is hazardous without qualifications. Some EC statistics are incomplete because not all national ministries, the source of Eurostat data, have the same scope or efficiency; others will not give certain information (e.g., on arms sales). U.S. agencies also use assumptions different from those of Eurostat. For example, we generally keep statistics by individual EC countries, which makes Canada, not the EC, our largest trading partner. Finally, even the best statistics are soon dated. Regular sources for both EC and U.S. statistics are indicated where available so the reader can update the information if desired.

Throughout the text the European Community's monetary unit, the ECU, is used. Because the ECU, as explained in chapter 6, varies in value with the national currencies it represents and with the frequent fluctuations of the dollar, it is not easy to give a single ECU/dollar value over a number of years. In the 1986-89 period the ECU was worth slightly more than one dollar.

NOTES

1. Walter Lipgens, *A History of European Integration*, vol. 1 (Oxford: Clarendon, 1982), 1:241. Lipgens has a comprehensive account of the extensive network of the pan-European organizations working toward different views of unification in the same work (see pp. 296-457). Richard Mayne's *Postwar, The Dawn of Today's Europe* (London: Thames and Hudson, 1983) also gives a good account of this period. Also see chapter 2, note 7, for a historian's account of the early ideas on European union and of a United States of Europe.

2. Monnet, *Memoirs*, 293.

3. Quoted in ibid., 283.

4. Konrad Adenauer, *Erinnerungen, 1945-53* (Stuttgart: Deutsch Verlags-Anstalt, 1965), 313.

5. Monnet, *Memoirs*, 296.

6. For the Schuman background, see Henry Beyer, *Robert Schuman, L'Europe Par La Reconciliation Franco-Allemande* (1986) and Henri Brugmans, *Le Message Européen de Robert Schuman* (1965), both in the Red Book series of the Foundation Jean Monnet in Lausanne, and his memoirs, *Pour L'Europe* (Paris, 1963).

7. There are still three communities (for coal and steel, economic affairs, and atomic energy), but a merger of governing institutions, completed in 1967, installed this three-part division largely in the Commission's directorates-general. The term "Community" is used here, as it is almost universally in Europe, to mean all three communities except where the context clearly indicates that only one is meant. The merger meant, in practice (and in these pages), that coal and steel and atomic energy are policies of the present single institutional structure, although they are important and separate elements in the early history of the Community.

8. Monnet, *Memoirs*, 333.

9. Ibid., 366.

10. The term "European Parliament" dates back to the 1952 draft treaty on a European Political Community. The Coal and Steel Community, however, used "Assembly," a practice continued by the other two communities. In 1962, the Assembly adopted a resolution calling itself the European Parliament, a practice soon adopted by the Commission and the Court of Justice. The Council, however, and the member states continued to use "Assembly" in official communications until the Single European Act of 1986 formally adopted "European Parliament."

11. The Community still functions from several cities. Agreement on a single site is still (with the language problem) the most irritating and costly problem the Community faces. Monnet tried several times to get agreement on one city for all institutions but national pride prevailed. In 1987 a private consortium began construction of a new office and meeting room compex near the Brussels headquarters of the Council and the Commission and close to the Parliament's Brussels outpost, now used only for committee and group meetings. A meeting place large enough for the Parliament's plenary sessions will be possible in the new area but whether the political problem of abandoning Strasbourg can be overcome is not yet clear. For more on this problem, see chapter 3.

12. The only vestige of the original ECSC is its Consultative Committee. Judged to be sufficiently different in scope from the Economic and Social Committee of the EEC and Euratom to remain separate, the Consultative Committee still discusses coal and steel problems for producers, users, labor, and consumers when it meets in Luxembourg. It remains a living monument to the modest beginnings of a uniting Europe.

13. For partition proposals, see Under-Secretary of State Sumner Welles, *The Time for Decision* (New York: Harper and Brothers, 1944), 345-56. On different views within the Roosevelt administration, see Secretary of State James F. Byrnes, *Speaking Frankly* (New York: Harper and Brothers, 1947), 182, 191. On the president's views and the Quebec statement of Roosevelt and Churchill on postwar Germany, see James MacGregor Burns, *Roosevelt, the Soldier of Freedom* (New York: Harcourt, Brace, Jovanovich, 1970), 440-41, 520.

14. The Commission of the European Communities has sponsored public opinion polling in member countries since 1970 in a series now called the

Eurobarometer. In 1982 a special poll of younger Europens was published under the title *The Young Europeans.* It indicated, among other points, that a slight majority of those aged 15-24 would be indifferent (as opposed to very sorry, or relieved) were they told that the European Community had been scrapped. Similarly, 44 percent never thought of themselves as citizens of Europe (53 percent did) but in this regard the young people were about the same as their elders. The editors of the study noted that "diffuse globalism" is one reason for young people's attachment to the idea of Europe. It may also be a reason for the large measure of indifference.

15. See the essays in Mauro Cappeletti, Monica Seccombe, and Joseph Weiler, eds., *Integration Through Law: Europe and the American Federal Experience* (Berlin: Walter de Gruyter, 1986), especially the final one by Eric Stein in collaboration with Louis Henkin, "On the Value of the Comparison," 79.

16. Cappeletti, *Integration Through Law,* xv.

17. Monnet, *Memoirs,* 371.

18. Most official documents and the treaty texts still refer to the "Communities." See, for example, *Treaties Establishing the European Communities* (Luxembourg: EC Publications Office, 1973 [and subsequent eds.]). Article 32 of the 1967 treaty on a single council and commission, however, refers to a "Single European Community." The Single European Act of 1987 also uses both the singular and plural forms.

2

The Foundations of the European Community

> Unity in Europe does not create a new kind of great power. It is a method for introducing change in Europe and, consequently, in the world. . . . [W]e are not in the 19th century. And the Europeans have built up the European Community precisely in order to find a way out of conflicts to which the 19th century power philosophy gave rise.
>
> —Jean Monnet

The effort to unite Europe in the second half of the twentieth century had several historical precedents, each of which enjoyed some success. But long before recorded history, the foundations of a single entity called Europe were being assembled from the geographical and human factors which create a distinct culture. Long before Europe was conceived as a political unit or even as a separate continent, an amazing variety of material and human resources slowly assembled on the western third of the world's largest land mass. Whatever separate races and pure languages ever existed in this area, which is only one-third the size of the continental United States, such distinctions have long been obliterated. Today there are many peoples but no races, many languages but none of them uninfluenced by others, and so many cultural influences from almost every other part of the world that Europe can fairly be called the world's most representative continent.

EUROPE'S PREHISTORY

Four times in Europe's prehistory the continent was subject to cataclysmic earth movements, each marked by mountain building, ice sheeting, and the folding and refolding of the earth's layers. After the last Ice Age, plants, insects, animals, and birds which had been driven into Africa in search of warmth, returned to Europe to join the few species which had survived the glaciers and the destructive earth forces. The appearances of men resembling our own species is quite recent in Europe, at least against the backdrop of geologic time. About 40,000 to 50,000 years of human history are available to scientists but most of this period belongs only to the archeologist, the paleontologist, and the geologist. The recorded history of human achievements, growth, and migrations is much shorter, beginning about 6,000 years ago after the final retreat northward of the mile-thick ice sheets which left Europe with the approximate shapes, including the remarkably crinkled shoreline, we recognize today. The British Isles were then separated from the Continent, and the Baltic—previously a large lake—opened to the North Sea.

One geographer has called this coastline "one of the most potent of the physical factors" in Europe's prehistoric development.[1] The length of the coast with its thousands of large and small indentations and its many islands—totaling over 47,000 miles by one calculation—was vital in encouraging and anchoring migration to the productive shore areas. The warm Gulf Stream made these coastal areas remarkably mild considering their northern latitudes.

This current of Caribbean water warms not only the British Isles and the continental coastline; it also penetrates the land mass in both northern and southern Europe. The prevailing southwesterly winds bring rain and moderate temperatures far inland because no mountain ranges block them until the Caucasus. (Rome, which sits at about the same latitude as Chicago, enjoys much warmer temperatures because of the Gulf Stream. So does Paris, which is at about the same latitude as Duluth, Minnesota.) This combination of extensive shoreline and warmed currents of moist air moving inland created ideal agricultural conditions beyond the fish-filled seas. The climate and the land, the same geographer notes, make most of Europe an agricultural land—quite different from territories of comparable latitudes elsewhere in the world.

A rich variety of natural resources resulted from these geologic and geographic circumstances. Although Europe has benefitted from a relatively warm and moist climate since the last ice age, the consequences of this climate varied with other factors. The greater part of western Europe, for example, was heavily forested after the last glacier receded. Over centuries this vegetation compacted to produce rich land, as well as useful timber for both firewood and the construction of homes and ships. Nature's bounty swelled from this fortuitous combination of human and material factors.

EUROPE'S ETHNIC AND RACIAL HERITAGE

Little is known with certainty of the human elements present as the Ice Age ended and the more benign landscape emerged. What is known is that some prehistoric forebears lived in what is now western Europe even before the ice melted from all land except the highest parts of the Alps. The indigenous Neanderthal man of this area was then assimilated by an eastern interloper, the Cro-Magnon man, in the first of many enriching penetrations at the western end of this Eurasian land mass. Why did Cro-Magnon man move west instead of Neanderthal man moving east? We simply do not know but can speculate that the great variety of land shapes and elevations in the west produced a comparable variety of plant and animal species which proved irresistible to an adventurous (and perhaps hungry) wanderer coming across the steppes of today's Soviet Union. Bones found in the past few decades indicate, upon careful reconstruction, that these two early *sapiens* types are similar enough to the present genetic pool that they could probably pass for some of the burly and broad-boned northern Europeans still seen today.

As early as 15-20,000 years ago, diverse racial types appeared in Italy. Since they apparently came by sea, were they attracted first by the very long shorelines which afforded mild temperatures, shelter, and sea food to those more accustomed to the hot sun and desert scarcities? There is firmer evidence that the Etruscans, who came from Asia Minor, landed in Italy during the tenth, ninth, and eighth centuries before Christ, bringing still other racial characteristics.[2] Farther north, hunting, which has been the principal means of survival during the glacial ages, now yielded to mixed cultures of nomads living in the increasingly rich forests and along lakes and rivers.

But in the distant east and south, a more advanced civilization had developed along the Tigris and Euphrates rivers in what is now Iraq. Here plants and animals were domesticated and health and survival enhanced. The burgeoning population sought new homes in the north and west. The dietary and climatic influences on these semitropical peoples made them smaller and darker than the native Europeans they encountered as they moved, perhaps in search of better land. Later other crop growers from the east, the Danubians, moved into present Central and Western Europe by land.

Aggressive Migrants

Others came by ship from the east, touching down in Italy and the Mediterranean islands. Still others, including animal breeders, went farther west by boat to penetrate the Spanish, Portuguese, and French coasts, moving slowly inland with their herds. By 2500 B.C., the Mediterranean also brought the sun worshipers who erected their stone monuments throughout much of western Europe.

At about the same time, other more powerful invaders, this time horsemen and stockbreeders, swept across the Russian steppes into present-day Germany and Scandanavia. These were tall, muscular migrants who were markedly more aggressive than Anatolians, Syrians, and Palestinians who came via the southern water route.

Adding to the colorful mixture of peoples in the western lands came skilled metal workers from the Aegean who arrived in Spain, a rich mineral-bearing land, to work the extensive copper deposits. These craftsmen eventually moved inland, probably seeking new ore supplies, penetrating the somewhat simpler cultures along their paths. Metal pots, beakers, and ornaments came with them and intermarriage spread the new skills widely. By 1800 B.C. these metal workers reached the British Isles.

Not all migration in Europe originated from the outside. The Kelts of the upper Rhineland and the Halstatters of central Europe brought their advanced metal-making skills into Italy, Greece, France, Spain, and, eventually, the British Isles during the Iron Age. From northern Europe came the tall, light-complexioned Teutonic peoples and from the east, the Slavs. These two movements came about the time of Christ and were followed by more extra-European incursions from the east, those of the Huns and the Avars. Each of these invaders left genetic and linguistic traces, some greater than others, by patterns and rules still not fully understood. These migrations are not simply something which happened in the past; they continue today with the arrival of African, Middle Eastern, and Asiatic visitors, workers, and students. The gene pot is constantly seasoned by this immigration which proceeds by jet plane, train, and auto instead of the boat, horseback, and footborne travel of the past. This variety of human stock in the European Community countries shows that there have been no "pure" races or languages in Europe for many centuries.

SOCIAL AND CULTURAL PATTERNS

If we begin to consider Europe as a unit from the middle to late periods of the Roman Empire (approximately the time of Christ), we see this somewhat vaguely defined territory now able to support the rising farm population and even to encourage its growth. From an early period, Europe organized itself into a productive if primitive economy with a specialized workforce. The agricultural economy soon expanded well beyond subsistence. The surplus was traded among farmers with the farm town emerging as the center of that trade. Growing prosperity brought further specialization with concentrations of workers in the town.

With economic growth, primitive political development followed. The desirable lands of western Europe were attractive to invaders who swept down from the frigid north and the less hospitable topography of the east. They soon met the outposts of the Roman Empire which extended to England, most of France, all of the Iberian peninsula, and parts of Germany. Sometimes with peaceful interplay of forces, more often with armed encounters, the outposts were pushed back toward Rome. The empire, itself weakened and divided by the fourth century after Christ, soon split into western and eastern halves, corresponding to the linguistic divisions of Latin and Greek. The western part was more rural, less productive in taxes for Rome, and thus less valuable. It became weaker and yielded more readily to the pressures from the east and north.

There were, of course, differences between northern and southern Europe as well as between the eastern and western parts of the empire. In the north, agriculture was more limited until better plows began to have an effect by about A.D. 900. Before then, the Mediterranean areas, with gentler climates, had advantages in productivity which induced population growth and urban development. Similarly, the milder climate of the south encouraged sea travel there much earlier than along the north Atlantic or the Baltic Sea. This advantage also disappeared eventually with the development of better sailing methods and stronger ships which finally brought naval superiority to the countries of the north.[3] This slow ascendency of the north was defined by 1600 and produced more wealth, greater trading networks, and thriving cities. Economic, cultural, and even political dominance by the north over the south in Europe has continued to be an influence.

This emerging pattern had several components, one of which was the capacity to produce and transport food from the areas of production to urban centers. Farmers, even in the Athenian period, has to be induced to release their surplus food in order to support the concentrations of skills, services, and wealth called cities. Force, barter, or sales networks were the most common forms of inducement. The precocious Mediterranean also led in this development which spread northward slowly and which favored the civilized centers over the rural areas.[4]

The receding of the Roman imperial tide left a cultural gap into which several new elements flowed, among them the Goths (actually several distinct groups of which the Visigoths were the most important). Of Germanic origin, the Goths had expanded both east and west at different times. Starting in the fifth century A.D., they pressed strongly with military forces against the empire. Yet at times they also negotiated for rights to imperial lands. Either way, they penetrated and determined (in the cultural sense) what would follow the Roman influences.

Similarly, Christianity, entering in parallel with the northern invaders, spread into Europe from the south bringing a different but equally forceful form of cultural imprint. Books, learning, education—all in somewhat simple forms—came with the dedicated believers. Monasticism, the form of Christianity nurtured in the earliest church in the Near East and Mediterranean areas, now moved to the north and west as the Romans faltered and moved back toward the metropole.[5] Christianity's diffusion throughout Europe from its centers of Rome, Constantinople, and Ireland was so complete and so integrated into the continent's cultural, political, and even economic life that the history of the religion can be said to be simultaneously the history of Europe.

Part of the cultural pattern of the early western Europeans was forceful thrusts outward into unknown or lesser known lands. These thrusts were motivated by adventure, a search for land to replace depleted fields at home and for woodlands for fuel and construction, and for the propagation and reinforcement of religion.

THE IDEA OF EUROPE

The two largest thrusts of this kind occurred from about A.D. 1000 to 1200 with eastward migration into present Poland and Russia and, at about the same time, when the Crusades brought Western political and religious values to the Middle East via Italy and the Mediterranean.

While these cultural outreaches proceeded, Latin Christianity's values prospered in politics, art, and economics. Combined with Italian mercantilism and naval prowess, pan-European trade expanded greatly by the start of the fourteenth century. Slowly, these internal changes transformed western Europe. As one commentator notes,

The upshot of these and other less spectacular developments was to integrate the everyday activity of a very substantial proportion of the entire population of all Europe into a single whole, regulated by market relations that focused in a few dozen cities, chief among them those of northern Italy. Strangers living hundreds or even thousands of miles apart combined to produce a result that some businessman, living perchance in still a third locality, planned and intended, though the participants in the process (including the business entrepreneurs) were not necessarily aware of how all the distant and necessary connections were in fact established and maintained.[6]

A functioning idea called Europe was underway.

Early Attempts to Unite Europe

The first attempt to form the disparate elements of what we today call Europe into a single political system was made by Charlemagne, the first Holy Roman emperor, who was crowned in A.D. 800. His attempt failed because his military skills were not matched by comparable administrative talents. His empire, like that of his Roman predecessor, Constantine VI, was held together by little more than a strong personality. But the extent of Charlemagne's empire corresponded approximately to the original six EC countries plus additional territory in the southeast now occupied by parts of Austria, Czechoslovakia, Hungary, and Switzerland.

Charlemagne was the first of the Holy Roman emperors and the most authentic; his successors bore the title but with decreasing credibility. There was a long interlude before another attempt was made to unite Europe by military force. But the growth of common European concepts continued after Charlemagne.[7]

By the fourteenth century, Europe had 50 million inhabitants and an established social pattern.

The same social classes had developed throughout the continent: the aristocracy, with their estates great and small, the well-to-do citizens in the towns, the merchants with their business contacts spanning the continent, the secular clergy and the monastic orders, and the serfs and freemen who had to perform unpaid services for their lords. The similarity of social structures across Europe was a major factor behind the recurring vision of a European unity, as in Dante's *De monarchia* (early 14th century), Pierre Dubois's *De recuperatione Terrae Sanctae* (around 1306), Enea Silvio Piccolomini's *Call to the Crusades* (1454) and in the treaty of George of Podebrady, King of Bohemia, with Louis XI of France and with the High Council of Venice in 1464.

But, as the same commentary notes, no matter what the literary or philosophical vision, there was a de facto unity in Europe in the Middle Ages:

In the 14th century Latin, which for centuries had reigned as the language of writers, poets, scholars and the Church, began to make way as the great vernacular languages gained currency—first Italian and Spanish, and later French and English. Despite the many languages and regional dialects, the knowledge of philosophers and scientists spread all over the continent, contributing to the cross fertilization of ideas. Artists travelled widely to meet, learn new techniques and try their skills in competition with each other. . . . The same is true in literature and music. . . . The symbols used by European writers and poets can be traced back to identical sources: Greek mythology, Nordic sages and the Gospels.[8]

Another and more complex attempt than Charlemagne's to unite Europe under a strong military leader was made at the start of the nineteenth century by Napoleon Bonaparte (1769-1821). The French general and emperor succeeded in directing the energies of the French Revolution into Europe but with the consequence of activating nationalism in Germany, Italy, Russia, and Spain. He destroyed the remnants of the Holy Roman Empire but could not replace it. At the peak of his influence, Napoleon could claim France and most or all of Italy, Portugal, Spain, Prussia, Russia, the Benelux countries, and Switzerland. His final battle at Waterloo, not far from Brussels, the Belgian capital and now the provisional capital of the European Community, marked a defeat (unfortunately temporary) of the idea that Europe could be united by force.

Napoleon's defeat resulted, in part at least, from a failure to recognize the tide of nationalism which confronted him everywhere outside the borders of France. His defeat is also a reminder that it was only in the late eighteenth century that the sharp divisions of nation-states began to separate European from European. Only in the late nineteenth century, for example, did passports become necessary for travel across the continent. Also in that century commercial rivalries sealed the national systems so well into trade and trade rivalries that diplomacy became an extension of commerce and war an extension of diplomacy. Instead of seeking a peaceful and democratic alternative to Napoleon, the reactionary forces which had prevailed against him restored and confirmed at the 1815 Congress of Vienna a tense system of power balances and spheres of influence without any democratic pretenses. It could succeed, like a skilled acrobat on the high wire, only as long as continued and skillful force was applied to it. This complacency was rewarded with "minor" but bloody wars of adjustment in the Crimea, along the Rhine River between France and Prussia and between Russia and Turkey, and with a continuous assault by persistent national revolutionaries against the smug attitudes of that Congress. These revolutions—in Spain in 1822, in Greece from 1821 to 1832, in France, Germany, Italy, and elsewhere in 1848, and in Poland in 1863—showed deeply rooted dissatisfaction with the reactionary and antidemocratic posture of the ruling classes who failed to recognize the changes which industrialization was bringing.

A Major Exodus

With these disruptive changes in European politics came other equally dramatic social and demographic alterations, some of which had a direct effect on the new American Republic. The growing nation demanded millions of immigrants to farm the expanding territories across the Mississippi, to build cities, and to staff factories and shops. Stories spread throughout Europe of the great promises of space, freedom, and prosperity in the New World. On the Russian steppes, in Scandanavian towns, and in German villages, the poor, the hungry, the ambitious, and the rootless heard and accepted these stories. When disaster struck Europe, as in the Irish famine at mid-century, millions more heeded the call to cross the ocean. All together, about 19 million immigrants, almost all from Europe, entered the United States as permanent immigrants during the nineteenth century. They formed about twenty-five percent of the total U.S. population in 1900.[9]

Even more impressive than the sizable numbers was the impact of these Europeans who arrived in the midst of a territorial expansion which trebled the continental land mass, pushed the western border to the Pacific, and terminated the frontier which had so appropriately symbolized the sense of expansion and freedom of the country. One American historian, writing at the time the frontier closed, drew a parallel between what was happening in the American West and an earlier frontier in Europe. "What the Mediterranean Sea was to the Greeks, breaking the bond of custom, offering new experiences, calling out new institutions and activities, that, and more, the ever retreating frontier has been to the United States directly, and to the nations of Europe more remotely." In another place in the same essay, Frederick Jackson Turner noted that the "effect reached back from the frontier and affected profoundly the Atlantic Coast and even the Old World. . . . The most important effect of the frontier has been in the promotion of democracy here and in Europe."[10]

Middle Class Revolt

Democracy was growing in Europe, in some places by violent revolution and in others by more peaceful reforms. Across the English channel from the French revolution and reaction an equally significant revolution occurred forty years later, this time of the middle classes. It produced the 1832 Reform Act in Britain. At the same time the French, still in reaction to 1789, were creating a bourgeois monarchy. Europe was progressing in material ways but its governance was only slowly moving out of the eighteenth century. Europe would eventually pay dearly in civil wars whose explosive force shattered world peace twice in a generation in the following century.

The first of those wars came in 1914 when an ambitious Germany, united under strong Prussian leadership, collided with an alarmed Britain and France which saw their sacred balance of power threatened by a kaiser not bound by their agreements. After a bloody four-year war of trench battles was finally decided by American intervention, a humiliated Germany sulked until Adolf Hitler was able to twist a fragile Weimar democracy to suit his megalomania. Using a military machine of power never seen before and with a fury which overwhelmed complacent neighbors, he exceeded the worst destructiveness of Charlemagne and Napoleon in a much briefer period. He foresaw a "thousand-year Reich," had aspirations as great as his two predecessors, occupied as much territory as did their empires, and caused death and misery which was only possible with twentieth-century war technology. Even before Hitler's end came, Europe began to think of ways to prevent another such war.

The early attempts to unite Europe failed, but they are instructive. Charlemagne might have succeeded if his knowledge of government and the means to extend it had been better developed. Napoleon's goals of glory and empire clashed with rising nationalism and was doomed by the general's confusion of military occupation with political control. Hitler came closest to success with a brutality which itself ultimately provoked and repelled the rest of the world. These failures provided some clues for those who tried in 1945 to pick up the pieces of Europe: make war more difficult, peace more attractive, cooperation more central to governance.

The events of our own century seem both complicated and immediate when aligned with those momentous but remote events in the ages of Charlemagne and Napoleon. Veterans of twentieth-century conflicts still live among us. A consequence of this immediacy is, sometimes, difficulty in assessing blame or assigning causes. We may know today why Charlemagne and Napoleon failed to unite Europe. Perhaps we are too close to the events to assign blame for the two World Wars or to be confident we know how closely Germany and France should be bound to each other. Nevertheless, Europe came out of both world wars with convictions that new ways must be found to prevent such civil wars. After the first war, however, there was a retreat into nationalistic explanations of the conflict and its consequences; after the second came a renewed, and so far, sustained search for ways to foreclose the rivalries and power balances which produced these wars. The history of this effort is the history of the European Community.

MAINTAINING A CONSENSUS

This consensus has varied, however, over the four decades since European recovery began in 1947. At the start of this period, support for political union was strong. With the rebuffs in the early 1950s to a political and defense community, energies were directed to economic integration. But with the variations in emphasis and tactics, a strong and consistent belief in a united Europe prevailed even when there was disagreement on the final form efforts should take.[11]

Who are these Europeans who show, by their history, both pronounced, consistency in their opinions and behavior, and yet an ability to adapt to changes in their environment? The Eurobarometer gives some insights into the contemporary European personality, a relative to that highly speculative and always tentative national character.

A European Profile

Here, in summary and somewhat simplified form, are some of the demographic and cultural highlights of the European Community:

• Europeans are a settled and mature people, marked by a diverse and advanced cultural life. They accept a larger role for government (and its higher cost) than do Americans. They count on the government for many services and exact a higher standard of performance from it than do many Americans. Europeans are not as inclined to strike out on their own in search of jobs or homes in areas they do not know, compared to their American counterparts. Europeans act as if they believe the social system will provide for them. Even when disappointed they do not easily change their ways.

• The perception of happiness or of satisfaction with life is quite high in most Community countries but surprisingly lower in France and Italy. Europeans seem to place considerable value on "quality of life" issues like town planning, environmental controls, high standards of public services in police, mass transit, and civil service, and elevated standards of health services. They expect to pay significantly higher levels of taxes for these services than is common in American states and cities.[12]

• They believe strongly in education and impose stricter standards on their children in school than do Americans. They value an established curriculum which must be mastered by pupils, strict and well-trained teachers, and a series of threshold examinations to stratify and direct children into further education or training principally according to their abilities, not by egalitarian principles.

• In the controversial areas of abortion and divorce, Europeans are more moderate than the highly individualistic Americans. There is a greater emphasis in European countries on the social consequences of both abortion and divorce with the results that Community countries remain less open to both. They also focus on the consequences of divorce on children while the United States seems more concerned about no-fault divorce with most emphasis on the adults involved.[13]

• The artistic and intellectual life is important to Europeans. They expect the government to recognize and support these values with subsidized orchestras, opera houses, and theaters, and by honoring artists and writers with appointments as diplomats and positions in the political hierarchy.

• The demographic trend in the Community is toward zero population growth, but with major differences among member countries. Overall, the causes are a declining birth rate which outstrips a gradual increase in longevity. Better health care has decreased infant mortality and extended life expectancy. Thus while population growth is diminishing toward zero, the age pyramid is starting to bulge at the older end. Later marriages, more divorces, and more working women account for some of the drop in fertility rates. Higher living standards, fears for the future, and more individual- rather than family-centered values seem to be involved as well.

• There are still important regional variations in the EC standard of living. In the prosperous northeast (Germany, Denmark) the per capita Gross Domestic Product is 1.85 times that of the Iberian peninsula. (This is more than comparable regions in the United States but less than among the Swiss cantons.)[14]

• Language diversity remains today a reflection of the Community's many ethnic and national groups as well as an obstacle to a more perfect union. The problems of the EC institutions in handling nine official languages is only a bureaucratic reflection of the larger political and economic hurdles which this linguistic variety creates. Of the nine Community tongues, German (78 million speakers), English (59.9 million), French (57.9 million), and Italian (56.7 million) are the most widely spoken. But Dutch (19.9 million) is an official language of both Belgium and the Netherlands, while Spanish is spoken by over 38 million in Spain and many times that number elsewhere in the world. Similarly, French has a global cultural role beyond its considerable importance in the Community in Belgium, France, and Luxembourg. Although Portuguese has only 10 million EC speakers, important areas in Africa and Latin America speak it also. Even Danish, with its 4.9 million speakers in Denmark, was the official language of Norway until this century and is still widely understood there and elsewhere in Scandinavia. Only Greek (9.9 million) and Gaelic (3.5 million) are restricted to a single country but in the case of Ireland, English, a principal Community language, is also used almost universally.

• Christianity is the religion of the vast majority of the citizens in all Community countries. Christianity's diffusion throughout Europe from its centers of Rome, Constantinople, and Ireland was so complete and so integrated into the Continent's cultural, political, and even economic life that for some time the history of this religion is simultaneously the history of Europe. Despite the serious splits between Eastern and Western Christianity and the later division of Protestants from Roman Catholics, the tenets of the religion are still broadly accepted and its moral teachings widely observed. Catholics outnumber Protestants about two to one (194 to 108 million) to which Greek Orthodox Christians add almost another 10 million. The remaining 25 million are distributed among other religions, including Judaism and Islam, and among non-adherents.[15]

• The role of food in family life is more important in Europe than in the United States. Even with comparable standards of living, the proportion of household income spent for food is higher in Community countries than in the United States. Further, more money is spent per capita in cafes and restaurants in Europe than in the United States.[16]

• Europeans are pet lovers but not to the extent Americans are. In the United States there are 39 cats and dogs for every 100 people. Only Belgium and France come close with 30 each. Other EC countries are Britain, 20; the Netherlands, 19; Italy, 16; and Germany, 11. But to show the gulf between east and west, Japan has but 6 domestic animals per 100 people.[17]

• When it comes to vacations, there are also important differences among Europeans. For example, 65 percent of the Dutch go away from their home areas on vacations but only 31 percent of the Portuguese do. Generally, the northern residents of Britain, Denmark, Germany, France, Luxembourg, and the Netherlands travel on vacations more than they stay at home. In the southern countries, a majority stay at home. But there are exceptions. The Belgians and Irish also stay at home while the Italians like to travel. Of the 56 percent of all EC adults who did go away on vacation in 1985, one-third did so more than once.[18] This is possible because, compared to Americans who often have only two weeks of vacation, Community citizens generally get four and often take them at different times of the year.

• Important European Community symbols are limited to an anthem and the flag of twelve gold stars in a circle on a blue field which became an EC pennant many years after it was adopted by the Coucil of Europe as its flag. Today it is used by both bodies. The anthem, Beethoven's "Ode to Joy" from the Ninth Symphony, has been used officially since 1972 and was also taken over from earlier use by the Council of Europe. Less well-established is Europe Day, May 9, commemorating the 1950 date when Robert Schuman made the announcement which eventually led to the European Coal and Steel Community as the first element in the European Community. Although an "official" Community holiday, May 9 is not yet a legal holiday in any EC country.

• Other Community symbols planned but still not operative include a European passport and a Community driving license, both of which are being introduced slowly by national governments with Community support. In neither case, however, will the Community be the issuing authority under present plans. Both help promote a Community "identity" which was the goal of a committee established at the 1984 EC summit at Fontainebleau. The Adonnino committee on a People's Europe, named for the Italian chairman, recommended several kinds of symbols and other images which the Community might encourage to help develop this identity.[19]

• Athletics are both an important pastime for Europeans and a source of Community identification. The Commission, in several instances at the urging of the Adonnino committee, sponsors, patronizes, or helps organize yacht races, cycling, swimming, tennis, and bicycle and walking tours in the name of the Community. The 1988 Olympics in Seoul, Korea, saw the Community emblem used for the first time by competitors in combination with their national symbol.

The European Community is both more than a title and less than a complete reality. When seen as if it were a single and sovereign power, its credentials are impressive: "Four of the ten highest gross national products in the world. Two members of the nuclear weapons club. Two permanent members of the Security Council. Four of the seven richest countries of the western world. Four of the International Monetary Fund's 'Group of Ten.' Two of the seven space powers. The strongest commercial power in the world. . . . Fascinating distinctions, but deceptive. For the Europe of the Communities is more impressive from the outside than experienced from the inside."[20] Yet even with these distinctions, the Community cannot solve its farm and budget problems and, thirty years after the Treaty of Rome and nearly forty years after the Schuman Plan, has still not achieved the "common market" which gave the Community both its original purpose and one of its informal names.

The rich variety of European geography and history has been incorporated into the Community's own tapestry of cultural, linguistic, and political traditions. But it has been a slow process. E pluribus unum is an appropriate caption for the European Community's efforts as it was of an earlier attempt, also still incomplete, to combine the disparate for newer purposes.

NOTES

1. George G. Chisholm, "Europe: Geography and Statistics," in *Encyclopedia Britannica*, 11th ed.

2. John Geipel, *The Europeans* (New York: Pegasus, 1969), 19, 33.

3. William H. McNeill, "Patterns of European History," in *Europe as a Cultural Area* (New York: Mouton, 1979), 10-14.

4. Ibid.

5. Kenneth Clark, *Civilization, A Personal View* (New York: Harper and Row, 1961), 7-10.

6. McNeill, "Patterns," 10-14.

7. For another historian's account of this question, see J. B. Duroselle in *World Today* (January 1966), where he notes the ambiguity and fluctuation in the meaning of Europe both as a geographical and a political concept. For another

Durocelle essay on the key year 1948 in the postwar decisions on unity, see "1948: Les Debuts de la Construction Européenne," in *Origins of the European Integration, March 1948-May 1950*, ed. Raymond Poidevin (Brussels: Bruylant, 1986), 11-22.

8. *A Journey Through the EC* (Luxembourg: EC Publications Office, 1985), 43.

9. Bureau of the Census, *Historical Statistics of the United States, 1789-1945*, excerpted in Richard B. Morris, ed., *Encyclopedia of American History* (New York: Harper and Brothers, 1953).

10. Frederick Jackson Turner, "The Significance of the Frontier in American History," paper presented at the American Historical Association meeting, 1893. Excerpted from Henry Steele Commager, ed., *Living Ideas in America* (New York: Harper and Brothers, 1951), 72-80.

11. See Eurobarometer series of public opinion polls, summarized in *Europe as Seen by Europeans, European Polling 1973-86*, in the European Documentation series (Luxembourg: EC Publications Office, 1986). This publication also summarizes data going back to 1952 which indicate a steady majority among EC citizens in favor of preserving and enchancing a united Europe. Because the Eurobarometer series only polls Community countries, that is the universe for this section on European beliefs and attitudes.

12. Eurobarometer surveys on "Satisfaction on the Conditions of Life in Community Countries," September 1973; "L'Europe Vue par les Europeens," September 1973; "Chomage et recherche d'un emploi: attitudes et opinions des public europeens," September 1979; "European Men and Women in 1983," March-April 1983. See also, *Long Term Trends in Tax Revenues in OECD Member Countries* (Paris: OECD, 1981), 11-12.

Related, perhaps, is the work of Richard Estes, research director of the University of Pennsylvania's School of Social Work, who conducted a study of 107 countries using 44 factors to measure the "quality of life." Nine of the top 11 countries were in Europe. Denmark was number 1; the United States, 41. Factors included health and welfare, literacy and education, political participation, and stability in the 1979/80 period. Estes explained the relatively low U.S. position by noting that his survey does not emphasize economic factors in which the United States leads (*New York Times* [September 22, 1985]).

13. Mary Ann Glendon, *Abortion and Divorce in Western Law* (Cambridge: Harvard University Press, 1988).

14. *Demographic Situation in the Community* (Brussels: Economic and Social Committee, 1986), 5-13. On regional variations, see "Regional Implications of Economic and Monetary Integration," in *Report on Economic and Monetary Union* (Luxembourg: EC Publications Office, 1989).

15. *A Journey Through the EC*, member country summaries, 5-42. Figures for languages and religions are adjusted for a unified Germany.

16. Eurostat, *Family Budgets, Comparative Tables, Germany, France, Italy, United Kingdom*, 1984.

17. *Economist* (April 26, 1986): 66.

18. "Europeans and Their Holidays," commission survey, 1986.

19. *European Identity: Symbols to Sport*, European File, 6/87 (Brussels: Commission, 1987). The Fontainebleau summit meeting in 1984 set up the Adonnino committee. It issued two reports the following year on efforts to encourage freer circulation of ideas, persons, and goods related to a united Europe. The European

Council adopted the reports and urged their implementation. In a typical division, a European Parliament debate on a People's Europe in September 1988 heard both those who thought these symbols important and others who felt the Community should instead concentrate on substantive issues like pension harmonization and investment policies.

20. Daniel Strasser, *The Finances of Europe*, European Perspectives series (Brussels: Commission of the European Communities, 1981), vii.

3

The European Community
Institutions in Operation

Europe will not be built all at once, or as a single whole: it will be built by concrete achievements which first create *de facto* solidarity.
—Schuman Declaration

There is no simple and brief account of the Community's constitutional history. But there is a straight and consistent historical line to be traced from the Schuman Declaration to the Single European Act (SEA). The treaties of 1951 and 1957 creating the three communities; the treaties covering the enlargements of 1973 (Denmark, Ireland, United Kingdom), 1981 (Greece), and 1986 (Portugal, Spain); and several conventions, acts, minor treaties, and decisions, today comprise the constitution of the European Community.[1]

If the "miracle at Philadelphia" was that fifty-five men could write the U.S. Constitution in one hot summer, keep it to 4,000 words, and make it last practically without alteration into its third century, the miracle at Brussels is that the European Community is still relevant today to political and economic unity in Europe nearly 40 years after the first steps, after the postwar ardor for unity has long cooled and after the endless alterations, adjustments, and compromises embodied in its "constitution."

The following account of Community institutions and their development concentrates on its main instruments: the Commission, the Economic and Social Committee, the Parliament, the Council of Ministers, the European Council, and the Court of Justice. Their interplay is indicated and their evolution outlined. A separate section on European

Union traces this concept of institutional growth with special attention given to the Single European Act (SEA), the most recent Community reform. This account only briefly mentions such important quasi-institutions as the European Investment Bank, which was set up under the Treaty of Rome for developmental loans within the Community, the Permanent Representatives of the member states, the Joint Research Centers, and the Court of Auditors.

THE COMMISSION

The Commission is at once the most exalted and the most humble of the Community's institutions—exalted because its initiating role and powerful staff i. charged with maintaining and fostering the Community's ideals, but humble because it has an unknown constituency, uncertain support from both the Council and the Parliament, and can even be removed from office (but not replaced) by the otherwise weak Parliament.

About 16,000 individuals work under the direction of the 17-member Commission, two-thirds of them in or near a large X-shaped building near the top of one of the few hills in Brussels. From the Berlaymont building comes a steady flow of regulations, opinions, and information. What the Commission and its staff propose usually becomes Community law after lengthy consideration by the Council and, usually, after review by the Parliament. In disputed cases, the Court of Justice may also rule on the Commission's work.

The Commissioners are often competent (sometimes even brilliant), experienced public figures, nominated by the member governments to serve a four-year renewable term. The five largest countries (France, Germany, Italy, Spain, United Kingdom) name two commissioners each, the other countries one each.[2] The Commission president, who acts as spokesman, is named by consensus and under informal rotation by the member governments. Six vice-presidents are divided among the "big five" and the remaining smaller countries. Although four-year terms are specified by treaty, the commissioners normally serve at the pleasure of their government. A few have served extended tours in Brussels when they felt especially comfortable with the Commission's workstyle or when their national government found them more useful in the Berlaymont than in the national political arena.[3] With the larger countries, one of the two commissioners is often from an opposition party.

The commissioners are forbidden by treaty provision to seek or to accept instructions from any government or from any other body. This mandate of complete independence is not entirely plausible since Commission members are appointed, not elected, and may be reappointed by their governments. Each member state explicitly undertakes, however, not to seek to influence commissioners. Finally, commissioners may not engage in any other occupation during their term of office.[4]

Over the 20 years of the single Commission, a variety of occasionally distinguished and some more ordinary people have served. (Until the 1989 Commission took office, all previous commissioners had been men. Two women are in the new Commission.) All have arrived in Brussels because of some previous commendable work but not all have succeeded in the peculiar combination of intergovernmental politics, an entrenched bureaucracy, and an international lifestyle which the job offers.[5]

From the start of the High Authority of the Coal and Steel Community, when Jean Monnet was president, the Commission has seen itself as the guardian of the treaties and of the traditions of a united Europe. Its natural opponents have become the Council of Ministers, the repository of national interests, and the member states themselves and their national bureaucracies. The Commission often finds common ground with the European Parliament, also mandated, especially since its first direct election in 1979, to represent Europe-wide interests.

If the European Community has institutional problems, the Commission does not seem to be their source. It has functioned as the founding treaties intended; the commissioners have remained generally independent of their governments. The Commission has created an international civil service of competent and disciplined experts who have produced a body of law which greatly affects how Europe lives, works, and trades.

But much of the substance of a united Europe has eluded the European Community and its principal agent, the Commission. It has been frustrated in reaching the treaty goal of creating a common market free of internal trade barriers. As agent, the Commission has also been unable to find sources of secure Community funding, to improve its competitive position in the world, or to project an image of a prosperous and united Europe. In each of these shortfalls, the national governments, either through the Council of Ministers or acting alone, must take the major blame for the failures of the Commission.

The Commission has a close relationship to its neighbor institution in Brussels, the powerful Council of Ministers. There is sometimes agreement but more often antagonism or at least tension between the two. Although the Council was also intended to view its responsibilities from a Community viewpoint, that perspective yielded early in the history of the Community to the urgencies of national politics, national constituencies, and national ambitions of political leaders. Until the Commission gets a clearer political mandate, its attempt to produce a single European market and a matching mentality seems destined to collide regularly with the nationalism of member countries as represented in the Council.[6]

National Traditions

From the Parliament's view, the Commission is a more ambiguous institution. While speaking for a stronger Community, the Commission must also find accommodation with member countries. (Some of this interaction takes place in the Council of Ministers where the Commission is represented and in committees on specific problems, including many in agriculture, some of which are established by the Commission and others by the Council.)

Both Commission and Council members come out of the national political traditions. Both are named by the national governments. Until the SEA reforms, the Commission and the Council often worked out solutions which were then presented to the Parliament for a perfunctory examination. In the process, the Commission sometimes became the defender of the Council. Quite naturally, this diminished the Commission's luster in Parliament's eyes.

But the truth is somewhat more complicated. Commission and Council members, despite their national political origins, represent increasingly diverse political traditions of pro- and anti-integration. These traditions are present within both institutions yet politicians find themselves increasingly forced to choose career paths in one or the other tradition. The SEA recently enhanced the institutional role of the heads of the EC governments or states as a Community institution.[7] The European Council, as this group of political leaders is called, may ease this split between national and Community political values by uniting the highest levels of the two spheres.[8]

The Commission's functions under the treaties are broadly described in two areas: initiating new measures under Council or treaty authority; and implementing Community policies, under the same authorities, by managing its programs. These powers of initiation and of administration mean that, except for a few specialized cases, the Commission does not itself make the major policy decisions of the Community. Those decisions are made by the Council of Ministers in its legislative function. The Commission's work is divided into 22 divisions, called directorates-general (DG), each of which generally is the responsibility of one commissioner. But while Commission presidents have reallocated responsibilities among the varying number of commissioners since 1967, the DGs are quite stable in number and responsibilities.[9] The member governments constitute the final authority on these allocations although "strong" commission presidents can resist these pressures more easily. (Walter Hallstein, who became the first president of the merged

Commission in 1958, and Jacques Delors, president since 1985, are considered the only really strong presidents the Commission has ever had.)

The Secretary-General

The head of the Commission's staff is the secretary-general, a position held by Emile Noël for the first twenty years of the single Commission (1967-87). Noël, who was a close aide to Prime Minister Guy Mollet during the 1957 French debate on the Rome Treaties, occupied the top commission post so long and with such intimate knowledge of the Community's origins, that it is difficult to predict the impact of Noël's successors. He was succeeded in mid-1987 by David Williamson, a close adviser to Margaret Thatcher and a former deputy director of the directorate-general for agriculture. Under Noël the secretary-general was a close adviser to the commission president as well as head of the commission's professional and technical staffs.

The secretary-general has a small, experienced staff, which serves both as a channel of information to him and the commission president and as a means of carrying out Commission decisions. Another part of this staff services the European Political Cooperation network (see chapter 8). The secretary-general also keeps members' embassies in non-EC countries informed of Commission work and monitors that work in those countries. Under the secretary-general's direction, the clerk of the Commission prepares the meetings of the commissioners and of their chiefs of staff who are charged with preparing the briefs their bosses discuss at weekly Commission meetings. Other aides to the secretary-general handle relations with member governments, including those with the Council and Parliament. In addition, an important internal inspection staff monitors the Commission's work in non-EC countries and the information flow between the directorates-general and from them to the member countries' embassies in those countries.

Aside from the large staff in Brussels, there are sizable contingents of Commission employees, including two DGs, in Luxembourg where the publications and statistical offices are located, and in the research centers and the information offices in the member countries. Commission offices in nonmember states function as embassies do for national governments except that they are called Delegations.[10]

National Representation

Proportionality among the Commission's staff by national origin is an important goal especially for the higher levels of the "A" or professional staff.[11] Disruptions from three enlargements and uneven interest in member countries in Community employment make this goal presently unattainable. The British, for example, are underrepresented in "A" positions while the Belgians, to take only one example, are overrepresented. Even with practices like the "golden handshake," by which early retirement with financial incentives is occasionally pressed on individuals whose grade or nationality is overrepresented, the uneven representation problem continues. The total staff has increased following each enlargement, reflecting both the problem of proportionality in numbers and the growing Community structure. Here the problem was to retain mastery of the ever more complex Community machinery while accommodating the principle that each new member should rapidly obtain its share of top jobs, partly to cement the Community allegiance of the new member's civil service as soon as possible.

Training and maintaining a high-quality staff puts the Commission in direct competition with the national ministries. From the beginning of the merged institutions in 1967, almost all of the top staff (positions designated A1, 2, and 3 and paying the equivalent of $75,000 to $128,000 in 1988) had or could expect to have employment at some time with their national government. The personnel DG has tried to overcome this problem by creating a career service instead of relying on recruitment from the national bureaucracies. Recruitment emphasizes, where possible, entrance at the lower grades by examination after university or other training. A carefully managed system of promotions, designed to retain the best staff, often fails however, when enlargement and other national considerations interfere.

Exact figures on distribution of positions by nationality and pay were only made public regularly starting in 1989. For example, on January 1, 1989, there were 2760 employees of all grades of Italian nationality; 1806 from Germany; 1648 from France, and only 1132 from the United Kingdom, yet these four countries are about the same size and are treated in almost every Community regard as equals in representation. At the same date, Belgium—with 4 percent of the Community's population—had 3521 employees which clearly shows the hometown advantage for getting jobs. Belgium had not only the largest percentages of the service and clerical personnel of the Commission but also over 13 percent of the "A" grades (more than the United Kingdom and almost as many as France and Germany).[12]

Language Barriers

Nine official languages in the member countries impose an extra burden on Commission staff. Practically every major document must be translated and distributed in each language. Every meeting of officials, commissioners, and citizens which the Commission sponsors must be ready to provide simultaneous interpretation into any Community language. One-fourth of the Commission's personnel is occupied with written and oral language requirements. The other Community institutions face, of course, the same problem but the production of so many documents at the Commission makes the language problem greater. Various proposals for a limited number of working languages have failed to identify which languages should be chosen. Like the question of a single site for all Community institutions, language seems an impossible political problem. After 40 years of living with this problem, the institutions have, in fact, adjusted to both the cost and the inconvenience. When the intolerable meets the insoluble, the latter seems to win.[13]

Model EC Schools

From the first years of the Coal and Steel Community, the importance of educating the children of the High Authority as future Europeans was appreciated. This project involved some tension with the Luxembourg government which initially anticipated that the children of the international staff would attend its local schools. Gradually, the idea of European schools with language sections appropriate to the Community's four original languages developed. Eventually the European schools in Luxembourg were dwarfed by the Brussels counterpart institutions as the staffs of the Commission and Council of Ministers grew in the Belgian capital. By 1990 there were nine EC schools with 15,000 students.

In both cities the principles of instruction include education in the primary grades in the maternal languages with an early requirement for students to master a second European language and, eventually, a third and even fourth. The European schools in both cities have high standards and function as model schools for local communities.[14]

A complicated network involving both national and Community elements links the Commission staff with the national ministries. Managing the Community's vast agricultural programs, for example, requires close cooperation between DG VI (agriculture) and the twelve national ministries of agriculture, each of which has different constituencies. Two-way communication by telephone, telex, and mail is supplemented by personal visits by national staffs to Brussels. Commission staff also travel, although they appear to be invited less often to the national capitals than the national ministry staffs are invited (or invite themselves) to Brussels.

Communications between the national constituencies of the directorates-general and the Berlaymont headquarters proceed primarily through the staffs of the Permanent Representatives of the member governments. The latter are the equivalent, in function and rank, of ambassadors from the twelve national governments. In addition, a large number of official EC committees operate, especially in agriculture, to represent the interests of constituents directly before the Commission.[15] Occasionally, the Commission staff hears directly from constituents. Farmers, for example, sometimes protest aspects of the agricultural policy in person in Brussels or at the Parliament in Strasbourg, complete with farm animals.

LOBBIES AND NETWORKS

There is no evidence that Monnet and the other designers of the ECSC institutions anticipated that interest groups and their lobbies would function in the Community. Yet the lobbyists came. The largest of these conventional lobbies is COPA, the agricultural producers group, now joined by many other sector interest groups. Besides EC industry and consumer representation in Brussels, other European and American businesses and their associations find it useful to have an office in the city which is gradually becoming the capital of Europe. The 1992 program to improve the internal market greatly expanded this corps of Brussels lobbyists.

Finally, elected representatives from national and regional legislatures, as well as from the European Parliament itself, appear in Brussels to seek information or to attempt to influence policy directions. Monnet himself left the presidency of the High Authority of the ECSC to establish a high-level lobby called the Action Committee for the United States of Europe. His goal was to support Community development by bringing top-level national political leadership together.[16]

The Economic and Social Committee

A special form of lobbying comes to the Belgian capital from institutional interest groups to both the Commission and the Council from the Economic and Social Committee (ESC), or the "other assembly" as the ESC calls itself in reference to the days when the official name of the European Parliament was the Common Assembly. Composed of 189 representatives of labor, management, agriculture, and consumers, the Committee is a descendant of both the Consultative Committee of the Coal and Steel Community (which maintains a separate existence in Luxembourg) and of the national economic and social committees which exist in some Community countries.[17] Its purpose in the ECSC was twofold: (1) to insure that those most directly affected by the common market for basic industries—mine and steel plant owners, managers, workers, consumers, and dealers—had direct access to the Community's decision makers, and (2) to serve as a conduit for those decision makers to convey the ideals of a uniting Europe downward through the committee's membership to the entire Community. The Consultative Committee thus differed from the Parliament which actually represented the six national parliaments.

The ESC and the Consultative Committee represented, in their earliest Community and national forms, a kind of directed democracy: interest groups would be incorporated into the institutional structure but would be used, in turn, by the institutions to instruct the masses. An additional goal was to provide a forum when the interest groups met and learned something about each other. This socialization contributed, of course, to the overall intent of building constituencies into the system, a preoccupation in the Community's earlier days.

Three Interest Groups

The two committees are referred matters by both the Commission and the Council. ESC, however, is considerably more active and broader in its scope of interests, corresponding to the jurisdiction of the Economic and Euratom Communities. They also have the right to initiate opinions. The ESC carries on its work through nine substantive sections. Each of the three interest groups—employer, worker, and consumers and others—is represented in each section which submits draft opinions to the Committee's plenary sessions, generally held monthly.

Members of the two committees are nominated by the member governments (which in turn rely on the interest group organizations for advice) and are appointed by the Council of Ministers. They receive no pay for their part-time services but are compensated for their travel and living expenses. The ESC has about 450 employees in Brussels and costs about 25 million ECU (U.S. $28 million) a year. (This is about four-fifths of the staff and of the cost of the entire Court of Justice.)

It is very doubtful if the original goals of the Consultative Committee and ESC are still valid. With interest groups able to represent themselves to the Community and with an ample information program operated by the Community, socialization among diverse groups seems the principal benefit of these committees today. Many members of the Parliament and the Commission staff privately dismiss the Consultative Committee and ESC as vestigial organs which could not withstand a strict cost-benefit analysis.

When the Assembly of the Coal and Steel Community met for the first time in September 1952, it was the center of a pro-European fever sweeping the continent. Presided over by a prominent European, Paul Henri Spaak, the first session of the assembly was asked by the foreign ministers of the six member countries to prepare a draft treaty on a European Political Community. The ECSC Assembly, the direct predecessor of the present Parliament, was thus conspicuously directed and dramatically called to action. At no time since has the Parliament, the Community's only truly representative body, ever had such centrality in the integration of Europe.

A DELEGATE ASSEMBLY

Nothing came of the European Political Community because its legal authority—the treaty to establish the European Defense Community—was rejected by the French Parliament in the bitter 1954 fight. The ECSC Assembly descended into obscurity. Eventually it was merged with those of the Economic Community and the Euratom Community to form the European Parliament in 1957. It would be 22 years after that before treaty provisions calling for direct elections were honored. During this long "delegate" period, the Assembly—now renamed by itself the European Parliament—was composed of part-time members delegated from their national parliaments to discuss European issues once a month. Neither its authority under the treaties nor the method of member selection contributed to a belief that Europe needed a genuine parliament.

Facing the Parliament, even in its first heady days as the political center of the coal and steel community, was the embarrassing absence of real power. The Parliament in Strasbourg never was, and is not now, the source of either legislative authority or political influence as is a typical national parliament. The European Parliament cannot initiate legislation but only give opinions in the form of resolutions from one of its 18 committees. This function was enhanced in 1987 with the SEA which strengthened the Parliament in several ways. This improvement leaves the Parliament still very far from true legislative authority, a reform which another constitutional conference will have to consider if it takes up the problem of the "democratic deficit" of the Community.[18]

The 518-member Parliament does have an important role in approving the Community budget and in supervising its execution. It has a Question Hour for both oral and written questions to the Commission and the Council. It also has the power (never used) to dismiss the entire Commission (though it cannot name a new one).

A senior leadership committee, the Bureau, is composed of the president of the Parliament, fourteen vice-presidents (with political and national balance), and five Quaestors, who are appointed to represent members' interests in handling administrative and organizational problems. An enlarged bureau adds the chairmen of the political groups and is increasingly seen as the Parliament's policy-making body.

The Parliament meets as a paying tenant in the Council of Europe's buildings in Strasbourg for five days in a single week each month, except August when no session is held and October when a second, and exclusively budgetary, session is added. Between 1967 and 1981 the Parliament alternated its plenary sessions between Strasbourg, where the ECSC Assembly also met, and Luxembourg, where the Parliament's sectetariat has its principal offices. A contest between the two cities for the Parliament's presence was won by France when it built private offices for each member in a new building adjacent to a new plenary hall, both completed in time for the second enlargement in 1981 and both large enough for the 1986 arrival of the Portuguese and Spanish delegations as well.[19]

The Committee System

The Parliament shares with the U.S. Congress a strong reliance on committees. All requests from the Council or the Commission are referred to committees. The 18 Committee Chairmanships are distributed among the political groups in proportion to their strength in the whole parliament but taking into account also their chairmanships of the interparliamentary delegations and other perquisites of political group strength. In the 1989-94 Parliament, the Socialists chaired seven committees; the Christian Democrats, five; the European Democrats (conservatives) and the Communists, two each; and the Liberals and the Gaullists, one each. The Parliament's members (MEPs) are assigned to at least one committee each as a full member and one additional committee as an alternate, to serve in the absence of the regular member.

The substantive committees of the Parliament, listed in their agreed order of precedence, are: Political Affairs; Agriculture, Fisheries and Food; Budgets; Economic and Monetary Affairs and Industrial Policy; Energy, Research and Technology; External Economic Relations; Legal Affairs and Citizens' Rights; Social Affairs, Employment and the Working Environment; Regional Policy and Regional Planning; Transport and Tourism; Environment, Public Health and Consumers; Youth, Culture, Education, the Media and Sport; Development and Cooperation; Budgetary Control; and Women's Rights. There are three committees dealing with parliamentary affairs: Institutional Affairs; Rules of Procedures, the Verification of Credentials and Immunities; and Petitions.

The Role of Rapporteur

The committee chairmen play a much smaller role than their congressional counterparts. In Strasbourg, the committee *rapporteur* (literally, report-writer) is the key figure in defining views on an issue, first within the committee, then in the plenary session of Parliament. The absence of a subcommittee structure enhances the role of the rapporteur who is named ad hoc for each report to be issued. He listens to the evidence (few congressional-type hearings are held but commissioners, Council members, and fellow parliamentarians offer views both in committee and plenary sessions), consults experts inside and outside of the Parliament, and drafts a report for the consideration of the committee and the whole parliament. Like the congressional subcommittee chairman, the rapporteur must determine where consensus lies within his committee and in the plenary hall. His skill in guiding his report to final approval brings a reputation which affects his long-term influences in the institution and in Brussels.

Committee meetings are not usually open to the public although this possibility was established with the first direct elections in 1979. Similarly, committees may invite outside experts for public hearings, a practice where MEPs acknowledge the congressional example. Wider use of both public sessions and investigative hearings might make the Parliament and its concerns better known to the public.

The rapporteur has far fewer resources than does the congressional committee or subcommittee chairman. His staff is limited to those civil servants of the secretariat assigned to his committee and to those staff members of his political group with relevant expertise. But since each committee has only four to six staff experts, each of whom has additional duties beyond any single committee report, the rapporteur does far more of the actual research and drafting himself than does his congressional counterpart. The Parliament's reports are thus more reflective of the political nuances within the institution but less comprehensive and authoritative than the congressional product.

Staff resources for the Parliament are generous by European national parliamentary standards but very small compared to the U.S. Congress. There are no personal staff members who are directly accountable to the ordinary member for parliamentary work.[20] There is also no counterpart to the Congressional Research Service of the Library of Congress which provides extensive and rapid information to members of Congress and their staffs.

There were about 3400 employees of the Parliament, including temporary workers, in 1990. This includes many service personnel and most of the translators and interpreters. It takes about 40 percent of the Parliament staff to provide these language services in written or oral form. Another 15 percent are involved in moving the Parliament and its members each month to three cities. Scientific and research personnel and facilities are almost nonexistent beyond a small library staff in

Luxembourg and a small data exchange facility which connects the Parliament by computer to other parliamentary centers (including most national parliaments of the Community).

The political groups have staffs which supplement the professional secretariat members serving the committees. From the political group staffs the members of Parliament can get tactical advice and political research not normally available from the secretariat which is politically neutral and subject to civil service hiring and tenure rules. Some of the group staff also serve informally as aides to group chairmen or its other senior members.

No Single Site

Complicating the work of the Parliament is the constant travel between national capital, constituency, and the Community cities of Brussels, Luxembourg, and Strasbourg. If we take a committee rapporteur trying to complete a report as our example, we can better see the problem. Since the parliament is in plenary session only one week each month, the rapporteur must use that period for intensive meetings with staff and parliamentary colleagues. Two other weeks each month are set aside for committee meetings in Brussels. The fourth week is reserved for political group activities. Weekends and odd days are free for visits home, national politics, and private activities. Included in the latter is whatever personal business or professional ties the member has retained.[21]

This peripatetic Parliament is due to the inability of the member governments to choose a single site for Community institutions. Debate on the single site goes back to the summer of 1952 when the six original members began the work of the Coal and Steel Community. The foreign ministers met from a Tuesday morning until dawn on Thursday, seeking agreement on the site of the High Authority. In desperation and fatigue, Luxembourg was chosen provisionally because no one had prepared objections against it. Jean Monnet threatened to resign the High Authority presidency if a decision on a site was not made. As compensation to France, which had proposed Strasbourg as the ECSC capital, the common assembly was located, also provisionally, in the Alsatian city. Later, the secretariat of the assembly was placed in Luxembourg to compensate that country for the decision in 1957 to place the Economic Community and the Euratom commissions in Brussels. This tricity distribution of Community institutions has resisted any reduction for over 30 years.

The Parliament pays the most for this anomaly. The Commission and the Council of Ministers, joined by the Committee of Permanent

Representatives (Coreper) and the press and diplomatic corps, spend most of their time in Brussels. (Only a few representatives from these groups must travel to the monthly parliamentary sessions.) They have all the advantages of a large capital city. The Parliament must move its files, which its secretariat maintains, and most of the service and professional staff, once a month from Luxembourg to Strasbourg. The committee staffs and members of Parliament must make a second move each month from their home bases to Brussels where most committee meetings occur. The political group staff, principally resident in Brussels, usually have two moves each month: to Strasbourg for the plenary session and once again in the fourth week each month to still another site for group meetings.

Travel dominates the life of every MEP but the successful Committee chairman or rapporteur must learn to use the interminable moves to his advantage, talking to colleagues in Strasbourg in person, consulting with the committee and secretariat staff in Luxembourg or Commission experts in Brussels, telephoning the doubtful members wherever he or she can find them, and assembling a report in taxis, airplanes, hotel rooms, and corridors. After presentation, the dazed look of colleagues may reflect more the same kind of schedule which they too have endured rather than any profundity or lack of clarity in the text.[22]

Interparliamentary Delegations

The Parliament has no foreign relations committee because a coordinated Community foreign policy is a gradual and irregular development and not a treaty obligation. Members of Parliament use the interparliamentary delegations to follow events outside the Community and develop expertise in foreign affairs (and to justify foreign travel which is more restricted in the Parliament than in Congress).

There are 26 delegations to specific countries and regions, with EP membership ranging from 26 (for the delegation to Washington, judged to be the most prestigious) to 8 or 10, the most common delegation size. Parliamentary delegations include those to eastern European countries which, in the Gorbachev period, have clearly grown in importance. There is also a superdelegation of 66 to the Consultative Assembly of the Lomé Convention countries of Africa, the Caribbean, and the Pacific. The Lomé countries are the former colonies or territories of the Community members and their treaty association represents a major commitment to their development.[23] The Parliament's delegation is also the forum for the members especially interested in Third World problems.

Several factors illustrate the discipline and the advantages which delegation membership provides an MEP. First, each member normally belongs to only one interparliamentary delegation. This concentrates his attention by limiting his overseas encounters. Second, delegation assignment is a political group decision; those who take the assignment seriously by regular attendance and careful work merit a move upward to a more important delegation when vacancies occur. Third, both national and group pressures operate to discipline members in both committee and delegation work; members resent those who let down their side. Together these elements make MEPs at least limited experts in the country or area they engage through delegation activities—limited, however, because the typical delegation meets its foreign counterparts only once a year, usually alternating between a European site (generally Strasbourg or Brussels) and a site in the partner country.

Political Groups

The Parliament is organized primarily by political parties which form multinational coalitions called political groups. The eleven groups of the 1989-94 parliament represent a political principle established in all western European countries but present in the American system in only the weakest form. This principle states that political party membership is the most fundamental measure of how society, the government, and the parliament should be organized. Party size in the European Parliament, for example, determines where members sit, how they vote, and how all chairmen of committees and delegations and all parliamentary officers are named. Party solidarity is usually much stronger than national ties in the 12-country body and generally more important than any single issue.[24] There are, of course, nuances distinguishing members by nationality but these are usually not significant for committee and floor activities.

During the week reserved each month for group activities, members discuss group positions on committee resolutions and reports; designate members for committee and delegation vacancies; and try to assess the prospects of member parties in national elections.

The political groups, and behind them, the national political parties of the member countries, are much stronger than their American counterparts. In the latter system, the elected members of Congress perform like heads of 535 individual political parties, raising their own funds and organizing and directing their supporters. Our nominal political parties confine their activities to the infranational officers although they are involved in some fund raising and in voter registration and mobilization in the national races. In the European system, the parties select the candidates, decide on their position on the crucial party list presented to voters, and raise the funds for both party activities and for elections. Without party support, candidates would wither away.

Intra-Group Differences

Occasionally, there are more serious differences within groups, sometimes (but not usually) along national lines. The elected group president and vice presidents, especially of the fractious Socialists, spend much time discussing internal splits on issues. Most groups also have "study days" once or twice a year away from the Parliament's hectic pace where outside experts lead discussions on issues.

Political groups existed before direct elections but were strengthened by them. Before 1979, the delegates to Parliament sat by political groups in both committee and plenary sessions, as now, but inevitably the issues (and the quarrels) in national parliaments tended to be carried into the European Parliament. With direct elections and the consequent decrease in national parliament members in Strasbourg, political ideology and solidarity are the principal focus of the MEPs within their groups.

The largest of the political groups are the Socialists, with constituent parties in every member country. The smallest is the Rainbow group, with 13 members and a group of 11 independents. The 180-member Socialist group obtains, by its size, the largest number of seats and the largest number of chairmanships in both committees and interparliamentary delegations.[25]

Next in size with 121 members are the Christian Democrats, now called the European Peoples' Party group, with members from every member country. Until 1976 the Christian Democrats were the largest group in the Parliament and have been the second largest ever since.

Third are the Liberals, with 49 members from 10 member countries. Fourth, with 34 members, are the Conservatives (called the European Democrats), largely a British Conservative group with two Danes. In the previous Parliament it also had 17 Spanish members who eventually joined the Christian Democrats. Both of these groups changed their names to seek wider membership as the Parliament (and the Community) grew larger. The Greens (29 members) and the European United Left (principally Italian Communists) (28 members) are the fifth and sixth groups in size, with representation from seven and four member countries, respectively. The next two groups, the European Democratic Alliance (EDA) (22) and the European Right (17), are essentially French parties. The EDA are the remnants of the once-powerful Gaullists while the European Right is principally the National Front of France with six additional Greek rightists.

The remaining three groups have only 38 members together, with no more than seven from any one party. They represent the conservative Communist parties and a sprinkling of fringe groups and independents. The largest, and most varied of these, is called, appropriately, the Rainbow Group.

Being the largest group does not mean the Socialists can control any single vote for they have barely one-third of the Parliament membership. They did elect the second president of the directly elected Parliament in 1981 when the right-center groups could not agree as they had in 1979 when they elected Simone Veil, a French Liberal, for the first term. Even if the Communists joined consistently with the Socialists, the two left parties would command only about 39 percent of the 1989-94 parliament.

The 11 political groups may seem an unmanageable number of parties for Americans used to only two parties in the Congress, but 11 represents a major consolidation of the 77 national parties and movements which sent members to the third parliament. The Parliament's rules make this contraction possible by requiring at least ten members from at least four countries to form a group.

Remuneration

How does the institution meet the member's own immediate interests? The pay of the Euro-MPs is the same as their national parliamentarians. This ranges from the relatively generous Bundestag salary of German members to the quite modest level of Westminster's MPs. Indecision of the member governments was again the cause of this pay arrangement when a single salary scale did not satisfy widely varying national systems.

Allowances paid by the Parliament itself cover members' travel to and from the institution's three official cities, official travel outside the Community, and a special allowance (2500 ECU a year) for orientation travel within the Community. A secretarial allowance may be used for both research and secretarial help although it is barely enough to employ one full-time worker. An office allowance helps cover costs within the constituency. Members are paid fairly generous allowances for their hotels and meals while on official business.

Office and staff allowances grew gradually during the delegate period as more and more time was required for the work of Europe which could not be charged to the member's national parliament. With direct elections, prospective members hoped for a single uniform pay and immunities act for all Euro-MPs but this is still resisted by some governments. Instead, there are 12 different systems of parliamentary immunity in the Strasbourg parliament and equally diverse pay and allowances paid to its members.

Direct Elections

Direct elections did not increase Parliament's feeble powers but tended to bring younger, more active, and less patient members to Strasbourg. The Parliament has, for example, twice delayed the Community budget since 1979 by initially rejecting it. It also proposed a sweeping constitutional reform which had important influence on the Single European Act.[26]

The citizens of Europe have voted three times for the European Parliament in direct elections which were without precedent in scope, complexity, and coordination in the continent's long history. Over 70 national parties and three transnational federations campaigned for seats in the first election in 1979.[27] Slightly over 60 percent of the voting age population participated. The national range extended from 92 percent in Belgium, where voting is compulsory, to 33 percent in the United Kingdom.[28]

There is no European Community electoral law so all elections were conducted under special national legislation which differed both among the member countries and from the national parliamentary laws. British law, for example, set up new EP electoral districts to match the country's single-member district tradition but a party list system, using proportional representation, was used elsewhere, including Northern Ireland. Voting time extended from Thursday through Sunday because of differing traditions. With national parties in charge and with no truly European issues, the campaigns tended to become referenda on national governments complete with party subsidies, campaign styles, and election themes.

National laws also determined whether, and when, Euro-MPs must give up their national parliamentary mandates. Many experienced members of the former delegate Parliament chose to remain national parliamentarians, judging that a national political career held more promise than the uncertain development of the European Parliament. Others hedged, running in the 1979 direct election while holding their national seats. Slowly the trend is toward full-time work for Europe. The combined pressure of party rules and national laws tends to force members to choose between Strasbourg and the national capital for their political careers.

The scope of the 1979 election was remarkable. A multilingual and multinational electorate of potentially 200 million is comparable only to elections in India or the United States. But in those two countries there was only one, not nine, electoral system and far fewer parties involved. For the European voter accustomed to an MP representing sixty to eighty thousand constituents, the EP member's responsibility for an average of 600,000 citizens was an enormous change.

Campaigning was complex for the participant and bewildering for the voters. The special national laws were similar but not identical to national rules. Only France used a completely different system but voters in all countries were exposed for the first time to party appeals to elect a national component in an assembly in another country. The number of seats for each country was determined by the Community's Direct Elections Act of 1976: Italy, France, Germany, and Britain had 81 seats each; the Netherlands, 25; Belgium, 24; Denmark, 16; Ireland, 15; and Luxembourg, 6. (Greece, when it entered the Parliament in 1981, got 24 seats while Portugal and Spain got 24 and 60, respectively, in 1986). This formula was not strictly by population but rather went back to early ideas of proportionality. The result benefited the smaller countries; Luxembourg, for example, received one seat for each 60,000 citizens while Germany had one for 750,000.[29]

THE OLD AND THE NEW PARLIAMENTS

When Britain entered the Community in 1973, hope rose that Westminister's traditions could somehow strengthen those in both Brussels and Strasbourg. When this did not happen, new expectations arose; perhaps direct elections could transform the European Parliament. A younger and less traditional parliamentary body was produced but the problem remains: the Parliament is given only an indifferent role in the basic treaties.

Yet when one examines the pre-1979 body and its directly elected successors, some important differences appear.

• The proportion of members of national parliaments dropped from 100 percent before 1979, to 31 percent in the first directly elected Parliament, to less than 6 percent in the 1989-94 body.

• About half of the 518 members elected in 1989 had never before served in the European parliament.

• Only 44 members or a little less than 10 percent of the 1984-89 parliament ever served in a delegate European Parliament; in the 1989-94 Parliament, the number fell to below 5 percent.

• More than half (244 out of 410) of the 1979 Parliament never before held a nationally elected political position.

• Of the 166 members of national parliaments elected in 1979, over half had never served in the European Parliament before. Of these new Euro-MPs, 61 were reelected in 1984, forming a group which has made a successful transition by choice from national to European politics. Most of them gave up their parliamentary mandates at home; by July 1988 there were only 31 Euro-MPs who were still members of their national parliaments.

The most recent Parliament on which detailed statistics are available, elected in 1984, has a broader educational and occupational background than its predecessors. Although the law was the favored training for a plurality of members (99 of 434), only 48 members actually listed themselves as lawyers by profession. The largest occupational category was teaching and lecturing, with 71, while journalism and writing were close behind with 60. Next were civil servants (41 from national governments, 13 from Community institutions). Thirty-three members were farmers but industry, with 13, and trade and finance, with 22, were close to the bottom.[30]

Parliament's functioning is intimately tied to its tentative political mandate and its frenzied and disjointed work habits. Often it is not taken seriously. Yet until Europe has a representative assembly with a constructive role, political Europe itself cannot be taken seriously.

The Parliament's Future

The Parliament will not get that power, of course, until Europe accepts that either parliamentary control or a change to balanced institutions with a kind of congressional control is an essential part of the Community. The comparison with the U.S. Congress is not gratuitous. The European Parliament, despite its name, is not a typical parliament which produces a government. Rather, like Congress, it is elected independently from the executive branch. It is the most representative institution of the Community, with a range of elected political viewpoints from the Communists to the extreme right and including the Greens. Despite that, the EP rule will not change until there is a wider popular interest in the Community itself as the chosen instrument for organizing the economic and political life of Europe. The real Community battles will remain those between the Commission and the Council of Ministers, with the Parliament as an expensive and harried observer if this change does not take place.

Now often seen as rivals, the European Parliament and the twelve national parliaments might yet devise a constructive relation under the pressure of converging governing responsibilities. The next phase of EC constitutional reform—perhaps starting with the 1990 intergovernmental conference—may take up this question of legislative authority that lies at the heart of the Community's "democratic deficit" reduction problem.

THE COUNCIL OF MINISTERS

German Chancellor and Foreign Minister Konrad Adenauer, at the first session of the ECSC Council of Ministers'[31] meeting in Luxembourg in 1952, described the Council's role as standing "at the crossroads of two kinds of sovereignty, national and supranational. . . . While it must safeguard the national interests of the Member states, it must not regard this as its paramount task. Its paramount task is to promote the interests of the Community; and, unless it does this, the Community will not develop."[32]

Monnet maintained as High Authority president, that "the Council's task is to arrive at a common view, not to seek a compromise between national interests."[33] Yet in practice, the Council is a forum for national interests. In this role, the Council appears to have changed the least of all Community institutions since the founding of the Coal and Steel Community in 1952. It is still the forum where the fiction largely prevails that member countries are equals. Here there is no talk of national rights since it is understood that each country relies ultimately on the national sovereignty which, 35 years after the signing of the Schuman Treaty, rests largely undiminished.

If there were serious doubts about the primacy of that sovereignty, the Luxembourg Compromise of 1966 resolved it in favor of national rights. This event was a statement by France reserving the right to say no. It climaxed nearly a year of conflict between Charles de Gaulle, who strongly resented Community institutions, and the Commission, led by Walter Hallstein, who believed strongly in expanding its powers. Although the "compromise" was a unilateral French declaration that vital interests of a country could not be subject to the qualified majority embodied in the treaties, the declaration, in fact, only confirmed past practice.

But since the statement ended a French boycott of Council sessions, the January 1966 restatement of national rights is cited as the terminus of political integration and also as a major obstacle to effective Community decision making. From 1966 to 1982, there was very little voting in the Council. A country would state that an important matter was before the Council and action would be blocked as long as that country refused to agree or, alternately, insisted on continued discussion. In 1982 Belgium forced a vote when the United Kingdom tried to block action on agricultural prices. Here other countries, normally inclined to go along with a dissenter for fear they might someday need the veto too, now insisted on action because farm prices were for *them* an important issue also. The British went along reluctantly.

The de Gaulle–Hallstein dispute was fought as the three separate communities prepared to merge their councils and commissions as they had already joined their assemblies and courts of justice in 1957. The French leader recognized that combined institutions meant combined strength. He was determined to limit what he called "a mostly foreign technocracy designed to trample on democracy in France."[34] De Gaulle resigned several years later but his suspicions on the course of Community development have deep roots in the nationalism of all member countries. His forcefulness and skills led some to think, mistakenly, that this national outlook was only a Gaullist or a French characteristic.

With the adoption, in 1967, of a single Council, emphasis fell on the central role of the national ministers, first, to coordinate the general economic powers of their countries and, second, to take decisions, normally based on specific proposals made by the Commission. The two Rome Treaties (on the Economic and the Atomic Energy Communities) thus reversed the procedure of the Schuman Treaty which had given the Commission the right to act, on coal and steel matters, with the assent of the Council. This distinction still applies when the Commission acts with the authority of the ECSC treaty.

How the Council Operates

The Council is the true legislature of the Community. Its work product takes several forms: (1) regulations, which are generally applicable to all member states; (2) directives, which bind the members concerned but leave them choices on how they will comply; (3) decisions, which oblige a member state, company, or individual to specific actions; and (4) recommendations and opinions, which are not binding. Normally the Council acts after receiving proposals or at least advice from the Commission. The Luxembourg Compromise confirmed the de facto veto which operated throughout the period following the Rome Treaties, and upon which de Gaulle insisted by France's absence from Council sessions in 1965. Not only were his actions consistent with that history but they underlined its implicit principle, as expressed by Robert Marjolin, a Commission member named by France, that "when it is a question of very important interests, the discussion should continue until a unanimity is reached." The result, as Marjolin notes, was that for the next 20 years, not only were important Community questions not decided by majority voting but very few secondary issues were so decided even when no serious interest of any member country was involved.[35]

The treaties refer to voting by majority, by qualified majority, and by unanimity. Qualified majorities presently represent 54 votes from these elements: France, Germany, Italy, United Kingdom, 10 each; Spain, 8; Belgium, Greece, the Netherlands, Portugal, 5 each; Ireland, Denmark, 3 each; Luxembourg, 2; for a total of 76. When acting on a Commission proposal, any 54 votes suffice; otherwise, at least eight countries must constitute that minimum number.

Reform proposals for the Community eventually address the need to end, or to limit strictly, the national veto. The German use of the veto in 1985 to protect its farmers from a one percent drop in farm prices was useful to this reform because it focused on the domestic pressures which can build when the veto is available for use. The steps taken in the 1985/86 intergovernmental conference of EC states, which culminated in the Single European Act, place some restrictions on the veto and make a number of other institutional changes.

Rotating Presidency

By a treaty provision, the presidency of the Council rotates every six months among the member countries. With the 1986 enlargement to 12 members, this means that each country assumes the chair only once every 6 years. Future national governments could spend over five years in office without ever chairing a Council meeting. The national civil services, as the institutional memories of their governments, will suffer the most from this lack of experience.

Longer intervals may also weaken the presidency itself through lack of continuity and correspondingly increase the influence of the Commission and, possibly, of the Parliament. Yet the growth of Community activity pushes EC concepts ever more deeply into each member government, gradually transforming them. As one close observer put it,

The existence of so many Council meetings reveals quite a lot about the extent of European integration. It also means that the machinery has become complex, cumbersome, and difficult to coordinate. And that, of course, is precisely where the Presidency comes in. Its main responsibility is to ensure that the necessary coordination takes place, which in turn means that nearly the whole government of the presiding member state is fully involved in the Presidency at all levels—ministerial as well as administrative.

The Council, in fact, is not one body but rather those representatives which the national governments send to discuss EC matters. Normally, the Council sits as the twelve foreign ministers, now called the General Affairs Council since it handles a broad range of questions. But the agriculture, finance, and economic ministers (or their equivalents) also meet frequently. By treaty provision, any one member of the national government may be sent to Brussels whatever the Council agenda item.[36]

The Council is assisted by two subsidiary bodies: its own secretariat and a Committee of Permanent Representatives (Coreper). The Council also has a number of committees which bring together national representatives with Council secretariat staff and, often, with Commission staff as well. The secretariat has about two thousand employees and is divided into seven directorates-general: administration, agriculture and fisheries, internal market and industrial policy, research, energy, transport and environment, external relations, institutional relations, and economic and social affairs (compared to 22 DGs for the Commission).

The Permanent Representatives are the ambassadors of the member states to the Community. They accumulate Council and Commission experience from the national viewpoint for the benefit of whatever government is in power and whatever ministers are in attendance. They have staffs appropriate to a large and important embassy, with specialists in substantive areas corresponding to the Council's secretariat staff. Much of the Council's preparatory work is done in committees and working parties, many of which are run jointly with the Commission. But the Permanent Representatives have the key role in watching over both Council and Commission staffs and supplying the indispensible national perspective, especially when their ministers are not in town. For while the Council and Commission secretariat staffs, as international civil servants, are pledged to neutrality, the Coreper staffs are national agents, principally civil servants, and thus obligated to their country's interests, not those of the Community.

Council–Commission Relations

The Commission, which has a representative in Coreper, also meets with the Council president before each month's General Affairs Council session to confirm the agenda and to anticipate any problems. Since the Commission has a key role in introducing legislation, it is the wise Council president who learns how to work effectively with the Commission.

The Council is not an intimate meeting place. Including interpreters and technical staff, there are over 150 persons present at every Council meeting, no matter what the agenda or which national ministers are assembled. Sometimes meals are used to reduce this crowd for more informal talk. Ministers may meet alone for lunch, perhaps accompanied by a senior Council aide. Larger functions may still limit attendance to the top three or four staff for each minister.

The gradual growth in Community scope (called the *acquis communitaire*) keeps the Council very busy in matching the work of the Commission. In the vernacular, the Commission keeps pitching proposals while the Council stays at bat. It was, however, really not designed for such activities. Reforms, including the Single European Act, are often designed to redistribute the burdens and some of these responsibilities among other institutions, especially the Parliament.

Even more of a problem than institutional overload for the Council is its frequent inability to reach agreement. Ministers are sent to Council meetings by national governments elected in national political systems where the ministers are active and dedicated participants. Their political futures lie more immediately in their own countries than in any nascent European political system. Despite the Adenauer–Monnet dialog, it is difficult to see how the Council could ever seek as its "paramount task" to promote Community interests.

A Triangle of Resistence

Together with the national parliaments and the national bureau-cracies, the Council's ministers form a triangle of resistance to further European integration, even when exceptions for the occasional prointegration policies of the Benelux countries are admitted.

The clash of interests between small and large member states is often played out in the Council of Ministers. Sometimes the differences reflect the relative support of member states for faster or slower integration, differences which can change greatly over time or with various issues. The initial impetus in creating the ECSC came from France and Germany while reluctance was the initial reaction of Belgium, Luxembourg, and the Netherlands. These three had formed the Benelux customs union during World War II while their govenments were in London exile. They feared domination by a Franco-German alliance and sought a "blocking minority" and other concessions to this fear.[37] These smaller countries always wanted British membership as a restraint on Franco-German domination. Britain, long wary to enter the Community because it still believed in its global role, was in this regard no different from the other larger powers which want to enjoy the benefits of Community membership while preserving maximum independence in other arenas.

The French, in 1950, wanted a proportional system of voting on coal and steel of which it and Germany were, by far, the major ECSC producers. The Germans had sought their own proportionality as the largest single producer. The solution, which Monnet considered a victory, was majority voting in the High Authority, a mixture of qualified majority, simple majority, and unanimity in the Council of Ministers (depending on the issue), and proportionality of delegates in the Assembly with France and Germany having 18 votes each which, together, equalled the votes of the other four members.

This complicated arrangement confirmed problems rather than solving them. Approximate proportionality remained the rule in the Assembly (later the Parliament) but this did not matter since nothing of importance was decided there. In the Council, majority voting yielded for many years to the practice, confirmed by the Luxembourg Compromise, that when important matters were at issue, no country could be overridden. The Benelux desire for a veto was ultimately sustained but by the 1970s, especially after the entrance of Britain eased the fears of Franco-German domination, the Benelux countries became the most fervent supporters of integration and, consequently, less supportive of the veto as a protector of national interests.[38] They found in the European institutions, as smaller countries generally find in the United Nations and other international bodies, that the only protection against the great powers is the institutional framework of a large organization.[39]

THE EUROPEAN COUNCIL

The idea of regular meetings of the heads of EC governments goes back at least to 1960 when Jean Monnet discussed with Maurice Couve de Murville, the French foreign minister, a plan for an EC confederation whose executive organ would be a Supreme Council of the Heads of Government. Monnet never abandoned the idea although he was aware that de Gaulle, who hinted at closer European governmental ties after he returned to power, might want to use meetings of heads of government to bypass, not strengthen, Community institutions. Monnet saw regular meetings of the European Council in 1974 with characteristic optimism as the creation of a supreme Community political authority, a kind of Council of Prime Ministers.[40] It is not yet clear whether he was right.

The occasional inability of the Council of Ministers to make difficult decisions was one of several motives for the heads of EC governments to hold regular summit meetings.[41] They had already met for the first time in 1957 when negotiations for the Rome Treaties faltered. They met again in February and July 1961 on political cooperation and in a largely ceremonial session in Rome in 1967 to mark the ten-year anniversary of the signing of the Rome Treaties. After meeting in the Hague in 1969 on an agricultural policy crisis and on Britain's candidacy for membership, a summit pause followed.

Difficult enlargement negotiations and a broadly held judgment that Europe was stalled led to a decisive summit in Paris in 1972. Here European Union by 1980 was established as the goal with monetary and regional programs and renewed "political cooperation" advanced as the means to that goal. But the summit communique was not specific about how progress toward this grand design would proceed. Would the rhetoric of the summit become a screen for the inability of Community institutions to act?[42]

In 1973, an indecisive Copenhagen summit centered on the energy crisis and the Yom Kippur war in an environment much more like an international conference than an intimate summit. In the next six months, the leaders of Britain, France, and Germany were replaced, disrupting plans for a spring summit. At a December 1974 session in Paris, agreement came on three summits a year. Giscard d'Estaing persuaded his colleagues that facilitation of Community goals, not their frustration, was now a French priority. The European Council was born.[43]

The Paris agreement confirmed that the country with the presidency of the Council of Ministers would host one summit in its home country during its six-month term of office. The third summit each year would be in Belgium or Luxembourg in mid-year. The leaders also agreed in principle to modify the practice of unanimity at Council of Ministers' meetings. Direct elections to the Parliament were set and a report on European Union ordered. This first European Council meeting moved at a pace which has been difficult to sustain or to implement fully.

Did the European Council now constitute a new Community institution? Initially, the answer seemed to be no but now this is an open question. By extending the concept of the Council of Ministers in the Treaty of Rome, the assembling of the top governmental leaders of each member country seems consistent with the treaty. Yet the heads of government clearly see themselves above the treaty when they meet. They are also, after all, the highest political authorities in their countries.

An Ambiguous Beginning

After a dozen years, the EC summit, which began as intergovernmental frustration with EC weaknesses has become an enlarged opportunity for Community action. The European Council began in ambiguity. Was it to be a regular Council of Ministers' meeting (with the foreign ministers doing the preparatory work), an intergovernmental overview of the Community, or a separate effort in political cooperation? Constitutionally, with the ratification of the Single European Act[44] which puts the European Council in the treaties for the first time, a separate institution, but without specified powers, seems to have been born.

A concept of the Presidency of the Community is developing, speeded, in part, by the growth of the European Council. Each member country has the presidency for six months in rotation by alphabetical order (in the country's own language), based on the treaty provision which established this procedure for the Council of Ministers. (There is no formal arrangement, like the EPC "troika," for continuity between successive presidencies.) For the two or three meetings of the European Council each year,[45] the format, participants, and agenda of the European Council differ sharply from that of the Council of Ministers' meetings.

First, there are far fewer staff at the summit meetings which are thus both exclusive and informal. The 12 heads of government are accompanied by their foreign ministers who prepare the agenda. The President of the Commission and one of his vice presidents attend, with a very small secretariat and the ubiquitous interpreters. This means less than 30 principals—far different from the platoons of experts and other officials who attend Community ministerial meetings.

Second, the agenda is limited. In some of the early summit sessions, the agenda got out of hand with either too many topics or too technical or too petty matters. Such an agenda was found to limit the spontaneity which the government heads obviously enjoyed in the closed door meetings.

Third, the prominence of the participants, the rise of personalized politics, and the ravenous media make the meetings newsworthy displays for naturally competitive national leaders. No comparable attention accrues to the Council of Ministers' meetings which are highly structured with careful preparations, detailed agenda and documentation, and a strong institutional continuity.

Personalities tend to dominate the public aspects of the summits but behind closed doors there is a formal equality of leaders of sovereign powers. There is a strong and growing tendency for the Council of Ministers, when they cannot reach agreement, to foist the problem onto their bosses who are normally even less likely by virture of temperament, publicity, and acquaintance with the issues to find the hard compromises which eluded their ministers. But it is also true that only the heads of government can ultimately find political solutions to Community problems. Some hope that the prestige and visibility of the European Council can eliminate or reduce the present divergence between Community and nation.

There are noteworthy examples. The British budgetary refund demand gnawed at the finance ministers and their chiefs for several years until the repeated public failures shamed the heads of government to action. Political cooperation itself owes much to the 1969 and 1972 summits when international crises exposed the inability of the Community to make reasoned response to events which affected it.

The greatest asset of the European Council should be its finality; by definition there is nothing higher than a summit and little but public discredit when its participants cannot agree. One result is that defeat is seldom admitted. When success is elusive, as in June 1987 when a confident Margaret Thatcher came from a striking reelection victory to reject a summit plan to raise new EC resources and expand programs, the heads of government tend to announce that the problem will carry over to the next meeting.

With the place and date of following summits now known well in advance, this postponement (or continued effort, depending on the viewpoint) eases the public aspect of apparent summit failures. But heads of government cannot for long appear impotent against Community problems. Decisions tend to be forced in summit spotlights.

Institutional Rivalry

The rise of the European Council can also create problems for other institutions, especially the Parliament whose specific advisory role involves examining Commission proposals to the Council of Ministers. Decisions made at the summit, especially when it supplants the Council of Ministers, can bypass Parliament. Summits also frustrate democratic procedures since they are extraconstitutional in scope and authority. They enshrine the exclusion of the public to important Community meetings. The substitution of private, intergovernmental summits for secret Council of Ministers' meetings is hardly a step forward. The two bodies contribute to what is called the "democratic deficit" of the

Community. The summits attract attention because their telegenic participants appear to be actually making decisions.[46] The Council of Ministers, a combined executive-legislative body, appears increasingly to be left only the role of preliminary consultation and agenda preparation for an intergovernmental, not a Community, procedure.

In early constitutional proposals and in the recent draft treaty proposed by the Parliament on European Union, the Council of Ministers became part of a bicameral legislature, with the Assembly/Parliament as the other part. In 1988, the *Economist* proposed a similar evolution.[47] Even if unrealistic, these ideas show a concept of the Council of Ministers as far from its present state as the dire predictions made for it because of the increasing role assumed by the European Council. The Council of Ministers, least changed of the EC institutions, now appears to be the least stable one because of differing views of what it should be.

THE COURT OF JUSTICE

The Court of Justice in Luxembourg is the only Community institution which, in operation, is completely divorced from the national governments (although it does have a direct relation to the national courts). It is also the most efficient and, by some measures, the most radical of all EC institutions in that it works without precedent in applying a supernational authority across twelve national legal structures.

Its judges are appointed by common agreement of the member governments but their deliberations and votes are secret and have never been challenged for national bias. There is no appeal from their judgments. The court, said one of its judges several years ago, "never gives political decisions but from time to time finds it necessary to remind politicians of what they have agreed to."[48]

The court—one of the four originial institutions of the Coal and Steel Community—has grown with the *acquis communitaire.* In the ECSC court there were six judges, increased to nine after the first enlargement and then to thirteen. Six advocates-general (originally two and then four until the third enlargement) present evidence and advisory opinions to the court. Both judges and advocates-general are named by agreement among the member states for renewable six-year terms, staggered at three-year intervals to avoid a complete replacement of the court at one time.

The court elects a President and also designates Presidents of the Chambers of the court which are smaller groups of judges assembled for preliminary hearings. In procedures, the court relies heavily on French judicial practice. The advocate-general is a direct adaptation of the *commissaire du gouvernement* who presents evidence before the *Conseil d'Etat*. But in the Court of Justice the procedures fall into two basic categories: direct actions, by which the court weighs the claims of an applicant and then listens to the defense before making a decision, and

Preliminary Rulings, in which the national courts ask the court a question concerning the interpretation or validity of a Community provision. For either type of action, the advocates-general prepare both a factual and legal analysis which cover legal doctrine, case law, and relevant national court decisions. This extensive brief follows preliminary stages where all sides in the case present first written and then oral arguments. Part or all of these two earlier stages may take place before a chamber or before the full court. An advocate-general presents both his analysis of the case and his proposal for a solution. After deliberation, in which the advocates-general do not participate, the court presents its opinion at a public session. The decision is served on the parties and is enforceable in all member states.

Functions of the Court

The Court of Justice has three functions: first, it is an administrative court concerned with the effects of Community regulations on national and legal persons of member countries. Various remedies may be sought here: annulment, judgment of the failure to act, or a judgment of illegality. Through the national courts, individuals may also bring actions involving Community law which may then be referred to the Court of Justice for Preliminary Rulings. Matters involving personnel of Community institutions also fall under this administrative court function.

The court is also a constitutional body when it rules on the respective rights and duties of Community institutions in their relations to each other and on the institutional balance between member states and the Community. Finally, the court is an international court because the treaties establishing the Community are pacts between member states and thus instruments of international law. Since the court also accepts cases brought by individuals, however, it recognized in one of its first cases that the "Community constitutes a new legal order of international law."[49] Failure of a member state to fulfil an obligation under the basic treaties can cause either another state or the Commission to seek judicial relief at the Luxembourg court. This legal standing of the Commission before an international court further illustrates this "new legal order" since the Commission is clearly neither an international organization in the traditional sense nor a nation-state, the two kinds of legal entities which normally appear before international tribunals.

The Court of Justice is not only the most efficient of Community institutions but also a quite radical one: the court directs the assimilation of Community law into the twelve legal systems of member states; it also produces a uniform system of interpreting Community law and itself constitutes the final stages of that system which begins in the national courts and from which there is no national appeal. In this way, the court achieves the most decisive step forward in construction of a supranational order.

Preliminary Rulings

In order to appreciate how this system works and why it is so important to the growth of the Community we must see how the basic treaties operate. They created rules for both member countries and for Community institutions. But the operation of these rules meant that individuals gain certain rights and obligations. In the first instance, these rights are protected in national courts which are thus required to apply Community law to their own citizens. Thus is Community law incorporated into twelve national systems. The national courts, in turn, function as Community courts when they apply, as they must, the laws and regulations of the Community. This is the legal linkage which ties the lowest national level of justice ultimately to Luxembourg and the court.

In one important case, the court firmly applied article 119 of the EEC treaty on equal pay for men and women. The court stated that courts in member countries must apply the article without awaiting either Community or national legislation.

Another famous case involved the export of a French liqueur, cassis, into Germany which barred the berry distillate because its alcohol content fell below the German standard. The court rejected this argument, affirming that national laws cannot be used, even when standards are reasonable, if the effect is to deny access to a product which meets the standards of another EC country.

The basic treaties gave detailed rules on this collaborative system of national and community justice. Preliminary Rulings are the heart of this collaboration. Lower national courts may, and supreme national courts must, refer to the Court of Justice any matter which raises a question of Community law. The Luxembourg court may only consider that Community aspect but there its judgment is supreme. It has no jurisdiction over national laws nor can it—within the context of Preliminary Rulings— assess their correspondence with Community law.[50]

The use of Preliminary Rulings has grown rapidly. From 1961 to 1966, only ten judgments were given, on average, each year. Ten years later, the number averaged between thirty and fifty. By the 1980s, the average was over one hundred a year. With this growth and the development of Community case law, the court altered its procedure to refer routine cases seeking Preliminary Rulings to a chamber rather than the full court.

What kinds of cases come before a chamber for this Preliminary Ruling procedure? Examples include specifying the meaning and scope of a Community regulation; determining if a provision of Community law applies to one or more national laws; and deciding which legal measures are governed by the Community and which by national law. In one interesting case (the "Hauer" ruling of 1979) the court confirmed that Community institutions have to protect fundamental rights but also that the institutions have the powers to lay down limitations on an individual's right of property. In this case the institution was the Commission and its right to forbid the use of land for growing grapes was confirmed by the court.

The Court of Justice proceeds efficiently, case by case, in making Community law an increasingly important factor in the twelve legal systems of member countries. Over the years the court has become very influential within its admittedly limited sphere involving what the basic treaties mean and what Community institutions may do.

Reform measures for the court, therefore, are usually limited to changes that adjust its jurisdiction accordingly, whenever other changes are proposed or enacted, as in the SEA, in the scope of the Community and the relations between its other institutions.[51] A subsidiary Court of First Instance was authorized in the SEA to take over some of the burden now on the Court of Justice. This new court will have the right to hear and make determinations, subject to appeal to the main court, on certain classes of actions involving natural and legal persons, but not matters brought by member states or by Community institutions or for Prelimiary Rulings.

EUROPEAN UNION

Reform of Community institutions is an idea as old as the effort at the first session of the ECSC assembly to write a constitution for Europe. More recently, reform has centered on two aspects of European Union, the term given in the early 1970s to the move toward a stronger successor to the European Community.

The first approach was taken by the member states after they recognized, following the 1973 enlargement, that forward movement toward integration had ceased. The arrival of Denmark, Ireland, and the United Kingdom not only failed to accelerate that integration but the larger Community experienced increased tensions when the British government threatened to withdraw one year after admission. Further, the Yom Kippur war and the oil embargo which followed disrupted members states' economies and postponed long-term thinking about Community goals. An earlier summit goal of economic and monetary union by 1980 was clearly unattainable.

The Tindemans Report

Community stagnation seemed to follow a period of national approaches to the social, fiscal, and monetary consequences of the energy turmoil.

The Community idea seemed adrift. Political leaders asked Belgian Prime Minister Leo Tindemans, at the 1974 summit, to discuss European Union with a range of people across Europe and then report back on its prospects. His report, issued early in 1976, set impressive but controversial goals: a phased approach to economic and monetary union, enhanced foreign policy coordination, and institutional rebalancing with a directly elected European Parliament matched with a more powerful European Council.

The Tindemans Report accurately portrayed the Community's weaknesses but in an inadvertent manner; its reception was both muted and divergent. Some blamed Tindemans for not addressing the most pressing problems of inflation, unemployment, and the environment. Other saw his economic proposals producing a two-class Europe, with the rich and powerful countries proceeding without regard to their weaker neighbors. Others said more vigorous reform was needed. The responses captured perfectly the mood of a divided and preoccupied Community.

The Tindemans Report was one part of the procession of steps, missteps, tangents, and restored direction which the Community has endured from Monnet and Schuman in 1950 to the 1992 deadline. Six years were to pass before an appropriate response was made to the report.

The Parliament Acts

Establishing a firm deadline to complete the internal market was a goal explicit in both the Paris and Rome treaties and thus has a long history. When the first Delors commission presented the 1985 White Paper on Completing the Internal Market, it responded not only to the call of the Community's own history but also to specific instructions by the European Council, the Community's highest political authority. The Council, in December 1982, had instructed the Council of Ministers to decide on the priority measures proposed by the Commission to reinforce the internal market. Eighteen months later, the European Council again asked the Council of Ministers to study how to abolish all police and customs formalities for people crossing internal Community borders.

At the same time that the European Council was concerned about the sluggish movement toward a single internal market, a second effort toward European union was developing as a consequence of direct elections to the European Parliament. A conviction soon developed among the new Euro-MPs that their first five-year term, which was to end in 1984, must address institutional problems or otherwise prove that a directly elected parliament would itself be judged a failed reform when reelections came in 1984. Leadership was assumed by a remarkable Italian, Altiero Spinelli, a former commissioner, and then a member of the Parliament elected as an independent on the Communist list. He chaired the Institutional Affairs Committee which carefully examined alternate reforms before proposing a draft treaty on European Union in 1983.[52] The Parliament passed the treaty by a wide margin the next year.

The draft treaty proposed the most sweeping changes in the European Community since the Rome Treaties took effect in 1958. A bicameral parliament would be matched with a European Council capable of action. Political cooperation would become more important and the national ministers less so. The national parliaments would be enlisted to bypass the national governments in the march toward a single market and an invigorated democratic structure. Spinelli's plan would also bypass the other Community institutions by being presented as a proposed treaty first to the 12 national parliaments which, as ratifiers of the basic treaties, could also presumably approve their amendment through this new treaty.[53]

The Spinelli Plan

If the Tindemans Report was finally dismissed as too timid and too oblique in facing European union, the Spinelli proposals were widely condemned as utopian doodling which no member government would support. But like the Tindemans Report, which mirrored Community indecision in its reception, the Spinelli plan had an effect different from that intended by the parliamentarians who wrote it. The member governments, aroused more by the internal dismay within EC institutions when nothing seemed capable of energizing the call for reform rather than by any vision of what that reform should entail, appointed its own study group, the Dooge committee.

Named for the Irish senator who chaired it, the Dooge committee produced a 1985 draft treaty which, not entirely by coincidence, was completed the same year Jacques Delors became the new and energetic Commission president. Upon approval by the 12 governments, the treaty—called the Single European Act—went into effect in 1987. Its modest reforms had the principal merit of implicit acceptance by the heads of member governments who named their personal representatives to write it. The Dooge committee demonstrated clearly once again that the national governments remain the ultimate determinants of what Community reform means.

The lack of progress toward European Union was thus the common source for both the Parliament's efforts and those of the European Council to relaunch the Community after the economic troubles of the 1970s and during a period of institutional malaise. The Draft Treaty induced the member countries, through the European Council, to find consensus in the Single European Act as a firebreak against more drastic changes sought by the Parliament.

Another Launching

The 1992 program, to take another strand of the history, represents not a constitutional reform of the kind intended by the Parliament and the European Council, but implementation of the long-established goal of a common market. In this way, the 1992 program was a third response to the doldrums of the 1970s. It was provoked, and is still led, by Commission President Delors, who embodies the same conviction behind the constitutional reforms: something was needed to relaunch the Community enterprise.

Thus 1992 and the Single European Act are quite different offspring of common ancestors: the SEA is a permanent treaty amendment while the 1992 program will eventually be fulfilled, if not precisely by December 31, 1992, then gradually, in smaller pieces, but with ultimate success.

There is one more important connection between the two: the goals of the 1992 program were explicitly but summarily included in the SEA and that treaty contains a number of changes in voting procedures relating to 1992.

The initial view of the SEA was that the member states had held reform to some modest and peripheral changes. The national governments seemed pleased that their leaders had given away little new authority to Brussels. But more careful study of the SEA brought resistance, especially in the national parliaments. Here it was recognized that important jurisdiction had already been given in agriculture, fisheries, and trade, not to the European Parliament which would have been bad enough, but to remote and collective decision making in "Brussels" (meaning the Commission). In fact, the SEA confirms a quite simple political fact: the heads of European governments, constituted in a quasi-Community institution called the European Council, hold the balance of power between national and Community institutions.

SEA Reforms

The SEA constituted more a second wind than a new start for a united Europe. But the institutional and internal market reforms of the late 1980s made clear that a genuine reinvigoration of the EC had begun with the arrival of Delors, the former French socialist finance minister and now committed Commission President.

Several important changes came from the new treaty, especially in institutional procedures. First, the SEA strengthens majority voting in the Council of Ministers especially in achieving the "internal market" by 1992.[54] Majority voting has been in the Council rules from the beginning of the Treaty of Rome but has seldom been important since the Luxembourg compromise. Renewed efforts toward completing the internal market became a specific justification for using qualified majority voting.

Second, the SEA gives the European Parliament an enhanced role in considering Commission proposals as well as a role in the admission of new member countries and in concluding agreements with nonmember countries. These rights, while important for the Parliament, tend to slow down the legislative process at the same time that qualified voting in the Council liberates it from the fear of certain vetoes.[55]

By the end of the second directly elected Parliament in June 1989, it was clear that the SEA had added significantly to the institution's workload. Its rules and institutional affairs committees proposed steps to speed up the Parliament's work, help it be a more efficient body, and put it in a more cooperative posture with both the Commission and the Council of Ministers. Even the modest reforms of the SEA eventually produced sharp and fearful reactions among the member states. Mrs. Thatcher's speech in Bruges, Belgium, in September 1988, sounded a warning to President Delors not to assume that the SEA meant full acceptance by all governments of his vision of an increasingly united Europe. For Mrs. Thatcher, the SEA meant liberation from old restraints on the free market, not the substitution of new ones from Brussels.

In response, Delors tried to smooth the institutional patterns for the post-1992 Community. He proposed "subsidiarity," a restatement of federalist principle, which would mean that no decisions or actions will be taken at a more central, that is, higher level of government than is necessary. It remains to be seen if this move will satisfy the critics of the activist president of the Commission.[56]

But not all of the fears about a more united Europe after 1992 come from Britain or even from those simply concerned about losing national sovereignty. A French survey showed that 58 percent of respondents were worried about a single market; only 33 percent were confident. A plurality (41 percent) also thought 1992 would aggravate French economic problems; agriculture was identified as the sector where France would be hurt most.[57] It seems possible that subsidiarity could mean more regional and local controls below the national level, a possible problem for unitary states like Britain and France.

How important the SEA will be judged after a few years depends on some or all of these factors:

1. Will the heads of government accept that Europe can only be important in the world if it is strong, and only strong if the European Council becomes, in effect, the Community's supreme governing body?

2. Is the Parliament's small step forward to be followed by a progression toward representative government in the Community?[58]

3. Will political cooperation eventually bind Community members into a reasonably coherent foreign policy on the basis of shared interests stronger than the ties which any one of them has with countries outside the Community?

4. Will the SEA suffice for the 1992 internal market to achieve the "free movement of goods, persons, services and capital" which the act foresees?

5. Will the SEA be followed by other incremental reforms or will it be seen as a final attempt to patch the Rome Treaties to be followed instead by the creation of a true Community constitution?

6. Will other events deflect the Community's concentration on its own development? For example, how would German reunification affect the Community economically and politically? Even if the danger of a united Germany is rooted in the fears of another age, problems of a single member considerably more powerful economically than the other larger members might be genuine.[59] A different problem would be that attention to the striking changes in eastern Europe distracts the Community from its own institutional development. For some, this distraction might be a useful tool to delay or discourage further progress under the SEA and the single market program.

7. Is the European Community an early form of what must become a true federation to survive or is it a confederation, comparable to the American states from 1781 to 1789, and destined to remain one?[60]

As is often the case, Jean Monnet deserves the last word. His *Memoirs* describe the efforts of 1973 to bring Europe to the next stage of joint political action. He recognized that new institutions were needed.[61] Once again the obstacles would become the means to progress. The failure of the Council of Ministers to make decisions meant that the heads of government must act instead. "No one," he wrote, "was challenging the sovereignty of the existing Community institutions; on the contrary, everything was now organized [with the agreement in principle on the European council] to strengthen their powers, make them work successfully and develop their potential . . . but they were not the institutions of a political federation of Europe. That would have to be established by a specific creative act which would require a further delegation of sovereignty. We should have to return again to the springs of power. . . ."[62]

Whether the Single European Act is the last draught from the old spring or the first from a new one is not yet clear.

NOTES

1. The last standard edition of these documents, issued in 1987, numbers over 1500 pages. An abridged edition of 500 pages is the present standard reference for the Community's basic documents. See *Treaties Establishing the European Communities* (Luxembourg: EC Publication Office, 1988). Same title and source for 1987 unabridged edition. See also Mauro Cappelletti, Monica Seccombe, and Joseph Weiler, eds., *Integration Through Law: Europe and the American Federal Experience* (Berlin: Walter de Gruyter, 1986), 106.

2. The number of commissioners has varied from nine to seventeen since a

single Commission for the three communities was created in 1967. Each member country names at least one commissioner and the larger countries, two.

3. Two commissioners set standards for longevity which may be difficult to surpass. Albert Coppé of Belgium started on the High Authority of the ECSC with Jean Monnet in 1952 and retired in 1972. His twenty years included five on the single Commission. Wilhelm Haferkampf of Germany lasted from the first single commission in 1967 until 1985. Several other commissioners served over ten years, including Claude Cheysson of France who served on four commissions.

4. To make this prohibition financially feasible, commissioners have been well paid from the beginning. In 1989 they earned well over $100,000 a year, slightly more than the head of government in Germany, normally judged the most generous employer of all EC countries. The requirement not to seek or accept instructions from "any other body" (Merger Treaty of 1965, art. 10) is designed to insulate commissioners especially from past or future employers.

5. Fifty-eight men have served as commissioners since 1967 when a single Commission began. Thirty-three were previously involved in national politics, in many cases as ministers, just before their Brussels appointment. Twelve of these thirty-three had also been involved in some Community institution, mostly as a commissioner of one of the three separate communities or as a member of the European Parliament. Of the remaining twenty-five commissioners, nine had been diplomats, four each had been in business and teaching, three each in law and journalism, and the rest in other professions or trades.

By education, these fifty-eight men had been predominantly trained in law, in some cases along with economics or politics. Graduates in economics and public administration followed, with the remainder in a variety of disciplines (military school, agricultural and forestry colleges, history, medicine, and chemical engineering). Each of these last-named produced one commissioner each. (In 1988, Greece named a woman commissioner for the 1989-94 term. She, and a French woman in the same second Delors Commission, became the first women in the Commission's history. By comparison, in the 1988 Parliament 85 of the 518 members were women.)

6. It is evident that the problem of nationalism is not diminishing but may be in a resurgent phase. One cause seems to be the receding number of World War II participants involved in political life. That war gave the idea of a united Europe its most vigorous push. Another is the increasingly painful conflict between national and Community governments in fields like agriculture and taxation.

7. See section below on the Single European Act and note 55.

8. Confusion naturally arises when two institutions of the Community have similar names and overlapping functions. The Council of Ministers is, by treaty, a full Community institution, with specified powers. It is usually called, in shorthand, the Council. The regular meeting of the heads of government or of state of member countries has been officially called the European Council since the Single European Act. It is still frequently called the EC or Community "summit." For more on the summit history and function, see "The European Council" below. For a list of summits, see appendix B.

9. See appendix A for the Commission's division of responsibilities and the directorates-general.

10. There were 9854 Commission staff in Brussels in early 1989, 2349 in Luxembourg, 2115 in the research centers, 157 in EC courtries (principally in the information offices), and 414 in other countries (principally in the Delegations). In addition, there are several thousand temporary and contract employees, principally in language services.

11. EC has a single personnel system covering all institutions.

12. *The European Commission and the Administration of the Community* (Luxembourg: EC Publications Office, 1989), 54-61.

13. In all institutions, informal conversation among staff of several nationalities usually is in French or English, but all official meetings and documents are subject to the nine-language requirements and its costs. Written documents in the Court of Justice may be provided in any language which is official in any member state (at present, a total of ten languages). The court thus deals in one more language than the other institutions which recognize nine "official" languages, dropping Gaelic which, however, retains its status both with the court and as a language in which the treaties were written and signed.

14. Several publications cover the history of the European schools. This research is summarized in Yves Conrad, *Jean Monnet et Les Debuts de la Fonction Publique Européenne.* (Louvain: CIACO, 1989).

15. Most of these special EC committees result from Commission or Council decisions requiring certain meetings between constituents and Community institutions. Examples include the Economic Policy Committee, many agricultural advisory committees, the Standing Committee on Consumers' Consultative Committee, and the Standing Committee on Employment.

16. Monnet's Committee, known by the acronym ACUSE, is described in Pascal Fontaine, *Le Comité d'Action Pour les Etats-Unis d'Europe* (Lausanne: Fondation Jean Monnet, 1974). Besides the institutional committees of the treaties and the private sector lobbies, some political subdivisions of member countries now seek representation in Brussels. Seven of the nine German *laender* (states) had Brussels offices by 1987, partly because of fears that Bonn does not, or cannot for constitutional reasons, represent them well in EC matters.

17. The models for these institutional committees seem to have been France and Italy which have had national social and economic committees since before World War II. The Benelux countries started similar national committees shortly after the war. Greece had a similar committee during its 1967-74 dictatorship but not before or since. Portugal has a comparable institution while Spain is starting one by regions. Britain and Germany have no counterparts in their national structures but they participate in the Community's committees.

18. See note 55 below for details on how SEA affects these procedures.

19. The race between Strasbourg and Luxembourg had comic aspects although it represents clearly the serious problem of a single site. Luxembourg worked day and night for months on a new plenary hall for the Parliament but the result did not please members who preferred Strasbourg for its location and amenities if they had to choose between the cities. The Luxembourg building, which was not designed to accommodate the Iberian countries, has been used only once for a Parliament session. Otherwise it remains unused by the Community, another monument to the fruitless quest for a single home for the European institutions.

20. Members received an allowance for clerical and research assistance which is usually devoted to constituency services or to contributions toward staff services provided on a pool basis by the political group. Group chairmen (comparable to the party caucus chairmen in Congress) and other members of the enlarged bureau usually have secretarial services provided by either the group or the Parliament in the official working places. But neither committee nor inter-parliamentary delegation chairmen have separate staffs. The only personal staff members in the congressional sense are provided for the president and vice presidents of all institutions; these are classified as "temporary" employees who do not have job tenure but otherwise receive the same benefits. Political group employees have the same "temporary" status but many spend an entire career in the Parliament in such positions.

21. A Code of Conduct for members is part of the Parliament's rules of procedure. It does not restrict outside work (as the treaties restrict commissioners and the staff regulations limit staff activities) but the code does require public disclosure if a member's business, trade, or profession is ever the subject of parliamentary action. Enforcement of the code is generally up to members themselves and their political constituencies.

22. By 1989, Belgian private enterprise, encouraged by its government and aided by a vote of a parliamentary committee, had facilities under construction near the Berlaymont which might help the Parliament reduce its travels. A Parliament resolution of October 1985 authorized its bureau to negotiate a contract in the Belgian private sector for occasional meetings in Brussels. In the delicate negotiations which followed, care was taken that member governments were not foreclosed from their treaty right to determine the seat of the EC institutions. Nonetheless, the French government, which began a new EP building in Strasbourg to counter the Belgians, filed suit against the Parliament for overstepping its authority in passing the resolution. It was unsuccessful. President Mitterrand added his voice to other Frenchmen opposed to leaving Strasbourg but history seemed to be turning slowly toward Brussels as the capital of Europe.

23. See chapter 4 for more on ACP countries.

24. This is in contrast to the high value placed in the U.S. Congress on individualism (versus party loyalty) and on fidelity only to the electors (as judged by the members of Congress themselves).

There are occasional issues and procedures which break down group solidarity and illustrate the national divisions, like fishery, dairy, and similar questions. In some political groups members meet first in national party groups before the whole group meets. Socialists are known for their sharp divisions among the many national components while other groups, especially the Conservatives and Gaullists, are more cohesive, probably because of one dominant national element.

The plenary seating arrangement puts the Euro-MPs in political groups, not country delegations (before March 1958, they sat in alphabetical order). Neither seniority, in the congressional sense, nor simple majorities are as important in the Parliament as party strength which is expressed through proportional representation. The principle operates in all of the national elections of Community member states (except for most of the British constituencies which have American-type electoral districts with majority candidates winning). Proportional representation also governs the selection of committee and interparliamentary delegation chairmen, quaestors, and almost all other groups composed of members.

25. Socialists, for example, as the largest group, choose first for chairmen of committees and also get more committee chairmanships. Election of the Parliament's president is by majority vote but the groups, in fact, form coalitions to win this vote since no group has ever had a majority of any Parliament's members. The center-right parties did this for the first and third presidencies (which are for half of the Parliament's five-year term) while the second president was a socialist who won when the center-right coalition broke down.

The election totals given in the section on the Parliament are from July 1989 right after the third direct election and subject to minor corrections.

26. For more on this revision attempt, see the sections below on European Union and the Single European Act.

27. The three federations were the Confederation of Socialist Parties of the European Community; the European Liberals and Democrats; and the European People's Party (Christian Democrats). There are also less formal ties between Conservative and Christian Democratic parties in the European Democratic Union which includes non-EC parties. For an account of the origins of both these federations and of the Parliament's political groups, see *Forging Ahead: Thirty Years of the European Parliament* (Luxembourg: European Parliament, 1982, 1989).

28. The 1984 and 1989 participation was similar but slightly lower, with approximately 59 percent and 57 percent, respectively. In these direct elections, voter participation was still considerably higher than the comparable congressional elections, but lower than EC national elections.

29. Enlargement and direct elections increased the size of the Parliament which originally (1953-58) had only 78 members. In the first single Assembly, the number increased in 1958 to 142. With the first enlargement in 1973, there were 198 members. At the first direct election, 410 members were selected which increased to 434 with Greece's entry. The present number of 518—increased from 434 with the arrival in 1986 of Portugal and Spain—seems likely to remain stable since no other countries are under serious consideration for Community membership.

30. The descriptions of MEPs and their numbers cover only the 434 members directly elected in 1984. They exclude the 24 Portuguese and 60 Spanish delegate members who were first appointed in 1987. The educational and occupational background of the Euro-MPs was derived from the *Official Handbook of the European Parliament* (Luxembourg: European Parliament, 1984), 289; for more on the characteristics of the MEPs, see *Forging Ahead.*

31. The proper name, since the 1965 merger treaty, is "Council of European Communities" which itself replaced the term "Special Council of Ministers" (ECSC Treaty) and simply the "Council" in the two treaties of Rome. The Council itself uses the longer title but almost everyone else uses "Council of Ministers" or "Council" when the context is clear. With the SEA designation of the European Council as a meeting of the heads of government, it is safest to use the term "Council of Ministers" to avoid confusion.

32. Quoted in Monnet, *Memoirs,* 381.

33. Ibid.

34. Ibid., 483.

35. Robert Marjolin, *Memoirs, 1911-1986* (London: Weidenfeld and Nicholson, 1989), 349-51. Translation by the author from the earlier French edition. Marjolin writes as an admirer of Monnet, but without the latter's attachment to a supranational European Community. He believed, for example, that the Commission's proper role was as a mediator between national and EC policies.

36. See Guy de Bassompierre, *Changing the Guard in Brussels* (Washington: Center for Strategic and International Studies, 1988), 48. This is an interesting inside account of how the Council of Ministers and the Presidency operate, including political cooperation. National civil servants like Bassompierre can also master EC ways—from secondment to the Commission or by assignment to their Permanent Representatives in Brussels—but these assignments are dwarfed by the tasks and staff involved in preparing and carrying out a member country's six-month EC presidency.

37. See Paul Henri Spaak, *The Continuing Battle: Memoirs of a European* (Boston: Little, Brown, 1971) on the origins of the customs union of the Benelux countries and the fear of small EEC countries of Franco-German domination. See Monnet, *Memoirs,* 327, on the "blocking minority" of small countries at the Schuman conference in 1950. This problem did not end with the Treaty of Rome. It reappeared, for example, in the early 1960s when British membership again became an issue. The Fouchet Plan on political cooperation proposed by de Gaulle faced continued opposition by, among others, the Dutch who continued to fear a French-German "tandem." On this point, see Hans von der Groeben, *The European Community: The Formative Years* (Luxembourg: EC Publications Office, 1987), 112-16. See article 149 of the EEC Treaty for voting provisions and below, on how the Single European Act affects them.

38. See the Eurobarometer series of opinion polls conducted by the Commission, especially nos. 17-25 (1982-86), which consistently show the Benelux countries leading all EC members in positive responses to Community membership in general and to their own countries' welfare in particular.

39. The small states which met in Philadelphia had fears similar to those of the Benelux countries 165 years later. The small states feared a popularly elected Congress would allow larger states to dominate them. The small versus large state split was the greatest threat to the U.S. constitutional convention in 1787. In Europe, in 1952, the issue did not have that same dramatic character since the Schuman Treaty was not the same far-reaching document which the summer of 1787 produced. If one imagines that a genuine constitutional convention for the European Community still lies ahead, it is possible that a similar small versus large member country split could arise. A bicameral legislature with one body representing the member countries and the other the population could be a solution for Europe also. The Council and European Parliament are the obvious candidates for these respective roles.

40. For the de Gaulle period, see Monnet, *Memoirs,* 437ff. When Monnet finally disbanded his Action Committee for the United States of Europe (ACUSE) in 1975, he justified the action by the creation of the European Council which he believed ACUSE had helped establish as the Community's highest political body. See *Memoirs,* 515-17.

41. The full designation is "heads of government or state" to allow for the situation in France where the president, as the head of state, also attends. In all other EC countries, the head of state is a nonpolitical position. Here the shorter version should be understood to include France also.

42. In the EC grammar, "political cooperation" means the coordination of foreign policies of the member countries. For the early development of the summits which led to the European Council as an institution, see Andrew Duff, "The Development of Summit Meetings," in *European Studies* 22, 1977.

43. For more on the development of the European Council in its role in European political cooperation, see chapter 8.

44. The SEA consists of specific titles and a final act, which together form a treaty; these titles contain amendments to earlier treaties, especially the Treaty of Rome, and a new treaty on foreign policy coordination (see chapter 8). The final act contains declarations for the record by the intergovernmental conference which produced the SEA, and by some of the participating governments and institutions. For the text, see *Bulletin of the European Communities, Supplement 2/86,* "Single European Act" (Brussels: Commission of the European Communities, 1986). See also the section below on the SEA.

45. The order of rotation for the EC presidency is: Belgium, Denmark, Germany, Greece, Spain, France, Ireland, Italy, Luxembourg, Netherlands, Portugal, and the United Kingdom. See also Appendix B.

46. The exact decision-making process of the European Council is not clear partly because its rules of operation and even its authority are not specified anywhere, even after the elevation of the summit to a quasi-institution in the Single European Act. For example, if the Council of Ministers is unable to reach agreement on a matter and it is referred to the European Council, does the latter proceed by unanimity or by the majority voting rules of the Council? (In December 1989, at the Strasbourg summit, an 11-1 majority agreed on the social charter for the internal market and the call for a 1990 intergovernmental conference for a treaty on monetary union, in both cases despite Mrs. Thatcher's opposition. But this was a political, not a constitutional, overriding.) Also, when exactly does the European Council act as the Council of Ministers and can it then propose specific actions to the Commission, a Council of Ministers' right under the treaties? Finally, will the formalized European Council in fact behave differently from its earlier role as umpire or from constituting the final authority when other institutions deadlock? At worst, the European Council could revert to serve only as an intergovernmental arbiter of Community disputes.

47. See "Don't Forget the Politics," *Economist* (July 17, 1988): 13-14. The earlier proposals from the two institutions were different both from each other and from more traditional bicameral legislatures. For a summary of the early plan from the 1952/53 ad hoc constitutional committee of the ECSC assembly, see Monnet, *Memoirs,* 382, 394. For the Parliament's 1983 draft treaty on European union, see Roland Bieber, Jean Paul Jacqué, and Joseph H. H. Weiler, eds., *An Ever Closer Union: A Critical Analysis of the Draft Treaty Establishing European Union* (Luxembourg: EC Publications Office, 1985).

48. Judge Andreas Donner, in a speech entitled "The Political Function of the Judge," presented before the legal faculty of the University of Freiburg i. Br., Germany, April 28, 1980.

49. Cited in *The Court of Justice of the European Communities* (Luxembourg: EC Publications Office, 1975), 5.

50. But it can take action for failure of a member state to fulfill a Community obligation under a procedure initiated by either another member state or by the Commission.

51. The Tindemans Report on European Union, for example, implies that the court's jurisdiction should simply be adjusted to any treaty changes since the Community already constitutes a functioning "state of the law." For the reports see *Bulletin of the European Communities 1/76.*

52. Monnet, *Memoirs,* 382, 394-95. See also *Ever Closer Union,* 7-17, for more on the Treaty background and the Tindemans Report.

53. See *Ever Closer Union,* 161-75.

54. The 1992 program and the Single European Act are often confused. The first is a complicated series of steps to achieve an old goal, the common or the internal market. The second is a permanent amendment to the Rome Treaties with important institutional consequences. For more on the internal market—sometimes called the single market—see chapter 4 on trade.

55. The following abbreviated schematic shows how Community legislation, previously a matter largely of Commission proposals being considered by the Council of Ministers, now has a larger input from the Parliament because of SEA changes:

Commission	Council of Ministers	Parliament
1. Makes proposal.	2. Adopts Common Position (CP) on Commission's proposal (QM) after getting Parliament's opinion.	
		3. If within 3 months, Parliament approves or fails to act, Council may adopt CP but if Parliament amends or rejects CP then:
	4. If CP rejected by Parliament Council may approve it only unanimously* or	
	5. If CP is amended by Parliament, then:	
6. Commission examines EP amendments and adopts	7. If Commission disapproves EP amendments, Council may	

Commission	Council of Ministers	Parliament
them in re-examina-tion or rejects them.	approve them only unanimously or Council may unanimously amend re-examined Commission proposal or,	
	8. by QM, may adopt re-examined Com-mission proposal.*	

Abbreviations: QM: Qualified Majority, EP: European Parliament, CP: Common Position

*If Council does not act within specified time limits, the proposal lapses. N.B. Excluded from Qualified Majority (QM) voting in the Council of Ministers under the SEA are: a) Any directive affecting the rights and interests of employed persons; b) Harmonization of legislation concerning all indirect taxes, including VAT, required for the 1992 internal market deadline; c) Legislation involving the freedom of movement of persons. These exceptions mean that each Member state has a veto on these matters when they come up in the Council of Ministers. In October 1988, the Parliament rejected for the first time a Common Position of the Council, requiring the latter to proceed unanimously on the measure.

56. See Delors speech, also at Bruges, on October 17, 1989, for a typical example of the Commission president's thinking.

57. Le Monde-RTL survey in *Le Monde* (March 13, 1989).

58. Two innovative interinstitutional meetings take place under the auspices of the Parliament. Its president hosts an informal monthly lunch for the Commission and Council of Ministers' presidents, the only time these three institutional leaders meet. An informal interinstitutional committee on the SEA was established in 1987 at the suggestion of Karlheinz Neunreither, a senior EP official. It has become an effective means for coordinating solutions to some of the institutional problems which the treaty reform produced.

59. A Germany composed of the present Federal Republic and the German Democratic Republic would exceed the other three EC largest members (Britain, France, Italy) by a population factor which might stretch the present system of parity among the four with equal representation in the Commission, Council, and Parliament. Taking France, the smallest of the big four with 55-million population, as the base of 100 percent, the present Federal Republic of Germany would go from 110 percent of French population to 128 percent if joined to East Germany. Spain, the next largest EC member after the big four, with a 39-million population, would be about half the size of a reunited Germany of 77 million. (Spain counts as a large member by having two commissioners, but as a middle-size one in the Council, where it has eight votes in the qualified majority system, compared to ten for the big four, and in the Parliament where it has 60 members compared to 81 for the four largest countries). These would seem to be manageable disruptions.

60. For more on the nature of the EC union and its possibilities for development, see Cappeletti, *Integration Through Law*. By the early 1990s, institutional pressures for reform were building again. A conference on monetary union became the forum of choice for these efforts.

61. Monnet avoided the debate about federalism; in fact, he avoided most debates about high principles, choosing instead a pragmatism which still irritates the federalist believers.

62. Monnet, *Memoirs*, 509.

4

Trade

Europe will rediscover the leading role which she used to play in the world and which she lost because she was divided.
—Jean Monnet to Konrad
Adenauer, 1950 (*Memoirs*, p. 310)

Jean Monnet believed that the nation-states of Europe must be replaced in this century with a superior form of organization.[1] That view is embodied most clearly in the European Community as trader. In no other field has elimination of national barriers among Community members been so complete. In no other field has the Community found such consistent and growing success. And in no other field of Community activity has European integration put itself on such a dramatic course as that embodied by the 1992 internal market deadline.

The Community's very origin came, as the history of the institutions shows, in the plan to turn "what divided France from Germany—that is, the industries of war—into a common asset."[2] Those industries of coal and steel became the first center of the Community's trading vocation. The Rome Treaties of 1957, which enlarged and extended the Coal and Steel Community, also expanded the successful experience of the original six as world traders. Community trade was built, in these formative years, on a heavy industrial base; on an intelligent, hard-working, but conservative labor and management force; and on a technology of considerable competence but declining innovation. The European Community became a prodigious world trader. It dwarfs the United States in its trading dimensions. It buys more from our country than we sell anywhere else and sells more to us than any other U.S.

trading partner.[3] Yet what the Community buys from us is only 8 percent of all its imports. Its success in trade is illustrated by these figures: The Community averaged 13 percent annual growth in inter-EC trade and 10 percent growth in its extra-EC trade in the 1976-85 decade.

Foreign trade is much more central to the economy of the European Community than it is for the American economy. The Community imports annually goods representing nearly 12 percent of its Gross Domestic Product (GDP); it exports goods representing about the same percentage of its GDP. This is more than 50 percent higher on the export side and about 25 percent higher on the import side as compared to the United States. According to OECD historical studies, these percentages are relatively stable with both imports and exports rising slightly as a percentage of GDP for the Community over the past ten years. For the United States exports have been stable over ten years but imports grew slightly as a GDP percentage (see table 4.4).

FOREIGN COMPETITION

Yet while integration proceeds in the internal market, it is in its foreign markets that the European Community feels increasingly less able to compete. This self-perception of weakness has a solid foundation. The Community has lost preeminent positions in several major export sectors to the mid-level technology and marketing skills of several Asian countries. Cameras, most consumer electronics, and smaller computers are increasingly seen as Asian specialities which are unlikely to revert to European (or American) manufacture. Automobiles have also become a specialty of several of the Pacific countries, although in Europe import restrictions, national pride, and local service networks combine to hold foreign penetration in the EC countries to below the one-third share they have in U.S. markets.

In the mid-1980s when the U.S. dollar was grossly overvalued, Europeans enjoyed renewed success in exporting to the United States. A surge of European Community manufactures, including autos, allowed profitable production to continue at home despite the Japanese (and later, Korean) competition both in American and other third country markets. Meanwhile, several European auto makers collaborated with their Asian competitors to introduce new manufacturing techniques in joint ventures in both established and new European auto plants. But the 1992 single market will almost certainly arrive before EC auto makers are prepared for the flood of Asian imported autos which the United States has faced for years. The European consumer may benefit but the costs of a single market will have to be measured in terms beyond lower prices. The new market will disrupt old trading patterns, encourage new enterprises, displace both workers and enterprises, and broadly remake the economic and, ultimately, the political patterns of the 12-member European Community. The single market may also recast the Community's place in the world trading picture by emphasizing its strengths and limiting or removing its weaknesses through enhanced internal competition. The result should be a more vigorous community as a global trader which may mean more competition for the Unites States.

It is not always recognized on either side of the Atlantic that the Community and the United States, two major trading powers, are natural competitors for each other's market and for those in third countries. They are condemned to compete.

But if the Community and the United States cannot cooperate too closely, they can also agree that they must each find solutions to productivity and competitiveness problems in a world trading structure which they no longer dominate. As they once struggled for domination, these two preeminent trading partners must now compete for second place in many industrial and consumer goods sectors.

THE INTERNAL MARKET

Three aspects of the Community's trading patterns must be distinguished for their differing economic and political consequences: intra-Community trading among the twelve; trade with the United States; and trade with the rest of the world.

Like the United States, the Community forms a mass market of several hundred million consumers with high purchasing power and a voracious appetite for goods, including those imported from other countries. Yet the Community is still some distance from being a "United States of Europe" in terms of its internal trade. The EC manufacturer lacks, for example, anything approaching the uniformity of consumer taste, the market size, or the ease of communication which define the American market. The Community markets are still sharply delineated by national and language divisions based on centuries of tradition, by fierce pride in local suppliers, and by conservative buying habits. Further, the Community still has many internal barriers to trade which never existed among the United States. These nontariff barriers range from custom clearances, to exchange and capital restrictions, to different health and environmental standards.

Three decades after the creation of a "common" market, the Community began a relaunching of the battle for its completion in a 1985 White Paper which listed 285 national barriers to internal trade—many created since the Treaty of Rome—and proposals to eliminate them by 1992. This effort to complete what is now called the "internal market" became, in the late 1980s, the test of fidelity to the idea of a European Community. The number of these barriers is not very great—compared to those already removed—but those which remain are very close to the heart of national identity in a modern trading society: taxes, border controls, government procurement and banking, insurance, and other business services. These barriers must eventually fall, or the Community may fail. The struggle over the internal market is truly and finally the test of integration.

The growth of the Community's institutions followed the lines of least resistance. National hostility to political and military integration led pro-European forces to move toward economic and, later, monetary cooperation. The Rome Treaties foresaw, with somewhat clouded vision, an elimination of all restrictions on trade among the member countries which would allow a flourishing new age of economic growth and partnership. Atomic energy would fuel this new era and political integration would eventually flow from the positive consequences of a single, powerful European economy.

Thirty years after the Rome Treaties went into effect, it is possible to assess their success in moving toward this integration. Only part of this assessment involves internal trade since it was also an original goal of the Economic Community to make Europe function more effectively as a world trader by making its industries more efficient, its workers more productive, and its products better conceived and marketed outside the relatively small and compact universe of the original six EEC members. But logically prior to this goal was the need to eliminate barriers between Community members and to create around them a common tariff barrier to form a single market for the outside producer and a single producer for the outside world.

A good measure of the considerable success achieved in three decades is the percentage of intra-Community trade within the total trade of member countries. In 1958, the original six members traded with each other, in both imports and exports, at a rate of 38.1 percent of their combined total trade. By 1987, this figure grew to 54 percent. For the EC-12 the comparable figures are 33.8 percent in 1958 and 58.4 percent in 1987. For the United Kingdom, the shift was even more dramatic. In 1958, Britain imported only 20.4 percent of its goods from the eleven other EC countries. By 1985 this figure grew to 44.3 percent. Comparable U.K. export figures are 20.3 percent in 1958 and 46.2 percent in 1985.[4]

One conclusion is that the Community has succeeded in tying its member countries closer together by important alterations in trading practices. These dry trade numbers mean, in sociocultural terms, that Germans were buying twice as much in woolens, scotch whisky, and other British products in 1987 as a percentage of their total imports as they did in 1958. The British, similarly, bought over three times as many German cars, machine tools, and wines in 1987 as they did in 1958, again as a percentage of total imports. The British and the Germans know each other, in consumer terms, two to three times better now than they did at the start of the Community. Comparable, if not quite so dramatic, changes mark the trading relations of all Community member countries with each other.

The initial assessment of intra-Community trade, therefore, is that the Community has succeeded quite well in reducing internal barriers and national prejudices, compared to those existing before 1958. But close behind comes another conclusion: 30 years have produced neither the common market which the Rome Treaties anticipated nor the investment and other decisions needed to support that market which now extends to 12 member countries. Evidence for this is the major effort underway until 1992 (or however long it ultimately takes) to eliminate many barriers, including some created since 1958, which still make the Community twelve different marketplaces and twelve different productive structures.

Background of the 1992 White Paper

In December 1982, the twenty-fifth anniversary year of the Rome Treaties, the European Council undertook a major effort to complete the internal market. Almost every summit meeting since then has restated this goal. Identifying, analyzing, and eliminating every important restriction initially involved a major Commission staff effort to compile nearly three hundred procedures, policies, and regulations of the national governments. These were listed in a June 1985 White Paper whose appearance closely followed the arrival of a new Commission under the presidency of Jacques Delors. A key portfolio assignment gave responsibility for carrying out this paper's goals to Lord Cockfield, a United Kingdom nominee who had extensive business experience but whose background gave no hint that he would pursue the elimination of these internal trade barriers with a single-mindedness which amazed his Commission colleagues and apparently dismayed his sponsor, British Prime Minister Margaret Thatcher.

The White Paper listed each obstacle with a date for both Commission and Council action for each of the seven years ending in 1992. These barriers consist of the continuing physical, technical, and fiscal obstacles to the "freedom of movement of goods, persons, services and capital" in the words of an amendment added in 1986 to the EEC treaty by the Single European Act (SEA). Successful completion of this program by its 1992 deadline "will be the Community's greatest single achievement" according to the Commission. It will also provide a 5 percent gain in its Gross Domestic Product, a 6 percent cut in consumer prices, and produce efficiencies in public sector purchasing. From 2 to 5 million new jobs may be created.[5]

By 1990, five years after the goal was announced, it was clear that the 1992 program, whether wisely or not, had become a measure of the vitality, even the viability of the entire Community.

Resilient Nationalism

Most Europeans, and many others who have followed Community integration, may have thought that ending internal barriers was what the whole venture was about and that it had been agreed to, without need for further amendment, in the 1957 treaty. What happened, or did not happen, in the intervening years to make a new declaration necessary and to establish, over nine more years, another timetable on the internal trade of the member countries?

The answer is that nationalism was and is still stronger and more resilient than the European movement anticipated. When economic troubles came, as they did in force in the 1970s and 1980s, the member governments thought first of protecting their own economies (and their voters) and then, if at all, about a united Europe. Even with a renewed commitment to ending internal barriers and a very specific list of these barriers to be acted upon by 1992, betting in Brussels is that the deadline will not be fully met. But most of it will be, and most of it on or near the December 31, 1992 deadline.

An anecdote illustrates the problem. In Italy, it is said, the customs service asked for three hundred more officers to carry out the Community program to simplify customs procedures at its borders. Hiring more national officials to reduce customs regulations only insures that the national bureacracy, as measured in terms of jobs, incomes, and careers, outweighs the Community on the political scales. The anecdote has the ring of truth whether or not it is historically accurate. And the problems are not limited to Italy or any other single EC country. There are about 15,000 national customs officers in member countries. Will all of them face disruption of careers if the internal frontier posts end in 1992? Will all of these officials be needed at the EC external frontiers? National politicians will be asked these questions. The administrative anguish from 1992 will be felt throughout the Community.

The EC treaties had always made freer movement within the member states an important goal. But its achievement depended not only on removing customs posts and speeding truck transit across borders but also involved the less visible borders which affect industrial standards, internal labor migration, professional qualifications, comparability of university and other training—all matters involving fundamental national prerogatives.

Physical Barriers

The most obvious national barriers to trade are physical ones—border crossings and international air and seaports. These are addressed in the first section of the White Paper in proposals to either eliminate national border inspections in favor of Community-wide rules or to move the inspection points away from borders to internal points of use, sale, or service of the goods involved. For those committed to Europe's integration, nothing is more ludicrous than cars and trucks lined up at the borders between Community member countries or people standing in a customs or passport line at an airport in one EC country after a short flight from another one.

But even with the 1992 program in operation, national priorities intrude. One example, which is not anecdotal, involves the United Kingdom. A US$28-million building is being planned by Her Majesty's Customs Service for London's Waterloo Station to examine travelers leaving the high-speed rail service connecting France and England through the English channel tunnel now under construction. The tunnel is planned for completion in 1993 or shortly after the proposed end of all customs barriers between EC countries. Does the U.K. government have plans not revealed to the Community about the 1992 deadline? Or is the British customs bureaucracy simply proceeding without taking account of the Community program?

Besides employment for customs officers, there are many reasons for national authorities to cling to inspection rights at their borders. National laws still govern immigration, terrorism, drug controls, and other police functions. Until the Community is given authority in these fields, or until there is better harmonization of national laws, this kind of justification for border controls is persuasive. Unfortunately, there are still dozens of national provisions which directly contradict the Community's mandate of liberating the internal market and which are maintained only through tradition, for fiscal reasons or as thinly disguised protection of national interests. These national laws, especially on taxation, constitute the principal justification for border controls, especially the costly delays of commercial shipments by truck.

Border Controls

The Commission's basic document on this problem cites both economic and political reasons for removing the physical barriers. For the political impact of border controls on Europe's citizens, the White Paper says that "there is no area in which progress, where it can be made, would be more visible or more directly relevant to the aims, ambitions and vision of the Community."

There is a quiet conviction in the Berlaymont that the doubters are wrong and that the timetable in the White Paper can be met. As the 1992 program proceeded within Community institutions, the pace increased, accelerated by the majority voting in the SEA. To produce an important directive on machinery safety took 12 months under majority voting while it had taken the Community nearly six years to accept unanimously the first EC standard on lawnmower noise!

Technical Barriers

The removal of technical and fiscal barriers, the second and third areas delineated in the White Paper, is more complicated than removing customs posts. The Commission has proposed harmonizing or eliminating many rules involving consumer health, public procurement, and construction and industrial standards which inhibit intra-Community trading. Freer movement of capital and access to better financial services are major elements in the EC proposals on technical barriers. These changes will allow banks and financial institutions from other EC countries, and perhaps non-EC countries as well, to operate in any EC country if they meet the standards of any one member country.

Restrictions on labor and the professions are also covered under technical barriers and promise to be among the most divisive issues of the 1992 plan. A special provision in the Single European Act protects national sovereignty regarding rules for the professions precisely because of the national sensitivities on the matter. Determining labor policies and judging how doctors, lawyers, and architects are trained and qualified have been national matters for centuries. Yielding to Brussels' standards can come only after many discussions, and undoubtedly, disputes, some of which will extend both beyond 1992 and, perhaps, the clear competencies of Brussels.

At its heart, the 1992 program is a formidable political undertaking with its goal the creation of a new level of governmental authority. Mrs. Thatcher is clearly right in maintaining that national sovereignty is jeopardized by the plan which certainly cannot be achieved without pain. Most of the suffering will be in the national capitals. In September 1989, the Commission reported that nearly half of the White Paper proposals had been definitively adopted by the Community. More than 90 percent of the original proposals had been formally proposed by the Commission. But only a handful had been implemented through legislation or other national action in the twelve member states.[6]

Gradually, the internal market is becoming a code word for making or breaking the European Community as a supranational entity. With physical barriers, the problem is convincing national authorities that the controls now made at the borders can be made as well or better internally or at the Community's exterior borders. But removing the technical barriers and the taxation obstacles demands what the White Paper calls "a radical change of attitude."

Health and environmental standards, sometimes representing cultural differences as well, are a major obstacle here. A German law, dating from the sixteenth century, for example, effectively prevented any other country from exporting beer into the Federal Republic. The Commission succeeded in 1987, after several years of litigation, in obtaining a favorable ruling from the Court of Justice, overturning the national law.

German brewers, however, planned a major campaign to support consumer resistance to the court decision. Whether it succeeds may depend on how strongly the "renationalization" of the Community proceeds. There are already pressures within Germany to resist Brussels not only on beer but also on more important matters.

The Community may ultimately lack both the will and the resources to contest all barriers. For when the German brewers insist that their medieval law which allows only water, barley, hops, and yeast in the brew is a health matter, they have broad support even outside Germany for the view that belonging to the European Community should not mean elimination of all cultural differences. Where culture ends and trade barriers begin is sometimes a political matter as the dispute over beer making shows.

Public Procurement

Public procurement—the purchase of goods and services for local and national governments or entities—is the most complicated and politically hazardous field of technical barriers, even dwarfing the consumer health disputes. It is a principle of public administration which most citizens accept that government should shop as efficiently as the most astute consumer. Yet it also seems evident to taxpayers in Community countries that the post office, the telephone company, and government offices should buy equipment and supplies within their own country and from their own citizens. Formidable local institutions, like labor unions and domestic industries, have better pressure points than does Brussels in this contest. "Buying at home" seems the moral equivalent to being faithful to flag and family, a belief not unknown in the United States as well. This concept of nationality must eventually yield to a larger loyalty to the Community if many of these technical barriers to commerce are to be overcome.

The Commission has been working on public procurement policies for nearly 20 years. Directives forbidding discrimination against foreign suppliers alternate with those requiring some affirmative action like the Community-wide publication of new contracts. Yet less than one ECU in four of public contracts covered by the directives is even published in the Community's official journal which is the minimal need of suppliers in other Community countries to prepare public procurement bids. The internal market timetable indicates specific measures which will be proposed against collusive bidding and in favor of greater "transparency" of the entire public procurement process.

One of the most complex areas of coordination of national standards involves the flow of capital and access to financial services. Restricting or controlling foreign banks and capital is an old tradition in Europe. Removing these controls means exposing local institutions and practices to competition and perhaps replacement by a distant company from another EC country or overseas. Outsiders, including the United States, are watching closely to see if the single banking license plan, approved in 1989, will make it more or less difficult for them to do business in the Community. This will not be known until the Community establishes firm rules on reciprocity—the principle that non-EC countries should give comparable access to EC banks and other financial services.

Fiscal Barriers

A history of the European Community could be written in terms of taxation. The first efforts of the Economic Community were directed to the abolition of national tariffs in favor of an external Community tariff wall. Thus the limited reform of taxation via tariffs was a Community organizing principle in 1958 as well as the standard, ten years later, when the Custom Union was declared completed. But a common external tariff replacing internal ones did not solve the problem of fiscal barriers, for complicated reasons including turnover, or value added taxes.

Each of the original six EC countries had a turnover tax applied at each stage of production or service, and each was different. In 1967 they agreed that a value added tax (VAT), levied on a common basis, was needed. A series of Commission directives on the value added tax system was aimed at harmonizing these taxes and, from 1970, assuring the Community a small share in the vast revenues the system produces. The EC share, referred to as its "own resources," has become the principal means of financing the Community and the center of conflict on each occasion when the Community faced a decision on a new program. Until the 1970 decision on EC's "own resources," Community finances were limited (beyond revenues from the common external tariff) to annual levies on member governments.[7]

This vexing problem of indirect taxation (taxes applied prior to the final transaction and not listed separately) slows harmonization and the end of physical barriers at the borders where commercial goods are counted for tax purposes and where tax fraud is discouraged by careful controls. Governments fear losing crucial income if physical control ends. Excise taxes on alcohol, tobacco, and perfume are another justification for border fiscal controls, particularly of commercial shipments. These taxes are a special problem for the Community since VAT rates are applied on top of the excise taxes. A multiplier effect thus works to exaggerate the differing rates on alcohol, tobacco, and motor fuels, the principal items covered by excise levies.

The White Paper faces this problem squarely by setting 1992 as the deadline for both reducing the VAT differences into two broad bands of 4 to 9 percent and 14 to 20 percent and for achieving identical excise tax rates. Pressure to reach these difficult goals comes primarily from the Commission's insistence, so far supported by the Council, that all frontier controls end by 1992. The White Paper proposes ways the Council and member governments can meet this revolutionary change. (The EC institutions do not enter the treacherous area of national budgetary consequences of the VAT changes. Some EC members will find that new VAT schedules will increase their income—constituting a tax increase—while others will run short of funds when their VAT income falls, requiring perhaps a tax increase there also!)

If the Commission prevails on this deadline on VAT and excise tax adjustment, the member states must also agree well in advance on how the differences in these indirect taxes will be reduced. Commission proposals in 1987/88 on changes in the number and level of rates and their scope met great resistance in the Council, led by an unusual national pairing of Britain and France. For different reasons related to their respective VAT structures, these two insisted on modifications of the original Commission harmonization proposal. While the Commission indicated a willingness to compromise on details and to allow a transition period for some special difficulties, this flexibility is within the overall goal of abolishing the frontier posts by December 31, 1992. Complete uniformity of VAT rates may not occur; the U.S. internal market operates with some variety of state tax laws which may, through competition, even hold rates down. Even after 1992, similar small variations in the Community could exist in a system where, for example, the French VAT rate was 33 percent on many goods and services which are taxed at 12 percent or 14 percent in neighboring Luxembourg or Germany. But the competitive effect is less likely when the taxes remain hidden which is often the case with VAT. Reducing these variations (England and Ireland, for example, have "zero-rated" categories in food and children's clothing) becomes the main conflict between national and Community authorities in the months before 1992, even if this deadline is ultimately postponed.

Without doubt, fiscal barriers are the most difficult challenge of the entire internal market reform; restricting national control of tax policy (and, therefore, over some part of national budgetary control) may constitute the most serious abridgement of sovereignty yet achieved by the Community.

Easing Nationalism

Although 1992 is often seen as a European regulatory system (particularly by skeptical outsiders), the facts are somewhat different. There will be some new regulation for the internal market but much more mutual recognition of national legislation and even more deregulation of national rules. An important Community contribution to this entire effort will be abstention from making new regulations. Several years ago, just as the 1992 program got underway, the Commission proposed a 350-page EC standard for mayonnaise. Abandoning such detailed regulations may concentrate the White Paper's effort toward easing national barriers without imposing rigid or lengthy EC substitutes.

Another example, of much greater policy significance, is "subsidiarity"— Jacques Delors' concept of EC federalism. By this principle, the Community has committed itself to finding the lowest level of government adequate to carry out any particular mandate or directive. If fully implemented, subsidiarity will mean more authority to national, regional, even local governments in carrying out EC programs.[8]

Yet a more apposite concern for the Community facing 1992 is what should be done with recalcitrant national governments. The 1989 Commission status report cited above showed that of 68 laws under the 1992 program (out of almost 300), only seven had been implemented in all 12 EC countries. Resistance, bureaucratic sloth, and lack of information at the national level were possible explanations. The Commission has only limited resources with which to combat this problem. Ultimately, if a national government really resists, the dispute may end in the Court of Justice but only after months and years of delay. The report made several proposals to avoid such delay which is due partly, but not entirely, to residual national pride.

THE EXTERNAL MARKET

EC and the United States

For outsiders, especially the U.S. government, the single market seemed at first to mean new trade problems with the Community. The charge that the EC was creating a "fortress Europe" flowed easily from both government and business speakers, many of whom had not paid much attention to the Community for years before the single market plan was announced in 1985. This meant that some Community policies, like its antitrust and competition programs, which we had once strongly supported or even devised, were now seen differently, particularly by U.S. firms less confident of their own competitiveness.[9] By the mid-1980s we felt more a victim than a leader in the trade field. Because we had so many and varied ties with Western Europe (compared with Japan) and because we had dominated those relations since World War II, there was a tendency for Americans to believe that Europeans were either ungrateful or complacent in not accommodating themselves more readily to our trade problems and our preferred solutions for these trade tensions.

This tendency can cause trouble on both sides of the Atlantic, for the Europeans have their own forms of myopia. The American inclination to blame the Europeans shifts attention away from specific trade problems and their causes. Instead, the United States focuses on past and current investments in Europe's security and prosperity. The Europeans, who share our tendency to link trade and security issues, then feel bound to remind us that these investments were undertaken for American as well as European interests. When the discussion gets down to specifics, as trade matters must, French farmers or German tool makers think it unfair that they should be asked to pay the price for the successes of NATO by accepting more American grain or by foregoing sales to Detroit. Americans think often that only their country pursues "free" trade and is thus at the disadvantage with less scrupulous foreigners.

But past trade negotiations clearly show odd linkages among unrelated elements; there is no reason to believe that the Uruguay round will be any different.[10] What seems to have changed is the role of the United States which has traditionally been both a free trader and a capital exporter. Since the Tokyo round, there have been important changes in the American role in the global economy. Where formerly we were dominant in that economy because of our size and the role of the dollar, this dominance yielded to a world where we are one of several large traders and where the dollar, at least in recent years, is a destabilizing element. These changes affect our relations with the European Community as much as with any other trading partner.

A Unique Relationship

It is only with the Europeans, in fact, that almost anything we do in one area of international affairs has direct and specific effects in several others. With Japan, for example, we have major trade relations and problems, but rather limited relations in other areas. With Latin America, we have long-standing political-security relations but little depth in our cultural or historical ties. With Africa, we have a deep and painful cultural linkage through the slave trade and its consequences but modest economic or political interaction. Only with Western Europe do we have such important trading relations combined with close security, economic, and historical ties. As a nation, we descended from the Europeans; the resulting cultural and historical similarities mean we have trading practices and polices which more resemble that of Europe than they do any other part of the world.

Despite the $9-billion deficit (1988) in our trade balance with member states of the European Community, there is a remarkable symmetry in our trade with them. In 1988, we sent 23 percent of our exports to EC countries; they sent 21 percent of their exports to us. (The deficit came, of course, because their world trade is much larger than ours making the same percentage yield quite different absolute numbers.) We received 19 percent of our imports from the Community; they received 16 percent of their imports from the United States. These figures fluctuate, of course, by year but if we go back to the last time (1980) we had a very low-valued dollar we find that, despite growth in exports from the Community to the United States, these two trading partners not only remain each other's best customers but have had that position for some time (see table 4.1).[11]

Table 4.1
U.S.–EC Trade as a Percentage of Total Trade
(Goods Only)

	1980		
For U.S.:		For EC:*	
Exports to EC:	26%	Exports to U.S.:	11.9%
Imports from EC:	15%	Imports from U.S.:	16.0%
	1988		
Exports to EC:	23%	Exports to U.S.:	21%
Imports from EC:	19%	Imports from U.S.:	16%

*EC consisted of 10 countries in 1980.

Sources: U.S. Department of Commerce; Eurostat (US$ basis).

On a worldwide basis, the Community is by far the most important trading partner we have. We export twice as much to EC countries as we do to Japan yet we import more from Japan than from the Community. We have a sizable trade deficit with Japan but a smaller and declining one with the EC. Aside from the similar fractions in our total trade with each other, the United States and the European Community each represent the most important trading partner for the other.

Total American trade (imports and exports) with the Community totaled over US$160 billion in 1988, well beyond our total trade with Japan which reached US$127 billion that year. (Our trade with Canada reached US$151 billion in 1988, but that figure is inflated by about US$40 billion in multiple counting of autos and auto parts which cross and recross the border in a free trade agreement.)

There are several other interesting U.S.-EC trading patterns (see table 4.1-4.3). First, there was a remarkable symmetry in U.S.-EC trade in 1987/88 when our exports to each other represented about 20 percent of our total respective exports and our imports from each other were both in the area of slightly less than 20 percent. (Although not shown in the tables, we also tend to import and to export many of the same goods to each other and to third markets.) Second, Japan represents a different kind of trading problem for the European Community than it does for the United States. Japan ranks behind the United States, Eastern Europe and Switzerland, as a supplier of imports and even farther down the Community list as an export market. For the United States, Japan represents by far the largest single element in our trade deficit, amounting to over US$50 billion in 1988; the Community's largest deficit is with Japan but it amounted to only US$24 billion.

Table 4.2
Major U.S. Trading Partners, 1988
(billions US$)

	U.S. Imports from:	U.S. Exports to:	Total
EC	84.9	75.8	160.7
CANADA	81.4	70.8	152.2*
JAPAN	89.8	37.7	127.5
EANIC**	63.2	34.8	98.0
MEXICO	23.3	20.6	43.9***

Source: Eurostat, ExTrade Yrbk 88, pp. 84-85 and USDC, U.S. Trade 88, pp. 83-84.

*Includes about US$40 billion in autos and auto parts counted more than once in the US-Canada Automotive Free-Trade Agreement.

**East Asian newly industrialized countries (Hong Kong, Korea, Singapore, Taiwan).

***Also includes some double counting in goods which move across the US-Mexico border in assembly operations.

Table 4.3
Major EC Trading Partners, 1987
(billions of ECU)

	EC Imports from:	EC Exports to:	Total
U.S.	56.0	71.0	127.0
SWITZERLAND	26.7	32.7	59.4
E. EUROPE*	30.1	19.2	49.3
JAPAN	34.8	13.6	48.4
SWEDEN	20.0	20.1	40.1

Source: Eurostat, ExTrade Monthly Stats, January 1989, pp. 16-17. ECU = US$1.15.

*Soviet Union, East Germany, Poland, Czechoslovakia, Hungary, Romania, and Bulgaria. The Soviet Union accounts for about 13.1 billion ECU in EC imports and 9.1 billion ECU in EC exports in these totals.

From the viewpoint of the Community, the United States is the principal cause of its own trade deficit. The enormous federal budget deficit in a period of steady economic growth is seen as irresponsible. This deficit, and the consequent higher U.S. interest rates, inflated the dollar's value and expanded imports, especially in an environment which discouraged savings and encouraged consumer credit. The resulting trade deficit was more than a singular phenomenon, many European economists believe. It represents an ingrained pattern of overspending by both the U.S. government and its consumers which eventually must end. As recently as 1980, we exported US$973 in goods per person while we imported US$1131 in goods. By 1987 we had increased imports to US$1676 per person while our exports fell to US$1044. By another comparison, the United States imports about one-third more per capita than Japan but that country exports almost 80 percent more per person whan we do. The Community also believes the United States ignores its own protectionist measures. In 1985 the EC started issuing an annual report on these U.S. trade barriers.[12]

In general, foreign trade is much more important for both the European Community and for Japan than it is for the United States (see table 4.4) and its engagement in such trade is in general balance (although this is not true for each of its member states).

Table 4.4
Foreign Trade as a Percentage of GDP, 1987

	Imports	Exports
U.S.	10.8%	7.4%
Japan	7.3%	10.5%
Greece	29.5%	22.4%
Canada	25.7%	26.5%
Germany	23.7%	28.7%

Source: OECD *Historical Statistics, 1960-1987,* tables 6.12, 6.13.

Note: EC members here include intra-EC trade. This table shows, therefore, the relative involvement of the countries listed in the foreign marketplace and also the relation of each country's exports to imports.

Finally, compared to individual countries, the United States in 1986 exported less per person than any OECD country and imported less than any OECD country except Japan. But the relatively small size of U.S. imports must be seen in the wide discrepancy between our exports and imports. The U.S. deficit is over 3 percent of our large GNP, a figure which has produced a trade deficit of over US$100 billion each year since 1984 and shows no clear sign, even in 1990, of falling below that number. To put these large numbers in more human terms, a US$100-

billion trade deficit means that each of our country's 241 million persons has spent, for most of a decade, about US$415 more overseas each year than what each earned abroad.

Fiscal Policy

The U.S. trade deficit, both global and with the European Community, causes anxiety for EC members but for reasons quite different from those expressed in Washington. The Europeans cite the failure of the Reagan administration to eliminate the huge budget deficit as the principal cause of this trade distortion. Community officials found satisfaction and relief, halfway through the Reagan presidency, when Washington accepted the view that management of exchange rates—previously rejected as inconsistent with the President's view of true market economics—was both feasible and proper. The rise and pitch of the dollar became the best argument available to Europeans for the worth of target zones and currency rate management not only for their own currencies but in some arrangement that included the dollar, too.

Although the ECU has reacted necessarily to these dollar movements, the European monetary system (EMS) has succeeded in modulating the effects of that movement within the Community (for more on the EMS, see chapter 6). Europeans hope that the lessons of the uncontrolled gyrations of the dollar in the 1980s will carry over to the successor administrations in Washington. Perhaps more conservative than their American counterparts, European banking experts believe that the increased interdependence of securities, money, and trade no longer permits one country to upset the global economy in the 1990s as happened in the previous decade.

The United States insisted, even after its acceptance of some discreet management of exchange rates, on German and Japanese stimulation of their economies to help reduce the U.S. trade deficit. This created serious tensions, especially for the Germans whose fear of inflation through such stimulation dates back to the collapse of its currency during the Weimar years. Bonn looked at the Washington record on inflation over the 1965-85 period and found only negative lessons. Although the Germans generally try to accommodate American views for security reasons, they resist when the pressure comes on the West Germany economy which many economists believe to be the best managed in the world today. The relatively independent role in that economy played by the *Bundesbank*[13] reinforces this tendency to disregard Washington's prescriptions for what is best for Germany. The *Bundesbank* and, to a lesser extent, the Bank of Japan, tend to listen only when Washington concentrates on its own budgetary and trade deficits. All else, these central banks believe, tends to distract the Americans from their principal responsibility. When, in the February 1987 Paris meetings on the dollar, the United States promised to reduce the budget deficit from 3.9 percent to 2.3 percent of GNP by 1988, there were hopeful glances among the European listeners. But back in Washington, it was clear by late 1989 that the federal deficit would still be above 3 percent of GNP when President Bush was well into his first term. If a recession comes, the Europeans believe, the U.S. deficit could double. It also seemed to mean that protectionist pressures in Washington would grow.

This prognosis also means that specific trade disputes with our principal trading partners will increase. The European Community, as the world's largest trader and the largest supplier to the United States, remains prepared to receive the heaviest blows when Congress starts to swing.

The Airbus, the Farmer, and the Auto

Among the targets of the congressional critics in the Community were the European aircraft industry where the Airbus consortium has been successful in competing with American manufacturers, traditionally both the leading designers and exporters of long-distance aircraft. The considerable European subsidies of the Airbus consortium partners are matched, the Europeans say, by American subsidies of Boeing and other U.S. aircraft manufacturers through defense contracts.

European farmers, protected by import restrictions and encouraged by export subsidies, continue to produce grains, dairy products, and wine for which traditional markets are unavailable. Disposing of these surpluses brings the Community into conflict with the American farmer in some traditional markets for U.S. products. More conflicts will arise here even with the gradual reforms of the Community's common agricultural policy (CAP).[14]

Until Detroit further improves its products, foreign auto makers, including those of Community countries, will continue to penetrate the U.S. market, particularly in the luxury and sport segments where higher prices do not seem to discourage buyers seeking the high quality and reliability which still seem to elude Detroit. In each of these areas of competition, Congress was implored to act by domestic interests when, by late 1989, the falling dollar still seemed to be without great effect in helping U.S. exporters.

Criticism of Washington's actions and omissions is not enough for Europeans, no matter how self-satisfying the delineation of American budget and monetary policies since 1981 may be for Community members and officials. The dollar's movements and their consequences, like the rain, fall on all beneath this currency's influence, without regard to innocence or guilt. By the early 1990s, the principal European fear was whether the damage of the 1980s was limited to that period or whether some permanent dispostion now ruled in Washington by which the strong and resilient American economic performance since World War II was no longer assured. Could American productivity, inventiveness, and flexibility no longer be counted upon as a Western model? Must Europe look instead to the Far East for new models?

EC and Japan–EANIC

As the world's leading trader, the European Community might have been expected to respond well to the tidal wave of Pacific imports which hit Western countries in the 1970s. The United States was struck first by this wave and ultimately suffered far greater penetration than did the Community. Neither the United States nor the Community has been able to increase exports significantly to Japan or to the East Asian newly industrialized countries (EANIC). Both the United States and EC consider their Asian trading partners a major, and so far, insoluble problem in their external trade picture but not to the same extent. For the Europeans, Americans remain their largest export market and principal supplier. However, Japan now sells more to the United States than the entire European Community. To this extent, the high level of Asian imports is a larger problem for the United States than for the Community.

Community trade with the EANIC (Hong Kong, Singapore, South Korea, and Taiwan) and Japan grew in imports from 5.7 billion ECU in 1973 to over 55 billion ECU in 1987, an increase from 6.7 to 16.2 percent of total imports. EC exports to these countries grew very little; in 1973 5 percent of Community exports went to these countries while in 1987 this figure had risen to only 8.4 percent of total exports.[15] Since Japan accounts for two-thirds of the exports of these countries to the Community and because it arrived earlier on the European markets, it is not surprising that Japanese trading practices became the center of EC concern.

But this concern is neither universal nor equally fervent among the Community member countries. Not surprisingly, the Germans, with a solid trading surplus, are among those least likely to identify the Asian countries as a threat against whom direct action is needed. The Dutch and the Irish, the other two EC members with a trading surplus, are both less influential and less affected by Asian imports. Reaction to the increases in market penetration by Japan and the EANIC countries in autos and consumer electronics tends to concentrate on two major elements of the problem: the lack of balance in overall trade and the isolation of this problem from any other major Community concerns in the Pacific.

EC Protectionism

An unfortunate tendency, for an organization founded in the Treaty of Rome to encourage free trade, is a protectionist cast in the Community's thinking, which has sharply increased in recent years. Especially in regard to Japan and the other Pacific trading partners, the Community's "anti-dumping" section in Directorate-General I has become a protectionist agent to which member countries make increasingly frequent appeals. As with most protectionist schemes, the antidumping rules are justified by the Community as reactions against unfair practices of others. The submergence of the Community's free trade ideals in this development dismays many of its supporters in both Europe and the United States. It also encourages similar American trends. In fact, the only negative side of the 1992 goal of improving the Community's internal market is the possibility that some member states, and some forces within them, will see a barrier-free domestic market as an improved opportunity to exclude outside competition, perhaps through continuation or acceleration of this antidumping approach.

Lack of balance in Asian trade is the immediate problem for political, business, and labor leaders in Europe. Japan, for example, went from a trade surplus of US$1.5 billion in 1973 with the Community to about US$24 billion in 1987. Even more revealing is the ratio of EC exports to imports in this period which dropped from .64 (that is, exports equaled 64 percent of imports) to .39 in 1987.[16] Although both Community and national leaders have identified Japanese trade as a problem for over a decade, little progress has been made in reversing the deficit or the export/import ratio, nor does anyone seem to have an idea where a solution can be found.

But the issue is actually larger than trade; it concerns Japan's role in the global economy, according to one Community study. The trade situation with Japan is "symptomatic of a deeper-rooted problem, which is that the Japanese economy is not sufficiently integrated with the broader international economy." This helps create a "lopsided pattern" which, within Japan, is based on a structural bias toward maximized export of manufactures and their minimized import. "The strategy pursued by Japan in its economic and commercial relations with the rest of the world—and from which it has had the greatest benefit—is largely based on this structure and now threatens to upset the whole international system of trade and finance, to the detriment not only of Japan's partners but of Japan itself."[17] This European judgment is in contrast with the assessment of the U.S. trade deficit which Europeans universally identify as caused by the American budget deficit. (They also see, as one of the few benefits of the Japanese trade surplus, its useful role in financing the American external deficit.[18])

This almost total frustration with Japanese trade reflects the second aspect of the Community relations with this Asian power: its isolation from other EC concerns. With the United States or with the ACP countries,[19] historical and cultural linkages provide a background against which trade, security, and other issues may be judged. With Japan and most East Asian exporters, the Community has had almost no contacts either in national history or through travel and education. Their products arrive in the auto sales room or the electronic shops as if from another planet.

Even for those in business and government whose responsibilities demand regular contact with Asian countries, there has developed little area expertise and no consensus on how to solve the trade imbalance.[20]

EC View of Asian Trade

There is broad agreement in the Community on these aspects of the problem:

1. EANIC and Japan are exceptionally aggressive and efficient at finding market opportunities in other countries and in exploiting them.

2. These countries are also characterized by layers of barriers to outside suppliers with whom they negotiate politely but without any real intention of opening their domestic markets.

3. The success of the Asians in entering our markets reflects primarily failures of the West. We became lazy and inefficient at producing what the market clearly wants. We are the problem which must be solved.

4. Stable or increasing trade deficits are a problem for the exporter as well as for the importer. Countries which do not understand this or who refuse to act upon it must become answerable to an international authority.

5. Japan, and to a lesser but undefined extent, the other Asian exporters, have developed business-government cooperation which is single-minded in its pursuit of overseas markets. Dealing with these countries is more like dealing with a state trading country (but without the rigidity and clear inefficiency of the eastern European models).

6. The European reaction to these Asian traders is milder than in the United States for both economic and cultural reasons. The degree of market penetration in Europe has not yet reached that in the United States nor, with minor exceptions, have sector or product competition in recent years matched what American manufacturers encounter. The Community has lost several sectors entirely to Asian imports but it still has some vitality in consumer electronics and in small autos, areas where comparable American manufacturers have almost entirely ceded the field to their Asian counterprts.

Europeans also have more experience than Americans in getting along with other countries with very different political and economic systems. Perhaps having their own cultural rigidities and having experienced their own attempts at strict central government planning (and being more skeptical of making unilateral demands on other governments), the Europeans are generally less agitated than the Americans in assessing and approaching the Japanese.

Table 4.5 tells part of this story of the penetration by Japan of the

American and European Community markets. The difference in 1987 between the 16 percent penetration of the Community's market and the 34 percent penetration of the U.S. import market is a clear indicator of the Japanese problem already faced by Americans and feared by Europeans.[21]

Table 4.5
Japanese-EANIC* Trade with the EC and the United States
(billions US$)

	1973	1980	1988**
EC IMPORTS:	5.7	23.0	63.5
% of all imports:	6.7%	8.4%	16.2%
EC EXPORTS	4.0	10.2	33.0
% of all exports	5.0%	4.6%	8.4%
U.S. IMPORTS	XX	51.0	153.0
% of all imports	XX	19.8%	34.6%
U.S. EXPORTS	XX	35.4	72.5
% of all exports	XX	16.0%	22.5%

Sources: Eurostat, ExTrade Yrbk 88, pp. 52-53; OECD Historical Statistics 1960-84, pp. 116-17; USDC U.S. Trade 88, p. 83.

*Hong Kong, Taiwan, Singapore, South Korea.
**1987 for EC. XX: Not available.

EC and the ACP Countries

The African, Caribbean, and Pacific (ACP) countries are former colonies of the member countries of the Community. They benefit from a special triangular relation to their former metropoles and to the Community which, in this context, defines both the development aid and the trading context of this triangle. The Community takes special care to play the role of the enlightened heir of a colonial past.

Four conventions signed by the Community and ACP bear the name of Lomé, capital of the former African colony now called Togo. The Lomé agreements cover aid, trade access, and other aspects of the relations between 68 former colonies and the Community. They are based on a provision in the 1957 Rome Treaty which defines the special relation between the Community and the countries and territories with which the EC members had been associated by long and sometimes bitter histories. Trade under a unique preferred status for the former colonies is the heart of this ACP relation. Reciprocally, the agreements also assure access for EC exports on a nondiscriminatory basis among member states and for the progressive elimination of custom duties for those members' exports into the former colonies.

The growth of special Community ties with the 68 ACP countries resulted from a coincidental and fortunate timing: the gradual end of the colonial period at the time of the birth of the Community, and the first EC enlargement in 1973 which greatly expanded the ACP countries by bringing in most of the former British colonies. The start of broader European trading policies in 1958 coincided, therefore, with a plan to define relations with present and former colonies. This constituted a radically different approach to global economics which Europe was constructing with a major segment of the developing world. The innovation by the Community with its ACP program eventually became an important part of political cooperation, the Community's foreign policy coordination.[22] When the United Kingdom joined the Community, the center of gravity of the ACP countries shifted from Africa, where most of the original six had concentrated their colonial ties, to the Caribbean and the Pacific where the more extensive British Empire's holdings had been prominent.

Table 4.6
EC Trade with the ACP Countries (millions ECU)

	EC Imports	EC Exports	E/I Ratio*
1960	2,826	2,392	.85
1970	5,472	4,068	.74
1980	20,744	17,048	.82
1987	16,374	13,843	.85

Source: Eurostat, ExTrade Yrbk 88, pp. 52-53.

*Exports divided by imports (less than 1. indicates EC trade deficit).

Trade with the ACP countries grew almost sevenfold in EC imports and sixfold in its exports from 1958 to 1987 (see table 4.6). While large, this growth is not as impressive when compared to considerably larger increases in the same period in EC trade with both Eastern Europe and, of course, with the United States. Community world trade volume, by a further comparison, grew in this period 14 times in imports and 16 times in exports. The relatively modest expansion in ACP trade is traceable to the low capacity of these newly independent countries to finance imports (except for the few oil producers among them).

Responses to the European Community's 1992 program has not been easy to detect in the Middle East, Africa, or Latin America except that the ACP countries will continue to expect favored treatment at the hands of the Community because of the long and sometimes bitter colonial relationship which these countries inherited. Since the principal export of the developing countries to the Community is commodities under a favorable preference arrangement, it may develop that the internal market program is of secondary importance to the Third World except for a broad interest in the continuing prosperity of the Community as a buyer of its exports.

EC trade with ACP countries appears to be out of balance with an export/import ratio of .85, significantly worse than the EC global ratio of 1.0. This deficit is a political price the Community readily pays to represent its past responsibilities and its commitment to future ties with these former territories. (With Japan plus EANIC, the EC trading ratio is even more out of balance—.52—with no compensatory political justification.) Table 4.7 shows the pattern of the Community's trade with these areas, by export/import ratios.

Table 4.7
Selected Export/Import Ratios

	Japan	ACP	U.S.	E. Europe	World**
1970	.68	.74	.72	0.96	.88
1980	.34	.82	.58	0.84	.76
1987	.39	.85	1.27	.78	1.00

**Extra-EC only. Numbers below 1. indicate EC trade deficit. Computed from ECU data in Eurostat, ExTrade Yrbk 88, pp. 52-53.

The EC and Eastern Europe

The value of the Community's trade with Eastern Europe (including the German Democratic Republic but excluding Yugoslavia) underwent important changes in the late 1980s because of the completion in 1984 of a natural gas pipeline from the Soviet Union to Western Europe, which boosted EC imports. Community trade with the seven Eastern European countries is, in fact, greater in total volume in merchandise than with either Japan or with the ACP countries. With both Eastern Europe and the former colonies, EC imports of raw materials are large trade components. EC exports to these two areas are relatively well balanced between food, semifinished industrial products, and medium technology in the form of machine tools and consumer items. The dramatic changes in the Soviet Union under Mikhail Gorbachev and in eastern European countries may provide new trade opportunities between East and West undreamed of since the end of World War II.

Because all eastern European trade has been conducted through state trading agencies in the communist countries, there is both a sluggishness and a predictability in this commerce (in contrast to recent trends in Pacific trade). How recent upheavals in Eastern Europe will change this trading relationship is not clear since the state trading agencies represent only a part of a much more extensive state control of prices, production, and quality. Changing these elements means changing the entire Eastern European economic and political structure, a process which, if fully undertaken, may require a long time.

A special trade relationship exists between the two Germanies. It was a condition set by the Federal Republic that its trade with the German Democratic Republic (GDR) not be seen as non-EC trade. This preserved the notion of a single German state with two governments temporarily in charge. Thus, goods from GDR could enter not only FRG but also the other 11 EC countries, foregoing the common external tariffs (although special quotas govern the volume of such goods). The Court of Justice in 1989 upheld this special relationship which several EC members had questioned. German reunification might mean, therefore, less in the trading relation with other EC members than some observers think. The political consequences of reunification, however, could be much greater than the strictly economic ones.[23]

NATO Coordination

Another characteristic of EC trade with Eastern Europe is that all medium- and high-technology items and other "strategic" materials are screened by the Paris-based Coordinating Committee for Export Control (Cocom) procedures of the NATO countries. Differences between the United States and some of its European NATO allies on the strategic value of certain exports to the East are often the cause of sharp disputes. Generally, the Europeans are more relaxed about trade with the Eastern European countries than is the United States. A 1981/82 dispute about whether the gas pipeline from the Soviet Union to western Europe should be completed formed the introduction for the Reagan administration into what has now become a tradition of disagreement with Western Europe on trade with the communist countries. In this instance, the European allies prevailed but in many other cases, less well-publicized but often quite important to European vendors, sales of modern technology have been vetoed by Cocom, acting under the strong influence of the United States. A January 1988 meeting in Versailles smoothed out some of these policy differences; in 1990 the Cocom controls were again reduced.

Until quite recently, the eastern European countries did not recognize the European Community, insisting on dealing in trade matters only with the member countries themselves. Brussels saw this exclusionary policy as a device to force reciprocal recognition of the Council for Mutual Economic Assistance (Comecon), which ties the communist countries of the world into a trading relationship. But Comecon functions only as a coordinating agency for its ten member countries; it has neither the capabilities nor the aspirations of the European

Community. The Commission has therefore consistently rejected all approaches from Comecon for reciprocity or any other form of mutual recognition.

On June 25, 1988, Comecon and the Community signed a joint declaration which recognized a primary EC role in both trade and political affairs. The European Parliament, at about the same time, also learned that its moribund delegation to Eastern European parliaments would now be received. Although not directly related to Gorbachev's policy of openness, these changes seem to represent an important movement toward realism by the Soviet bloc.

There is also evidence that individual Comecon members want better access to the Community. In December 1989, the Soviet Union and the Community signed a 10-year trade agreement, giving both sides increased market access. The German Democratic Republic sent an ambassador to Community headquarters in Brussels for the first time in 1989 even before the turbulent events in that country. Direct relations with other Comecon countries will certainly follow.

The EC and EFTA

If we consider Community trade with the United States, Japan, EANIC, the ACP countries, and Eastern Europe as a single group, EC still does more trade with the remainder of the world. These named groups constitute only about 40 percent of EC imports and 35 percent of its exports. Where does the rest of Community trade take place?

About 25 percent of EC exports go to the Western European countries outside of the Community, principally the members of the European Free Trade Association (EFTA). Of these EFTA members, Sweden and Switzerland alone take 13 percent of all EC exports. The other four—Austria, Finland, Iceland, and Norway—are not quite as important but together the EFTA countries trade with the EC at a significantly greater level than either the United States or Japan.

EFTA was created under British leadership in 1960 as a counterpoise to the European Community. Its original members, besides Britain, were Austria, Denmark, Norway, Portugal, Sweden, and Switzerland. As EC membership eroded EFTA, the latter sought a trading relationship with the Community. Both Norway (which rejected EC membership narrowly by referendum in 1972) and Austria began internal discussions about Community membership by the late 1980s. If this happens, EFTA could become a small group of neutrals plus Iceland, an unarmed NATO member. This would further erode the significance of the group which functions largely to negotiate trade access to the Community. Some in Brussels believe that the EFTA countries want the rights of EC membership without its responsibilities. Yet they, and perhaps the Eastern European countries, must find a new relation to the EC after 1992. In December 1989 the EC and EFTA countries announced an agreement in principle to negotiate a new relationship termed "the European economic space." Difficult negotiations with EFTA began in 1990.[24]

Finally, to complete the EC global trade picture another 30 percent of EC exports are destined for the Mediterranean basin countries, OPEC, and Latin America. The remaining 5 percent covers Canada, China, and a few other countries.[25]

THE NEW EUROPEAN COMMUNITY AND THE WORLD

How will a more perfect union in the Community's sense of a single internal market affect its relations with the rest of the world?

To begin closest to home, the 1992 program coincides with momentous events in the Eastern European countries. It is quite possible that, by the turn of the next century, our perspective will indicate that those internal changes in the communist countries close to the Community will be considerably more important than the 1992 program. For example, if the Gorbachev era is not repudiated, how will the relaxed internal controls in Eastern Europe affect its relations with the Community? Will the long anticipated and sometimes feared reunification of the two Germanies upset the 11 other EC members?

Can Eastern European countries find a stable economic and political relation with Western Europe, including the Community, to replace the institutionalized tensions of the NATO-Warsaw Pact era? This is not only a problem for communist countries; there will certainly be limits to the number of economic refugees which the Community countries can accept from the East. Would a united Germany still be treated as the institutional equal of France, Britain, and Italy in EC even when it included the 17 million East Germans and that country's impressive industrial sector? Or would the arrival of a united Germany so upset the Community that its fragile unity would be threatened?

Not only are answers lacking to these questions but we cannot be sure that these are even the proper questions for the 1990s. But the 40-year history of the European Community should give it some confidence that survival of past crises has adequately prepared it for those of the future in dealing with its eastern neighbors.

The role of the Soviet Union is, of course, a key element in how the Community faces Eastern Europe. In the late 1980s, the Soviet Union finally appeared to recognize the significance of the EC role in Western Europe. In parliamentary relations also, and even in introducing the concept of a "common European house," Gorbachev initiated ideas whose audacity seemed to baffle Western Europeans. Whether Gorbachev and his counterparts in Eastern European countries survive the economic and political strains they induce is still not clear but they have found, by the early 1990s, a responsive audience in the EC countries.

The principal countries of the Far East, especially Japan, follow Community affairs closely only in the narrow but voluminous trade relations which largely mark their global roles. Since the 1992 program involves principally a more efficient and larger internal EC market, its impact on Asian traders could be double-edged: efficient exporters will have an even better chance to succeed in the EC market where they will have to meet only one, not twelve, sets of technical and marketing obstacles; this should first of all benefit the EC domestic firms which presumably know their home markets better than anyone else. The past skill of these Asian traders, however, pushes Community firms increasingly toward protection by transitional or other exclusionary devices for some time past the December 31, 1992 deadline.

Economic Welfare First

The interest in a "new" Community after 1992 seems tied generally with this question of trade penetration and disruption. Even in the European countries which are not EC members, the interest in a reinvigorated Community is seen largely in the traditional EC trading partners like Sweden and Switzerland in terms which contemplate EC membership or other extraordinary measures only because the internal market seems to threaten their economic welfare. There is little in the history of countries like these two, or even of Austria or Norway, to take two other possible EC candidates, to indicate that profound political changes are inducing this new (or, in Norway's case, renewed) consideration of EC membership. Economic protection, not political union, seems the goal of the countries.

Trading may be the prime vocation of the European community; it is certainly its most developed skill. Today there is still no European political or defense community and only the skeleton of a monetary system. But there is a mature, sizable, and generally efficient trading community. When it perfects its own internal market sometime in the 1990s, the Community may improve its efficiency in intra-EC trade and position itself for improved exporting. Two major problems stand in the way of this optimistic prospect: the CAP (which inhibits internal fiscal reform) and the Community's inability to date to stay competitive in high technology. The next two chapters look at these problems.

NOTES

1. See Monnet's account of his disputes with Charles de Gaulle in 1960 in his *Memoirs*, 433-34, and his final words in the same work: "Like our provinces in the past, our nations today must learn to live together under common rules and institutions freely arrived at. The sovereign nations of the past can no longer solve the problems of the present: they cannot ensure their own progress or

control their own future. And the Community itself is only a stage on the way to the organized world of tomorrow."

2. Monnet explaining the Schuman Plan to Konrad Adenauer in 1950 (Monnet *Memoirs,* 310).

3. These comparisons are derived from Eurostat, *External Trade Yearbook, 1988* (hereafter cited as Eurostat, ExTrade Yrbk 88), 52-53, and U.S. Department of Commerce, *United States Trade, Performance, 1988* (hereafter cited as USDC, US Trade 88), 83.

Unless otherwise indicated, when the Community is compared to its trading partners, the 12 members are considered as one unit, which is both the imperfect economic reality of the Community and its final goal. Therefore, trade between EC members is not counted as foreign trade. The U.S. Commerce Department still considers the EC members principally as individual countries in compiling and reporting trade statistics although it does do some EC comparisons. This practice matches the political analysis in Washington in the 1980s that while the Community is a trading mechanism of 12 countries, we still treat them as individual entities for most of our purposes. For more on this, see chapter 9.

4. Eurostat, ExTrade Yrbk 88, 52-55.

5. *Second Report of the Commission to the Council and the European Parliament on the Implementation of the Commission's White Paper on Completing the Internal Market,* May 11, 1987 (No. Com[87]203 Final). For more on the Single European Act, see chapter 3. See Commission White Paper, "Completing the Internal Market" (Luxembourg: EC Publications Office, 1985). For the costs of "non-Europe," see the study sponsored by the Commission and produced by Paolo Cecchini, *The European Challenge, 1992: The Benefits of a Single Market* (Hampshire, England: Wildwood House [distributed by Gower, Brookfield, Vt.], 1988).

6. See the September 1988 issue of *Target 1992,* the Commission's newsletter, p. 1. The full Commission report on implementing the 1992 program was issued in September 1989 as COM (89) 422 (final).

7. For more on turnover or value-added tax and on "own resources," see appendix C.

8. For more on subsidiarity and its relation to both the internal market and European integration, see the section on the Single European Act at the close of the preceding chapter.

9. An American law professor, Robert Bowie, drafted the two articles in the ECSC treaty on antitrust and decartelization. See Monnet, *Memoirs,* 352-53. The EC policy on competition is summarized in *EEC Competition Policy in the Single Market,* European Documentation series (Luxembourg: EC Publications Office, 1989).

10. Two earlier trade rounds, held under the authority of the General Agreement on Trade and Tariff (GATT), were the Kennedy round (1964-67) and the Tokyo round (1973-80).

11. Best customer means, in this context, the highest total of combined exports and imports to the other as a percentage of the total foreign trade of the Community and of the United States (extra-EC trade only; Eurostat, ExTrade Yrbk 88, 58; USDC, US Trade 88, 35-36.

12. Eurostat, *Basic Statistics,* 26th ed. 257, 266, 268. The 1989 report of U.S.

trade barriers listed, for example, about 40 tariff and nontariff measures the United States takes to reduce foreign competition.

13. See chapter 6 on EMS for more on the role of the *Bundesbank* and other central banks.

14. See chapter 5 for the operation of the common agricultural policy (CAP) and its conflicts with the United States.

15. USDC, US Trade 88, 83; Eurostat, ExTrade Yrbk 88, 51-55. See also table 4.8.

16. Computed from Eurostat, ExTrade Yrbk, 88, 58. See also table 4.5.

17. *Japan and the European Community, A Stocktaking* (Brussels: Commission of the European Communities, 1986), 1-2.

18. Ibid.

19. Asian, Caribbean, and Pacific countries are former colonies of the EC member states which have a treaty relationship with the Community governing trade and development. This relation includes a program (STABEX) to stabilize the export earnings of the ACP countries, whose economies depend largely on the export of commodities which often fluctuate in price with disastrous effects on poorer countries. The EC considers its relations with ACP countries to be the central feature of its approach to the Third World and a major function of the coordination of its members' foreign policies in what it terms political cooperation. The importance of the ACP relation for both the Community and the former colonies is often unappreciated in the United States.

20. The Commission, however, has sponsored a successful program to bring young executives and managers from member countries to Japan for language, area, and management studies. There is no comparable U.S. government program.

21. See Dick K. Nanto, *European Community-Japan Trade Relations, A European Perspective* (Washington, D.C.: Library of Congress-CRS, 1986), 11-12.

22. For more on the ACP relation, see below and chapter 8. The fourth Lomé agreement was signed on December 15, 1989, took effect in February 1990, and will run for ten years instead of the previous five-year terms.

23. The Belgian and Dutch governments asked the court to interpret the Community's treaties to require that the GDR be treated as a non-EC country. On September 21, 1989, the court upheld a 1957 protocol on intra-German trade, stating that the GDR is not a third country even though it is not an EC member.

A reunited Germany would exaggerate the already predominant position of the Federal Republic as the largest, and, by many measures, the strongest of the "big four" of the Community: taking only population, and starting with France, the smallest of the four, as 100 percent, Britain attains 103 percent; Italy, 104 percent; Germany today, 110 percent. A reunited Germany would reach 128 percent. Still, an enlarged Germany would not be out of line in a Community where the smallest country, Luxembourg, has only one-one-hundredth of the population of Ireland, the next largest member. Denmark, the third smallest EC member, is 50 percent larger than Ireland, and so on. A France which was 28 percent larger than the next largest EC country would not excite fears, an indication that the problem with a reunited Germany is political, not economic. For some institutional consequences of a united Germany, see note 59 in chapter 3.

24. The EFTA countries felt, with good reason, somewhat threatened by the 1992 single market program which could make EC trade more difficult for them. EFTA represents an unresolved residue from the British attempt to thwart the original six EC members from their course toward political unity. When Britain abandoned that course by joining the Community, it left the other EFTA countries in their awkward state. Some EFTA countries may eventually enter the Community; others will try to find a stable trading relationship with it. The emergence of market economies in eastern Europe may help this EFTA adjustment under the concept of a central EC group committed to closer integration, with concentric circles of other countries in defined trading relations to the core group. Eventually, countries in these outer circles might apply for EC membership. Jacques Delors hinted at such a system in a speech to the European Parliament on November 21, 1989. See "Delors' Dream" and "Westward Ho," *Economist* (November 25, 1989): 57-58. For the December 1989 agreement, see "A New Trade Zone Seen for Europe, Adding 6 Nations," *New York Times* (December 8, 1989): A1.

25. Eurostat, ExTrade Yrbk, 88, 80-101.

5

The Common Agricultural Policy

> It would have been inconceivable to set up the European Economic Community without including an economic sector as important as agriculture. In order to create a large single market, sweep away tariff barriers and other obstacles to trade, it was necessary that the more agriculturally developed countries should benefit just as much as those centered on industrial activities.
>
> —Commission policy statement, 1987

From the outside, the Community's Common Agriculture Policy (CAP) is an expensive, contradictory, and self-destructive form of protectionism. From within, the CAP is the magical adhesive which has kept the Community together when other forces tended to pull it apart. Both views exaggerate some essential truths.

The Community could not have developed without some arrangement to unite its members around the traditional European values of land, family farming, and food. Yet the political weight of these values has made it extremely difficult for the Community to move beyond this support for traditional farming at a time when global agriculture is being radically transformed. Instead, a system of payments and protection attempts to isolate the Community's farmers from the global economy. The Community entered onto a long, convoluted, and expensive route which seems to allow for no reversals and no fundamental reconsideration. The more money that poured into the CAP, the less the inclination of its beneficiaries (both the farmers and political leaders) to see the course altered.

THE EC FARMER

The direct beneficiaries—the EC farmers—are more numerous, hold less land, and earn less than their American counterparts. The average agricultural gross value added per farm worker in the Community was US$11,500 in 1984; it was US$28,300 in the United States. The comparable figure for each nonfarm worker in the same year was US$20,800 for the Community and US$35,400 for the United States. The EC countries have one farmer for each 18 people. The United States has one for each 69.

Italy still has one million farms of less than 5 hectares (12 acres); the United States has almost none. The average EC farm size (Spain excluded) was 60 acres in 1986; it was 438 acres in the United States. There are about 9.8 million farms in the EC-12 and about 2.3 million in the United States which has an area four times that of the Community.

These figures show how strikingly different the agricultural situation is for the European Community, compared to the United States, and also illustrates why the painfully expensive CAP is tolerated politically: nearly 18 million farmers (and voters) live in the 12 EC countries (although many are part-time farmers) while only about 3.2 million U.S. workers are in agriculture. By another measure, U.S. farm employment in 1985 was about 3 percent of total civilian employment; in the EC, farm labor was about 8.5 percent of the total employment.[1]

The growth of the Community may provide the means for extrication from the agricultural program which, by 1985, consumed 70 percent of the EC budget. The 1986 enlargement to include Portugal and Spain increased Community cultivated land by almost one-third. France, Greece, and Italy were natural competitors, for many products, of the two new countries. A condition imposed by the three member countries for assent to the enlargement was a major new EC Mediterranean program to allow them to meet the Iberian competition, together with special assistance to restructure Portuguese agriculture over ten years. The Community committed over 6.6 billion ECU (about U.S.$7.6 billion) to help those areas of the three members threatened by the approaching Portuguese and Spanish membership to adjust by modernizing their own agriculture, infrastructure, services, and small industries.[2] With this commitment went a goal of making agricultural prices, not quantitative restrictions, the controlling factor in farm production. But even in 1988, it was still not possible to find Community agreement on how a new price structure would operate.

To see how this long-term goal might be met, the beginnings of the CAP must be examined and its crucial role in building the Community assessed in both its economic and political dimensions.

When the Community started, farming was a major occupation. There were still 19 million farm workers in the six EC countries in 1960, comprising about 21 percent of the total civilian employment. By 1984, less than 9 percent of the workforce was in agriculture. In individual countries, the change was even more striking. Italy went from one-third of its workers on the farms in 1960 to 11.9 percent in 1984. In Greece and Spain, the percentage of farm labor in the whole labor field dropped by approximately half.[3]

But a larger movement was underway to thin the European farm population long before the Community was even a dream. The Industrial Revolution had, by 1900, already reduced the farm population in western Europe to about 43 percent of the working population.[4] Much earlier, before the steel plow and the thresher, most of the population had been either on the farm or directly involved with the products of the land or their distribution. The move away from the land in recent years, therefore, is part of a larger movement separate from the CAP but related to the Community's dilemma in agriculture: fewer and fewer people were needed to feed the population but their integration into the larger national or Community economy precipitated a farm policy which devoted an increasing proportion of the total budget to a smaller and smaller population segment.

THE GOALS OF THE CAP

By the single measure of self-sufficiency of domestic food production, the CAP can be judged a success. From 1962, when the CAP began, the Community has become self-sufficient in many key commodities. By 1980, for example, self-sufficiency was reached or exceeded in dairy products, beef, pork, sugar, and temperate fruits and vegetables. By the late 1980s, self-sufficiency had also been achieved in cereals, wheat, and potatoes.

By other measures, however, the CAP has not been a great success. As laid down in the Rome Treaty, the five goals of the Community agricultural program were:

- to increase agricultural productivity
- to improve agricultural worker income
- to stabilize markets
- to obtain secure food supplies
- to achieve reasonable food prices[5]

The middle three goals have been generally achieved; the first and last objectives have not yet been reached although productivity is slowly rising. EC food prices are usually well above world prices despite sizable stored surpluses in many products. The beneficiaries of this system have been farm owners and their labor force. A stable market and secure food supplies have been assured but at a very high price of market restriction, consequent high costs to the consumer, and some disruption of the world marketplace.

The CAP goal of achieving secure food supplies was understandable even as late as the 1958 Stresa conference which established the direction of the CAP. But greatly improved agricultural productivity went forward in the postwar years without regard to the political or economic policies pursued by a united Europe. One result of this technology was to bring self-sufficiency for key commodites within reach of Europe ahead of when anyone at Stresa could anticipate and without regard to the programs that conference judged necessary for such a dramatic expansion of production.

Once self-sufficiency is attained, there are only three possibilities for any agricultural producing country: (1) find new outlets for the surplus by sales in an increasingly competitive world market; (2) store the surplus and reduce it where possible through international stockpiling arrangements for future famine areas or by "fire-sale" disposals at prices far below production costs; or (3) reduce production. Each of these options has budgetary or political obstacles which the Community must face. But the problem is not limited to the EC or to Europe.

The balance sheet, however, must measure not only the monetary but also the political cost. Confidence in the Community ideal erodes when over two-thirds of its funds are devoted to financing the farm sector. The EC citizen might well ask, "Is the Community to be merely a means of financing our farmers?" For reasons we shall see later, this is far from being the case but we cannot blame the Community taxpayer for being confused.

CAP Operating Principles

Within the broad goals of the Treaty of Rome, the CAP operates under three basic principles: market unity, Community preference, and common financial responsibility.

Market unity means that farm goods circulate freely among all member countries. Like the "common market" for industrial goods, a united agricultural market requires an external tariff wall for goods originating outside the Community.

Community preference is conceived by the Community as a "logical consequence"[6] of the single market. This principle is not entirely at ease with the basic free trade and competition rules which apply to all other Community goods traded on the world market. This preference principle means, in practice, that prices of imported agricultural products are raised at the Community borders by a variable levy which adjusts the incoming price to the internal EC price level. The Commission sets that level high enough to insure adequate compensation even for the small and inefficient farmer who still dominates important geographic sectors in the Community. The result is high consumer food prices.

Financial solidarity, the third CAP principle, means that all costs of the agricultural program are borne in common. This does not mean that all farmers benefit equally (or even fairly) or that each member government pays an equitable share of the CAP costs. Nor does it mean that each member government pays for farm programs only through the Community since various aids are still available under national programs. Solidarity simply means that all common agricultural spending and receipts pass through the Community budget.

These principles were discussed and elaborated at a landmark conference in Stresa, Italy, in July 1958. Building on the Rome Treaty goals for agriculture which were accepted the previous year, Stresa contributed some important, if not entirely consistent, secondary principles.

Stresa participants agreed that Community agriculture, for example, should become more competitive; it should also, however, protect the tradition of the family farm. Because of higher production costs in the small and less efficient farms, uniform EC prices would have to rise above world prices. But participants also warned against overproduction. Total self-sufficiency should not be the Community goal in farm goods but the internal market must be protected from disruptive global competition. With this agenda, the CAP was destined for some difficult decisions along a zig-zag course for nearly thirty years.

Adapting these contradictory principles to specific market mechanisms involved, from the start, the most delicate balance of national and regional tensions. Northern industrial Italy, for example, or the port of Hamburg might care little for the principle of protecting family farms in the southern parts of their respective countries. But political leaders in Rome, Bonn, and every other member country recognized the strength of small farmers. When conflicts came in Brussels between the principles of competition in agriculture and the politics of maintaining the existence of small farms, there was little doubt where political truth lay.

The Market Organization

The CAP works through market organizations, the earliest of which (1962) covered cereals. Within each market organization, a system of support prices and market intervention operates to maintain production at fair prices for the farmer.

Take wheat as an example. A target price is set by the Commission at the start of each crop season in consultation with the Council of Agriculture Ministers. This is the price at which farmers will earn a fair return on their investment, including their labor, taking account of inflation and other factors beyond their control. Set below the target price is an intervention price which is the guaranteed minimum the producers will receive.

When the EC domestic price stays below the target price, Community farmers are given an opportunity to supply the market for wheat at a price below that possible to outside suppliers, for whom the world price must be raised to the target level upon arrival in the Community.

When, in other cases, the EC domestic price rises to the target price, outside supplies enter the Community market to stabilize prices around the target price. EC farmers thus sell all of their wheat around the price determined by the Community to be fair to them; EC consumers benefit from a stabilized (but high) price even if domestic production drops. Figure 5.1 illustrates this price support system.

Figure 5.1
Levy and Refund System for Wheat

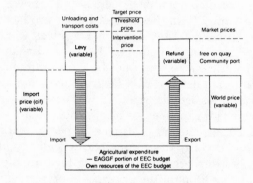

Source: The Common Agricultural Policy and Its Reform, European Documentation series (Luxembourg: EC Publications Office, 1987), 20.

This system of support prices and intervention is the most common type of Community market organization, covering over 70 percent of EC farm production. About 25 percent of EC farm products are protected only by levies, custom duties, or both. No market support devices operate here. The principal commodities involved are bulk wines, poultry, eggs, and flowers. A few products—about 2.5 percent of total EC farm production—get specific assistance because of the nature of the crop. Examples are durum wheat and olive oil, both limited by geography and climate to small areas of the Community and to small quantities. Less than one percent of EC products get acreage or quantity benefits without regard to support prices. These products are cottonseed, flax, hemp, hops, and some forms of fodder.

THE UNITED STATES AND THE CAP

The United States has a special interest in the CAP for several reasons. First, we have considered Community countries prime markets for our agricultural exports for many years. Any negative change in these export patterns, no matter what the ultimate cause, upsets American farmers and their supporters. Second, the structure of the Community's agricultural subsidies is different from ours. We tend to view with suspicion the export subsidies and the variable levies which do not match our farm support system and which, we believe, unfairly reduce our competitive advantages. Finally, the CAP has become, to some Americans, a functioning symbol of the effects of European integration which we fostered for several specific political reasons at the end of World War II and which now seems often to embody principally problems for our country. The CAP is the most visible and, to some Americans, the most painful manifestation of European solidarity which some think should yield to American appeals for gratitude, for fair consideration for U.S. farmers, or at least for common sense to reverse a worldwide escalation of farm subsidy costs. Much transatlantic shouting is the result.[7]

The Europeans quite naturally see the situation differently. The large American farm exports to the Community in the 1970s are judged in Europe to be exceptional historically and produced largely by a fortuitous combination of an undervalued dollar and a seller's market in a world hungry for imported foodstuffs. This temporary situation ended by the mid-1980s and probably will not resume. Further, neither in costs nor in scope of agricultural support is the CAP much different from what other countries, including the United States, do for their farmers. Besides, EC spokesmen say, the Community remains the world's largest customer for the American farmer.

Some figures shed light on these contrary contentions. U.S. farm exports *did* rise sharply since 1960 but in an interesting pattern which shows the problems which American farmers faced in adjusting to the rapid changes in exports in the late 1970s and early 1980s. Our farm exports rose slowly and steadily from 1960 through 1971 when exports exceeded 1960's total by about 53 percent. In the next 11 years, however, exports rose by 151 percent, propelled by a cheap dollar and other factors. In 1986 for the first time, agricultural exports of the EC-12 exceeded those of the United States.[8] One reason was that U.S. farm exports fell drastically when the dollar began to rise in value. Even with that decline, exports in 1985 were double those of 1971 and, in the 1988/89 fiscal year forecast, the farm trade balance was already triple that of 1985 which seems to have marked the export low point for the decade.[9]

Largest U.S. Customer

Two points can be noted from these data. First, the Community remained the largest outlet (and the most important competitor) for U.S. farm products even though it declined somewhat as a percentage of our worldwide exports. Second, in 1980 we exported almost four times as much to the Community as we imported from the EC-10. In 1985, we still had a farm trade surplus with the Community but our exports were only about 28 percent higher than our imports. The American farm community was very happy with the exports to the EC in 1980 and very unhappy in 1985 but the reasons for the change had very little to do with the CAP and very much to do with a worldwide fall in U.S. farm exports. This decline came both because of the exalted value of the dollar in 1985 and because the world agricultural trade system may have experienced some fundamental changes which showed up in that five-year span but which actually relate to much longer trends in food production, especially in the developing countries. The revival, after 1985, of U.S. farm exports tended to mute the unhappy memories of that year for American farmers.

The CAP and the American farm program represent fundamentally different approaches to the problem of how to insure stable food supplies and a fair return to the farm sector in a largely unregulated world trade in farm products. The CAP, conceived in national traditions of food scarcity and a sizable farm labor segment, emphasizes protection for its workers even if that requires higher food prices. The United States starts with considerable comparable advantages for high production, low domestic prices, and aggressive export sales. The clash between the two systems comes when new factors—like fluctuating currency values, generalized prosperity in nonfarming sectors, and new competitors in the global farm market—combine to disrupt both the assumptions of the U.S. and EC systems and the benefits to the two societies. Table 5.1 illustrates the effects of these influences on worldwide agricultural exports.

Table 5.1
World, U.S., and EC Agricultural Exports*
(billions US$)

	WORLD	U.S.	EC	% OF WORLD U.S.	EC
1971	57.77	8.22	5.25	14.2	9.9
1976	140.47	24.13	11.65	17.2	8.3
1981	225.26	39.0	28.45	18.9	12.6
1985	225.5	32.0	24.21	14.2	10.7

Source: U.S. Department of Agriculture, Economic Research Service. EC data based on UN Commodity Trade Statistics Series and is extra-EC trade only.

*Includes Standard International Trade Classifications (SITC) 0,1,2, and 4, but excludes divisions 081.42, 03, 24, 25, 27, 28, and 411.1.

CAP AND THE BUDGET

If the Community were a fully articulated government, judgments about the cost and the direction of the CAP might be quite different. For example, the cost of the CAP appears reasonable as a percentage of GDP if compared to Japan and the United States. Both of these countries are first-rank industrial powers with small but politically powerful agricultural sectors. These two countries have farm programs of similar size to the CAP in terms of GDP percentages and with comparable protectionist features. The magnitude of the Community's farm program, however, dwarfs all other activities financed from the same budget. If the Community were a more complete system of government, with broad social programs and external relations, there would be little reason to call so much attention to its quite ordinary means of protecting food supplies and their producers.

High costs are the first and, often, the only form of constructive criticism of the CAP. In absolute numbers, the Community estimated net expenditures of about US$30 billion for farm programs in 1988, with about the same amount foreseen for 1989. The United States spent about US$22 billion in 1987 on about one-third as many farmers, but its costs fell to about US$13 billion in 1988, with the same net cost estimated for 1989.[10] In budgetary terms, U.S. farm policy expenditures constitute about 1.2 percent of the federal budget. For the Community, the comparable figure is 1.5 percent, taking into account both EC and national government expenditures. Often the Community and the United States can agree on little else in farm policy except that each spends too much money on agriculture support programs.

A Distorted Budget

The Community spends far too little on other important matters. For example, the total EC budget for 1988 was about 41 billion ECU (US$46 billion). The CAP took about 66 percent; the next largest programs were the regional and social funds. Each received about 2.5 billion ECI (US$3 billion) or about 7 percent of the entire budget for each of these important activities. For a population one-third larger than that of the United States, these are very modest sums even when they do not cover the large national outlays for these activities.

Agriculture was put into the EC budget as part of the original political bargaining which created the Community. When the CAP was developed, in the years after the Treaty of Rome became effective, the national differences on agriculture had to be accommodated within the CAP. This meant, for example, that France and the Netherlands, both exporters of farm products who wanted free intra-Community trade in these products (behind a high external tariff), insisted on equal treatment of agricultural and manufactured goods. Germany, which favored a controlled farm market system, yielded because of its strong and dominant industrial base. There was also agreement that the existing national systems of protecting farmers would be maintained. Finally, because

Britain, which had a different farm sector because of its Commonwealth imports, did not enter the Community at the beginning, the CAP became a continental compromise, starting with the Franco-German accommodation.

The financial burden of the CAP was undertaken under these circumstances of compromise and mutual accommodation, without full awareness of how the system's cost would grow. Protecting farmers' incomes was an early principle which soon took the Community far beyond either its expectations or its reach for the financial welfare of any other segment of its society.

REFORMING THE CAP

The EC and the United States both have a federal system for financing farm support with most of the direct expenditures undertaken by the Community and the Washington administrations, respectively. In both the Community and the United States, the subsidiary units of government also conduct some farm programs but these are dwarfed in cost and scope by those cited above which are exclusively those of the Community and the U.S. federal government. In any construction of total governmental costs, the CAP is a small item which should not be discussed as the fiscal catastrophe which one hears it called (often for national political purposes both in Europe and in our country).

The Community today has been given, for understandable historical reasons, the full responsibility for Community agriculture. If, and when, it assumes other responsibilities of comparable scope, the emphasis on the large portion of the Community resources spent on one item—agriculture—will fade away. The Community's problem is not too much agriculture but too little development of a real community beyond the farm and marketplace.

From this perspective, the CAP represents an inefficient and unproductive use of Community resources. There is a broad, if still disparate, consensus within Community institutions and even inside most member countries that fundamental changes in the CAP are needed. In 1985, the Commission presented a Green Paper on restructuring the CAP. This, and other proposals to reform the CAP, focus on these elements: (1) reducing total cost of the program; (2) reducing total farm production for budgetary but also political reasons to avoid desperate measures to minimize disposal of surplus commodities in markets already established by EC trading partners; and (3) redefining CAP goals in terms of EC self-sufficiency in most foodstuffs, enhanced environmental sensitivity and more realistic farmer income standards.

Restraining and ultimately reducing the cost of the CAP in both absolute terms and as a percentage of the EC budget is indispensable in political terms even if the Community could manage the expense. The Community was not established simply to administer a farm program, even if it had one of superb efficiency and at reasonable costs. The Community must enlarge its resources and expand its scope so that agriculture assumes a more modest share of resources and thus its proper place in the EC budget. Failure to do this may erode the still strong popular support for the Community ideal.

Some new factors may help alter the course of the CAP, as well as reduce its costs. Part-time farming in Germany and several other EC countries already provides a chance to reduce farm income support through production controls. If nonfarm income can be taken into account more accurately, and if further growth of part-time farming can be encouraged, the need to maintain high internal food prices to support farm income may diminish.

The 1985 Commission proposal made a start with steps to trim supply down to demand levels through increasing market influence as a stabilizing element. One institutional change under this plan gives the Commission final authority for determining when support payments can be reduced if supplies exceed the maximum EC guarantee support level. After stabilizing the markets, the Commission proposed reducing the "butter mountains" and "wine lakes" which accumulated under past programs of surplus storage. By 1989 important progress on these goals was being made.[11]

A longer-term goal, not yet undertaken, would find alternate means, perhaps of greater direct farmer income support, to be substituted for the high internal food prices which now encourage overproduction.

Pressures on the CAP

As the Community gradually exceeds self-sufficiency in most of its major farm products, problems of two kinds arise. For domestic reasons, resistance grows to the increased budgetary costs to buy and store surplus commodites which cannot find a place on the internal marketplace; as a result, pressures increase to move the surpluses out of storage onto the world marketplace no matter what the cost or the consequences of dumping them.

A related global problem of increasing importance to the Community is how surplus food can be directed to the hungry of the world without undue disruption of global markets and without discouraging appropriate levels of agricultural self-sufficiency in developing countries. This linkage of the Community's farm program with world hunger is increasingly explicit with the "green" political movement now represented in several national parliaments as well as in the European Parliament.

Increased commodity self-sufficiency for the Community puts the CAP under international pressure—starting in the GATT round—to reduce production immediately while referring the question of world food shortages to another forum. This is also the budgetary message which the Community began to receive in earnest in 1986-88 when its limited "own resources" faced their most serious shortfall since the EC budget began.[12] Whether this crisis, the latest of many, will focus finally on changing the CAP or simply on finding new budgetary resources is not yet clear.

The Cairns Group

Besides internal pressures to reduce costs and achieve some proportionality, external forces operate to restrain the CAP. A consensus which emerged to emphasize agriculture on the agenda for the Uruguay trade round is recognition that the Community's farm programs (and others like them) are seriously disruptive to world trade. Fourteen agricultural exporting countries led by Australia and New Zealand (called the Cairns group for the Australian city in which they first met) have promised joint action to encourage freer trade in farm products. The Community is acknowledged to be the first on the unwritten list of offenders, from the Cairns viewpoint. The United States, however, and Japan are close behind. The problem is that agriculture can no longer be kept separate from other trade issues which was the assumption underlying previous GATT trading rounds.[13]

The Community's defense of the CAP has always begun by an assertion that it only follows the pattern set by other countries in protecting its farmers and food supply. Now this pattern itself is recognized as a major problem which the comprehensive trade round talks must address. This decision will have implications for nonfood trade matters also since it is now the established pattern that any matter under consideration in a GATT round is open to sectorial tradeoffs.

Self-sufficiency developed gradually for technological reasons, not only because of specific CAP actions. Farm production in Europe is now part of a global growth and sales network which has changed greatly in the past 40 years. Each of these changes points to changes needed in the CAP principles themselves. A related problem is that once self-sufficiency is attained in a given commodity, a surplus—to be stored or sold in a new market—will shortly follow with attendant budgetary or political consequences.

Other changes, not directly related to agriculture, affect the assumptions under which the CAP was adopted. For example, the goal of making farmer income comparable to that of nonfarm workers may no longer be realistic or even sufficient under an enlightened approach to rural poverty. The danger in 1958 was that farmers might be left behind in the growing prosperity of industrial Europe. But today part-time farming and industrial farming are well established as part of that broader prosperity in the Community, although these nontraditional elements are distributed unevenly among the member countries. Thus, regional inequalities must be addressed better and farmer income must be redefined at the same time that a continual reduction in the number of farmers proceeds. Maintaining the farm population may be a social or an environmental matter; it is no longer simply a question of food production.

Environmental Worries

Production and enhancement of the environment are now major issues in all Community countries but are not related, as they should be, to the CAP and its costs. Proportionality of expenditure must become an issue in the environmental area when its meager EC outlays are compared with those of the CAP. In several EC countries, these concerns are represented by successful and apparently stable political parties and movements. Any revision of CAP goals should consider incorporating these environmental issues not merely in broad terms but with specific reference to retiring farmlands, creating new "greenbelts" around urban areas, and protecting threatened forests. A possible tactic here is to combine environmental concerns and global food aid in the same forum with trade in order to maximize the political strength of these diverse constituencies.

If successful, these expanded goals could well alter the CAP constituency in both electoral and budgetary terms. A failure to contain these elements creatively could have political consequences which member states may soon find very uncomfortable.

NOTES

1. Eurostat, *Basic Statistics,* 26th ed.; *Review 1975-84, Europe in Figures,* 1988; *The Agricultural Situation in the Community, 1988 Report* (Brussels: Commission, 1989) and *Agriculture in the United States and the European Community. A Comparison* (Washington, D.C.: Economic Research Service, USDA, May 12, 1987), 13-15. The ECU was worth about US$1.20 in these 1988 calculations.

2. *Europe's Common Agricultural Policy,* European File series, 2/86 (Brussels: Commission of the European Communities, 1986).

3. *Eurostat Review,* various years.

4. Compiled from B. R. Mitchell, ed., *European Historical Statistics,* 2d ed. (New York: Facts on File, 1981), 167-73.

5. Article 39, EEC Treaty.

6. *The Agricultural Policy of the European Community* (Luxembourg: EC

Publications Office, 1983), 15. For another account of the CAP, see the International Monetary Fund's Occasional Paper # 62, *The Common Agricultural Policy* (Washington: IMF, 1988).

7. To cite two examples of this shouting, the European Community considered a Reagan administration proposal to end all farm subsidies worldwide by the year 2000 to be a form of "dreaming," according to a *New York Times* story on March 8, 1988. The Bush administration softened and limited the proposal; it also eliminated the deadline which had sounded like an ultimatum. It proposed a substantial and progressive reduction of many, but not all, subsidies to farmers. It was still aimed, however, at the EC form of market intervention which it believes distorts world farm trade. The 1990 Houston economic summit continued this deadlock.

Another episode involved growth hormones which the EC forbade in all meat sold in the Community. American cattlemen use these hormones in about half of the $200-million worth of meat sent each year to the Community. After a series of threats and counterthreats, the United States imposed retaliatory tariffs of 100 percent on certain EC exports to the United States. In May 1989 a joint task force recommended an interim measure to accept EC certification as hormone-free American beef began to enter the market. A GATT panel was asked by the EC later to review the U.S. retaliations.

8. U.S. Bureau of the Census; cited in USDA, *Desk Reference Guide to U.S. Agricultural Trade,* 1986, 15; Mark Newman, Tom Fulton, and Lawrene Glaser, *A Comparison of Agriculture in the United States and the European Community* (Washington, D.C.: USDA, 1987), 10-11.

9. For an account of the reasons for sharp fluctuations in U.S. farm exports, see the 1986 monograph by Donna U. Vogt and Jasper Womach, *The Common Agricultural Policy of the European Community and Implications for U.S. Agricultural Trade,* 13-14; and *Agricultural Trade* (October 20, 1989): 9-10, both by the Library of Congress-Congressional Research Service, Washington.

10. USDA, *Comparison of Agriculture,* 5, 12, 53 (updated by conversations with USDA staff) and Commission, *Agricultural Situation, 1988,* 104. Comparing farm labor numbers is difficult because there is a growing part-time sector in both the United States and EC. By one EC estimate, there were about 17 million farmers in the Community in 1985 who constituted the equivalent of 9.4 full-time workers. According to USDA, there were about 3 million U.S. farm workers in 1986, supplemented by temporary and foreign workers.

11. For a summary of the 1985 Commission proposals as actually implemented up to 1989, see Commission, *Agricultural Situation, 1988,* 13-19.

By the end of 1989, there were some encouraging signs from programs begun several years earlier to cut dairy costs through concerted pressures to reduce the number of cows held for milk production. The German finance ministry announced in June 1989, for example, that the Federal Republic would save several billion marks in the 1990 EC budget year because its total Community contribution was falling sharply from the CAP dairy reform. See *This Week in Germany* June 24, 1989 (German Information Service, New York).

There was also relief in Washington when the Community agreed at the end of 1989 that its controversial program to encourage domestic soybean and other vegtable oil production would be altered after a GATT panel agreed with a U.S.

contention that the EC program unfairly favored its domestic oilseed producers. A Dillon round agreement in 1962 gave U.S. soybeans tariff-free entrance into the EC but the oil producer plan diminished these U.S. soybean exports (*New York Times* [December 21, 1989]: D1).

12. See appendix C for more information on the EC budgetary process.

13. In April 1989, the GATT member countries agreed to a negotiating framework for the next twenty months. The Cairns group includes Argentina, Australia, Brazil, Canada, Chile, Colombia, Fiji, Hungary, Indonesia, Malaysia, the Philippines, New Zealand, and Thailand. When they met in Bariloche, Argentina, in February 1988, they proposed a compromise position under which the short-term subsidy cuts which the EC had proposed to reduce overproduction be counted as a down payment toward the broader goal of eliminating all subsidies by a definite date. The Cairns group, which has yet to prove its effectiveness as a farm bloc within the world trade round talks, supported the U.S. goal of eliminating all farm subsidies but wanted the ban effective before the year 2000.

6

The European Monetary System

The European Monetary System is the embodiment of a determination to preserve all that has been achieved so far in the Community and . . . an essential pre-condition for any future development.
—Commission Vice-President Ortoli, 1984

At several points in the postwar history of the European Community, a relaunching of the whole venture became necessary; at one crucial intersection, the rarified subject of monetary reform became the vehicle for a renewal of the European spirit.

It was as if the whole effort to make a unified Europe out of many national and cultural elements was too much for the people involved. The project seemed to falter, the old patterns started to reappear, old fights were resumed, but then, each time, something happened to restart the engine of Europe:

In 1954, when the European Defense Community was rejected by the French National Assembly, many thought that a united Europe was a postwar hallucination which was now over. Yet Jean Monnet and Paul Henri Spaak could somehow collaborate in the winter of 1954/55 to redirect energies toward an effective trading system instead of the political-military bonding which was now seen as clearly premature. In the late 1960s, impatience with slowed economic integration discouraged many believers. But the frustration inspired a move toward a more perfect European Union with a ten-year goal. More recently, the Parliament's draft treaty on European Union, the Single European Act, and the 1992 program constitute three aspects of still another move to restore and rededicate the Community.

Another important and highly successful relaunch came in 1979 when, after several false starts and with the caution appropriate to bankers, the European Monetary System (EMS) began. To date, it is the EMS more than any other Community program which shows clearly, though imperfectly, how a united Europe will transform the lives of its citizens. The short history of the EMS also shows the pains which accompany the unifying process.

Like every other major EC venture, the EMS has political undercurrents. Here the struggle was for European mastery of the field dominated by the dollar and by one of the most vigorous forms of nationalism, that of the European central bank authorities. To understand how great the transformation already achieved by the EMS, we must return to the formal origins of monetary planning in the 1957 Treaty of Rome.

There the principle of freedom of capital movement is expressed as a fundamental means of achieving the European Economic Community. When it came to details, however, the treaty was much more explicitly concerned with ending impediments to trade than with prescribing common policies in any detail. The treaty, for example, gives only general monetary principles on the objectives of balanced export and import payments, stable currencies, and coordinated capital and currency movements.[1] How to achieve these complicated and revolutionary goals for six different countries was left to time, the ingenuity of the successor generations, and some unanticipated help from disruptions in the dollar-centered monetary system of the world's leading trading countries.

BRETTON WOODS AND THE BIRTH OF THE EMS

The European Monetary System, like the Community itself, has roots in the Second World War. But in the case of monetary policies, what came out of wartime experience was ultimately rejected in the altered climate which the war itself produced. In 1944, less than one year before the war ended in Europe, representatives of 44 countries met in the New Hampshire resort town of Bretton Woods. There, in the shadow of Mount Washington, they fashioned a pact which lasted a quarter of a century for certain key monetary provisions and which still prevails today in its institutional forms of the International Bank for Reconstruction and Development—known as the World Bank—and the International Monetary Fund.

Bretton Woods, the place, also become the shorthand expression for a system of relatively fixed exchange rates governing the values and the relationships between the major world currencies. This system worked so well for so long that its limitations only slowly became evident. But by the late 1950s and increasingly in the 1960s, the name "Bretton Woods" came to signify restrictions on the dynamic growth of the Western economies.

The Exchange Rate System

Fixed exchange rates rested squarely upon the continued determination of the United States to express the price of its dollar as 1/35 of an ounce of gold. When other currencies, with a fixed rate of exchange with the dollar, deviated from that rate through inflation or other disruptive influences, it was the responsibility of that government to readjust either by internal changes of a monetary or budgetary nature or to alter the exchange rate with the dollar. As long as the value of the U.S. dollar remained relatively stable and as long as the U.S. economy remained both robust and largely isolated, the Bretton Woods system worked. But as the economy of the United States became internationalized, its currency became subject to the same pressures felt by its trading rivals. Tensions arose between the dollar as the standard measure of the world's currencies and the dollar as a fluctuating value, dependent on the policies of its government and the whims of currency traders.

By the late 1960s, the United States was regularly running deficits in its balance of payments. These deficits, although modest by the standards of the 1980s, were judged serious and persistent by the prevailing conservative standards. A growing lack of confidence developed in other countries in the American management of its currency which led to attempts, first moderate, than less restrained, to trade in their accumulated dollars for the gold which stood behind them. European treasuries led these efforts. When U.S gold reserves were threatened and efforts at reform failed, political turmoil caused President Nixon to react with a harshness which Europeans still use as a measure of the episodic American failure to discuss solutions to common ailments.[2]

Nixon slammed down the window on gold exchanges for dollars. The convertibility of the world's primary currency into its standard precious metal was over and the pact in the New Hampshire woods had to be replaced with a new monetary system.

From the rigidity of Bretton Woods, the money system shifted over two years to the other extreme. Market conditions would now allow the free and continuous adjustment (called "floating") of all exchange rates. Many economists supported this change. They had long advocated a global system which could easily respond to differing exchange rate pressures and domestic economic goals by immediate and automatic fluctuations on the foreign exchange markets.

Oil and Inflation

The first oil price crisis, coming just two years after the Nixon shock of detaching the dollar from its gold backing, tested this new flexibility. Greatly varying inflation rates were an early result of the irregular oil supplies and their fluctuating prices. Oil prices rose everywhere so inflation was a generalized threat but it grew with the variations determined by how much oil a country produced, how it taxed energy, its conservation policies, and other national characteristics. In the United States, inflation was fueled by the underfinanced Vietnam war.

The European Community countries ranged from Britain, which was becoming a net oil exporter with a large economy, to Belgium and Denmark, which both imported all of their oil and also had small economies which were especially sensitive to the exchange rate movements allowed by free-floating currencies.

Flexible rates in this crisis period certainly relieved pressures which otherwise might have disrupted international trading even more drastically. But the longer-term advantages expected from flexible rates, principally the ease of adjusting skewed payment balances, did not occur. Economists found that several other factors beyond exchange rates caused the persistent payments problems. Markets were rigid in some ways, even if exchange rates were not. Oil was imported, for example, regardless of its price, at least in the short term, because there were no convenient substitutes.

More broadly, flexible rates helped balance trade shortfalls and surpluses only when other measures were taken by national authorities to support the desired change. Rate fluctuations alone could become a dangerous crutch for weak or timid national governments. On the other side, governments were often unwilling to accept the consequences of large exchange rate movements which included economic problems and a declining "prestige" of their currency.

Another unappreciated element was the growing ease of moving capital across national borders. These movements now dominate the foreign exchange markets which trade, like the stock exchanges, 20 hours of each working day. Trading action moves with the sun from European markets, to New York, then Chicago, and on to the West Coast markets. After the Pacific market day in Tokyo, Hong Kong, and Singapore, there is only a brief pause before trading starts again in Europe. Money can move as rapidly as the electronic signals which express it.

Closing the Gold Window

Even before the U.S. gold window closed in 1971, the European Community countries began to see themselves as victims of a monetary system over which they had little control. The swing from Bretton Woods to floating rates still left the Europeans subject to a dollar-centered world. And flexibility itself tended to tolerate the economic problems of individual countries which, collectively, inhibited further integration of the EC economies. Clearly Europe needed something else even if the United States preferred the volatility of the exchange markets to all known alternatives.

The world of monetary policy and exchange rates, especially for a Europe trying to integrate, did not exist in isolation from trade, agriculture, and the regional problems of the Community. Internal trade policies of EC countries were slowly bringing their economies together and freeing the movement of capital between them. The share of intra-Community trade in total foreign trade climbed from 30 to 50 percent for the original six between 1958 and 1972. Growing interdependence, while a fundamental Community goal, created new tensions, especially in the period of freely moving exchange rates.

Balance of payments problems grew when the six EC governments found fewer means of controlling their economies. Capital crossed their borders by phone calls, dissipating or at least complicating traditional controls by finance ministers over their monetary stocks. There were also problems when major EC currencies, like the French franc and the DM, tended to get out of proper alignment with each other. It slowly became evident that the freedom of the post-Bretton Woods period was not fully compatible with the provisions of the Rome Treaty which provided, without specification, for the monetary integration of Europe.

This realization did not come easily or in a single insight. As early as 1968, with Bretton Woods still in force, the Council and the Commission exchanged ideas on how to move toward the goals of a firm fixing of EC exchange rates, establishing a European unit of account or currency, and instituting a European Monetary Fund.[3] An elaborate system of restricting the fluctuation of each member country's currency within a range of movement was devised even before the 1971 action by President Nixon which finally, and clearly, focused the attention of Europe. But the Community efforts failed to produce a separate system before the dollar's gold convertibility ended. For a time after the Nixon "shock," no possibility of joint European action existed. What progress had been made in the discussions after 1968 evaporated in the national anxieties of the moment.

The Benelux Plan

The Benelux countries[4] presented a plan to the Council shortly after the Washington announcement on gold. This plan would limit fluctuations of connected EC currencies within a "tunnel" formed by their margins of fluctuation against the dollar.[5] This idea of relating EC currencies both to each other (in a "snake") and to the dollar was not new. Pierre Werner, Luxembourg's prime minister, and Raymond Barre, Commission vice president, had led the 1968 exchange of ideas which produced such a plan. Now, under pressure, the small EC members wanted it to start.

Their three larger neighbors could not agree as readily as the Benelux members did. The latter then instituted their plan alone in August 1971, creating, in effect, a demonstration project for the rest of the Community and for the world that a middle ground between Bretton Woods and free flotation was possible. The Benelux model, although representing only a tiny fraction of the Community's total economic and monetary weight, was persuasive but not yet decisive.

Put aside for less tense times was the long-standing debate between the "monetarists" and the "economists," that is, between those who stressed "pure" monetary solutions to exchange rate problems and those favoring concentration on the coordination of members' basic economic policies. This debate had slowed every earlier discussion of how a European monetary system should proceed. Both approaches were clearly needed, but the "little three" believed that members needed to unite to survive. The Benelux example would reemerge at several painful points later in the 1970s as something the other Community members might profitably adopt.

The Search for Stability

Near the end of the tumultuous monetary year of 1971, the major financial powers sent their finance ministers to a meeting in the Smithsonian Institution's red brick castle on the Washington mall. The December sessions established fluctuation margins against the dollar which were broader than the version the Community had considered earlier but still consistent with the Benelux plan both in itself and as a model for future EC cooperation. But the end of dollar convertibility into gold and its devaluation at the Smithsonian meeting made the U.S. currency suspect. Europeans were now reluctant to begin accumulating more dollars. Their search for their own currency stability began again.

A further devaluation of the dollar in 1973 and the American tendency toward a policy of nonintervention to support it on currency markets convinced the Europeans that improved joint EC action, however difficult to achieve, must become their goal. From 1973 to 1977, there was much painful confusion but finally the six central banks agreed on a "snake in the tunnel" after the Basle Agreement of April 10, 1972. At one point, several Community members arranged a joint floating of the currencies centered on the German mark. This was the "snake out of the tunnel'' which the Commission had at first proposed but which France and Italy could not accept.

Several important restatements of the principle of Community monetary management occurred in this difficult period and from these efforts the construction of the EMS must be dated. In September 1974, the French finance minister proposed coordination of all nine Community currencies (those already in the snake and those of the three new EC members from the 1973 enlargement). This plan, which included joint currency intervention and an EC unit of account or currency unit, failed but it had a stimulative effect.

Seeking European Union

The European Council, in 1974, asked Leo Tindemans, the Belgian foreign minister, to report on how to transform the Community into a European Union, including the economic and monetary union foreseen at a summit meeting two years earlier. The resulting Tindemans report on European Union in December 1975[6] proposed several alternate ways of strengthening the snake.

A third consultation plan emphasizing economic coordination was suggested by Dutch Finance Minister Duisenberg in 1976. These antecedents coalesced in a brilliant speech in Florence in 1977 by Commission President Roy Jenkins who said only monetary union could promote full recovery and growth for the Community. This speech achieved, through perfect timing and precise ideas, the real start of the European Monetary System. Yet even after four years of hesitation and a growing conviction on the part of political leaders that the Community must act, it was two more long years before the EMS began.

The political push began when French President Valery Gisçard d'Estaing and German Chancellor Helmut Schmidt (both finance ministers who moved up to chief executive) proposed, at the Copenhagen summit in April, 1978, the details of an EMS in which all Community countries could participate.[7] The Bremen summit three months later instructed the finance ministers to devise a new currency unit, to continue the snake, and to provide a fund to support the system. The December 1978 summit in Brussels approved the entire plan with operations actually starting in March 1979. A major step in the ''cumulative logic of integration''[8] was about to begin.

OPERATION OF THE EMS

The EMS had, from the start, two major goals: to provide greater stability of exchange rates among Community members and to promote a convergence of their economic policies to promote internal stability. Because the EMS was launched just before the second oil price shock in late 1979, it is difficult to measure its performance by a simple before-and-after analysis. What must be estimated is how well the Community countries stabilized exchange rates and coordinated their economies under the extraordinary difficulties from 1979 to the present.

Before that analysis, we should look at the EMS mechanisms available for this ambitious two-part goal and how these tools differed from the previous system.

Stabilizing exchange rates under EMS is achieved by an active and mandatory mechanism which relates the basket of currency values of the old unit of account, the interrelationship of EC currencies of the former snake, and a grid of bilateral exchange rates based on a parities system. The second device marking the EMS is a divergence indicator which shows when a country should intervene to maintain its currency in relation to the ECU[9] by making policy adjustments as opposed to short-term market interventions which are required to maintain the grid limits.

Like the previous system, EMS is optional in its rate mechanism. Britain has not participated in that program since it started in 1979. Greece, Portugal, and Spain also abstained initially although both the pound sterling and the drachma are included in calculations in the currency basket. (Such inclusions reflect market realities, not political decisions.) The peseta was added under the 1989 agreement when Spain joined EMS. Eventually, monetary union is expected to require all EC members to commit themselves fully to the rate mechanism and to the private use of the ECU. For a country to have its currency included in the ECU basket has no direct effect on policies but entering the rate mechanism does oblige actions to keep within the divergence limits.

Intervention requirements are the heart of the EMS. They are achieved through the use of the ECU, a currency unit of greater use and versatility than its predecessor, the unit of account. The ECU is a composite monetary unit made up of fixed quantities of each member countries' currencies. Thus the ECU has had, since 1984, 140 Italian lire, 1.15 Greek drachma, 71.9 pfennige, and so on. Total value in terms of any one currency in the basket, or against any non-EMS currency (like the dollar), can vary daily. There is, as yet, no paper or metal version of the ECU but it is traded on several European currency markets like any other foreign currency. Private investors can buy and sell ECU bonds and the invoices of some European companies are written and paid in ECU. In the United States, the ECU is traded as a currency future in both New York and Chicago commodity exchanges.[10]

The Rate Mechanism

Within the EMS, the ECU expresses the central rates in the exchange rate mechanism, the intervention indicator, and the credit mechanism which allows the central banks of member states to lend and borrow funds for their interventions. The ECU is also used to settle accounts between the monetary authorities of the Community including the central banks. Finally, it is used for the construction and execution of the EC budget.

There is considerable flexibility in the EMS system, both in allowing for movements of exchange rates within limits and through adjustments or realignments of the central rates. A number of these realignments have been made, showing that both speed and calm could accompany what under Bretton Woods often caused domestic political and financial crises. The EMS has not eliminated the pain of adjustment but it has eased the path of these domestic measures.

An Incomplete System

The EMS, in institutional terms, is an incomplete structure. When the Council gave final approval to the system in 1978, it was with an understanding that the credit devices for the operation of the existing snake would be consolidated into a European Monetary Fund (EMF) within two years. This has still not happened a decade later. Instead, the European Monetary Cooperation Fund, established at the Paris summit in 1972, operates without the strength and the commitment of the central banks which a genuine EMS would require. The resistance of these central banks, especially the *Bundesbank,* which first wanted much greater convergence of economic policies by member countries, prevents the creation of the EMF and the wider use of the ECU, particularly within Germany.

There are also EMS short-term and medium-term financing and credit mechanisms which will, eventually, be incorporated in the EMF.

Two other functions of the EMS concern the regional and program-matic sides of the Community. The first helps less prosperous members when they fully participate in the EMS exchange rate system. Interest rate subsidies enable these countries to strengthen their basic economic structure and bring them closer to the Community average.

A second special EMS function allows the agricultural sector protec-tion from the periodic adjustments of national currencies. This device, called the Monetary Compensation Amounts (MCA), dates to the 1969 devaluation of the French franc and was intended to prevent the infla-tionary effects of such currency devaluations on imported food prices and on farmers' incomes.

Floating currency rates complicated the MCA device but during this period the Community remained committed to unified agricultural prices. Originally, it was thought that the CAP would promote exchange rate stability. Instead, it forced the monetary system to adjust to national farm prices. This required creation of "green" currencies which were translations of the unit of account into national currencies for agricultural purposes. When EMS started, further adjustments of MCA were needed. It became very awkward for Brussels to seek an integrated market for agricultural products without having fully integrated currencies to pay for them. EMS advocates hoped that this lesson was not lost on the national governments.

There are differences between EMS and its somewhat simpler predecessor. There is now an emphasis on economic convergence which was a mere hope before 1979. There are still tensions between the "monetarists," who tend to see much in monetary devices which others miss seeing, and the "economists," who believe, with the *Bundesbank* approach, that if all countries behaved as they should in the strict management of their currencies, there would be less need for monetary approaches. EMS represents a tender compromise between these two positions but the compromise now emphasizes more economic coordination than the snake could ever induce. Thus EMS, as a step in the logic of integration, also became a political act.

The role of the European Currency Unit is much more important than that of the unit of account under the snake. The ECU, for example, aspires to become a reserve currency in the world financial community as well as a genuine foreign currency on world markets. The conservative *Bundesbank,* which retains doubts about the ECU until it is backed by a strong and independent European central bank (like itself), resists both measures but it is slowly being moved away from rigid opposition. The ECU has also developed a modest life in the private monetary sector, something which never occurred with the unit of account. This development, however, is limited until there is a central clearing bank for ECU transactions.

Britain and the EMS

It is important to note these differences between the EMS and the former snake because critics often note only the similarities. The latter include the currency basket, the exchange rate structure, and the optional nature of national participation which were folded into the EMS intact. Britain, for example, although a member of the EMS, continues to stay out of the rate intervention mechanism. Indications by Margaret Thatcher that eventually the pound would join are accepted in Brussels as a domestic political statement and not as any commitment to a full EMS by the British leader. Increasingly, Brussels seems to accept that nothing other than a fundamental shift in British politics will break the impasse in London. By tying the pound to other EC currencies in the rate mechanism, Britain would acknowledge that its currency's former global role was now circumscribed by the European partnership. This recognition will presumably prompt criticism of whatever British government is in power for allowing a further decline of Britain as a world power. Britain is, in fact, the only EC country which still witnesses this kind of criticism pitting national values against those of the Community.

The British pound is still a global reserve currency but this role may be declining. It still floats, strictly speaking, but the British economy is gradually becoming so firmly tied to that common one of its eleven EC partners that the pound is certainly on its way to inclusion in the EMS rate mechanism. Since there will be undoubtedly some partisan criticism of any British government entering the ECU rate mechanism, the timing will depend on managing and isolating this criticism and insuring that the change has as little effect as possible on domestic economics. Its entrance into the rate mechanism will signify, from the viewpoint of these domestic U.K. critics, that the pound's global role has ended.

The United States and the EMS

For most of the first decade of the EMS, the United States was firmly opposed to managed exchange rates. Even when an important exception was begun in 1985 by cooperating with several other countries to reduce the dollar's value, the American government since 1981 has opposed the concepts behind the EMS and resisted any suggestion that the U.S. dollar might either participate in such international management or by other means be subjected to even U.S. government controls on its market value against other currencies.[11]

This firmness has persisted against the sharp deterioration of the U.S. balance of payments and especially against the component of that balance represented by trade. Until the "Plaza" meeting,[12] the U.S. administration refused even to discuss exchange rates with other countries. With the New York meeting came the admission that the U.S. Treasury wanted the dollar's value to fall but without either an explicit policy statement or a tactic announced toward that goal. After September 1985, there were suggestions, usually by anonymous Treasury Department voices, that the highly valued U.S. dollar should fall to ease the country's trade deficit. But could this take place by itself? Would the United States continue to cooperate with the other major economic powers to manage exchange rates? While there were occasional suggestions from the Secretary of the Treasury that Germany and Japan should stimulate their economies to absorb more U.S. exports, there was tacit recognition in Washington and other world capitals that the problem was in U.S. economic practices, not in the habits of foreigners. The traditional prescription for a trade imbalance remained an increase in exports or a drop in imports, or both, with a decline in the value of the currency the method of choice.

A different problem—an undervalued U.S. dollar—was the occasion—not the cause—of the creation of the EMS in 1979. In a review of the EMS after seven years, the International Monetary Fund (IMF) noted that "periods of weakness of the dollar tend to coincide with increased tension in the EMS" while "a strong dollar had . . . often been coincident with a lack of tension in the system."[13]

Although the Europeans succeeded in creating a zone of relative tranquillity in their exchange rates, they remained bound to a dollar whose movements they could neither predict nor influence. The EMS was, in the late 1980s, still under great strains from this dependence which was made much worse, in European eyes, by an administration in Washington which recognized neither a problem nor a responsibility. Since an ideological commitment to nonintervention in the currency market was, by definition, not subject to negotiation, Europeans waited for a change in ideology. They were gradually joined by many (but not all) international economists who found the evidence of 1971-88 more and more difficult to match with the now-extremist view of totally free floating rates.

The same IMF report noted that the Europeans have confounded their critics who thought that the EMS could not endure. Although the international organization did not say so explicitly, the American government was, for much of the life of the EC system, strongly, if quietly, sympathetic with those critics.[14]

The turbulence of the dollar caused several adjustments in the EMS. There were two general alignments of exchange rates in April 1986 and January 1987 and a less extensive one in January 1990. There were also minor steps taken to increase the use of the official ECU.

More significantly, there was a tendency in EC countries, as they watched the gyrations of the dollar, to recognize the need for better economic coordination, leading toward convergence of macroeconomic policies, to protect themselves and the still fragile EMS. The move to liberalize capital movements in the 1992 program originated in these deliberations.

Substantial improvements to the EMS came in the Basle-Nyborg agreement of September 1987 which recognized this increasing convergence. Steps were taken to refine the intervention mechanism. Short-term interest rate differentials narrowed after the agreement even though the dollar's abrupt movements continued. (The dollar's value dropped from about 1.5 ECU to .80 ECU in the 33 months from February 1985 to December 1987.)

A Commission report in 1989 noted these accomplishments and said, concerning the future of EMS, that its accomplishments, especially in establishing operating rules on exchange rate differentials and interventions, prepared the way for the SEA and the internal market.[15]

As the EMS passed its tenth anniversary in 1989, there were still skeptics in the U.S. Treasury Department. They had once doubted that the EMS could ever work. When it did, they seemed dismayed that it might be working so well in Europe that it could serve as a putative global model with a firmly structured exchange rate system.

SIGNIFICANCE OF THE EMS

It is widely, if not universally, admitted by some that the European Community has achieved a notable success with EMS. What is its longer-term significance both for Europe and the rest of the world? Those who see EMS as the largely untold story of the Community winning the monetary stability which has eluded the United States believe that these lessons of a carefully constructed and moderate mechanism can now be applied with care but confidence to the world monetary system. The remaining skeptics, even while admitting that EMS works in Europe, see both political and functional problems with its global application.

For EMS supporters, the principal question is whether its principles can be applied to cover the two key world currencies, the dollar and the Japanese yen, which still float. It is probably impossible for Japan to resist a global currency grid if the United States both advocates and participates in it. The central question is whether, even with a change of ideologies in Washington, the United States could accept a fixed rate currency system, no matter how flexible, which required institutionalized cooperation and some form of majority voting. Bretton Woods unilateralism cannot be revived but it is not easily forgotten either.

Also, a worldwide monetary system with EMS features would not necessarily mean a return to the dollar-centered system of Bretton Woods. The German mark and the yen have become global markers since 1971 and the pound sterling, while greatly altered, is still an important one. A reconstruction of a world monetary mechanism would need all four major currencies in some form of parity grid and, depending on EMS developments, the ECU as well. Some important regional currencies might have to be related to this global grid either by direct participation or through regional subgrids. Devising and operating such a plan would require an enormous commitment from the four reserve currency countries. It would also need a special leadership role by the United States which is unlikely, as least as far ahead as economists or political observers can see.[16]

The Future of the EMS

Whether the Europeans ultimately succeed in the Community monetary system has implictions for the United States, for Japan, and, indeed, for the rest of the world. A return to managed exchange rates after nearly twenty years of floating the dollar could amount to a definitive change in American economic direction for two reasons.

First, the United States remains the principal engine of the Western economic structure; our willingness to cooperate more closely with our major trading partners would signal our dependence on their cooperation and good will. We have not been obliged to demonstrate such dependence since the end of World War II. Our readiness even to discuss the problem of exchange rate misalignments and volatility would acknowledge that we can no longer determine the rules of the international monetary system.

Second, the use of the EMS as a model providing such stability and flexibility in currency rates would acknowledge for the first time the success of the Community (as distinct from individual members) in monetary management. The EMS would necessarily become a model if the world moves toward a restructured monetary plan.

While the present resistance of the United States is the strongest reason why a new global monetary system cannot be created, it is not the only factor limiting the application of the EMS model. Diversity in the world economic order is quite a contrast from the high degree of economic integration in the Community which, while imperfect, is much greater than exists between non-EC countries. Even with the addition of Portugal and Spain, and the presence of Greece and Ireland, these relatively low-income countries are far better meshed in the EC's economy than the debt-ridden and commodity-dependent Third World countries are in the world trading system. A manifestation of this closer integration is seen with the problems the Community experiences in trade among its members whenever monetary tensions arise.[17]

A second difference reflects the political power distribution in the Community. The Council of Ministers and central bank authorities, working closely together, created the original snake, the monetary cooperation fund, and finally the EMS itself. No legislative authority was granted and no parliamentary action was involved since the Rome Treaty granted sufficient power for this kind of decision to Council and banking officials. A comparable acquiescence by the Congress, for example, is impossible to imagine.

Until the world sees a movement toward greater institutional cooperation, the EMS seems destined to remain a somewhat incomplete and imperfect model of multinational monetary cooperation. It could be an even more effective example if it could overcome a number of problems.

There is still too little strength in the EMS structure to resist truly great national movements against it. The refusal, for example, of France or Germany to cooperate in fiscal or monetary policies could collapse the system under certain assumptions. Such a refusal would produce both a fierce reaction in capital movement and significant exchange rate misalignment which EMS would be unable to solve. For European monetary coordination to remain stable, it must, like the bicycle, move forward. The next step was, clearly, movement toward a European central bank and a single EC currency.

Strong National Pressures

Macroeconomic policy coordination is still too weak within the entire Community structure. National pressures are still strong throughout member countries where inflation, unemployment, and threatened trading patterns continue to become domestic political issues easily. These pressures soon manifest themselves in Council meetings where the veto still operates under some circumstances. On the positive side, it is now accepted within the Community that a member's domestic monetary and fiscal policies will be critically studied by other EC members.

The development of a European Monetary Fund, as proposed in 1978, and ultimately, of a European central bank, remains essential if the EMS is to be judged complete and fully capable of action. Resistance, especially in the powerful *Bundesbank*, seemed, by 1990, to have been worn down or at least restrained, partly under the realization that the conservative monetary and fiscal policies of the Germans would almost certainly dominate any EC central bank, as least as thoroughly as the *Bundesbank* itself had dominated the EMS in its first decade.

Overcoming or reducing limitations on the use of the ECU in the private sector must proceed. Important gains have already been made. The ECU is now the third major currency on the Euro-bond market after the dollar and the mark. But a superior clearing house system must be established. Again the resistance of the *Bundesbank*, which fears less discipline among some of the EC members, is a major obstacle. The German central bankers would not want to rely on any currency less conservatively managed than the DM. For the ECU to reach this level of acceptance (and for the other EC members to reach comparable levels of self-discipline) may take many years.

The Delors Committee

Solving these problems[18] gradually became a top agenda item under the Commission presidencies of Jacques Delors, starting in 1985. He recognized, and set out to convince his colleagues on the Commission and the political leaders of the Community member states, that the gradual alignment of monetary and economic policies was both the ultimate goal of the EMS and the logic of the entire Community.

The European Council, meeting in Hanover in June 1988, set up a high-level committee to study these EMS problems in the light of the 1992 program and the Single European Act. Delors, who had been a French finance minister before being president of the Commission, chaired the group consisting of representatives from each of the members' central banks and three outside experts. Their report was issued in April 1989, recommending a federal central banking system which incorporated the 12 central banks in a European System of Central Banks (ESCB).[19] The ESCB would itself be an autonomous Community institution, requiring a new EC treaty both for its creation and to allow a central management of economic and monetary policies.

This audacious proposal by the Delors committee induced a properly conservative response from the members' central banks. Karl Otto Poehl, president of the *Bundesbank*, seemed to recognize the logic of the Delors report but cautioned that the desired result of a monetary union should not be pushed too fast. He suggested that the 1992 internal market program itself did not demand an EC central bank to succeed, at least immediately.

Delors' report proposed three stages, each with economic and monetary phases, in moving toward monetary and economic union. Phase 1 would seek greater convergence of economic performance by member countries through existing institutions and mechanisms. This phase assumes the successful completion of the internal market program. The structural funds (social, regional, etc.) would be reformed and doubled in size in this phase. In monetary matters, obstacles would be eliminated to financial integration. Banking, securities and insurance services, and their instruments would circulate freely. All EC currencies would have to be in the rate mechanism under the same rules in this phase. Finally, the Committee of Central Bank Governors would express nonbinding but authoritative opinions on monetary and exchange rate policies, including those of individual member countries.

An interim proposal by several committee members favored a European Reserve Fund (ERF) which would facilitate "concerted management" of exchange rates, possibly with increased market intervention. The ERF could also serve as a training ground for a board of directors and staff to improve coordination of monetary analysis and decisions. Finally, the report noted, an interim ERF would symbolize the Community's political will to proceed toward full monetary and economic union. Several committee members, however, opposed an ERF both on institutional and policy grounds.[20]

Phase 2 could come about only after an intergovernmental conference produced a treaty which was then ratified. The treaty would specify institutional changes needed for full economic and monetary union. In this phase, which is both a training and transition period for full union, there would be some majority decisions but most options would remain with national authorities. In the monetary phase, ESCB would be established, incorporating all earlier institutional entities. Here the key will be the gradual transfer of decision making from national to Community institutions.

Phase 3 would see the rules in macroeconomic and budgetary matters becoming binding. The Council of Ministers could take enforceable decisions on national budgets to maintain monetary stability and to supplement structural resources to member states. Exchange rates would become irrevocably locked with the ESCB exercising control over monetary policies and on exchange market interventions in third currencies. Official reserves would be pooled and managed by ESCB and plans would be made for a single EC currency.[21]

The 1990 Treaty Conference

Several years will stand between the 1989 proposal of the Delors committee and definitive action on its report. The Strasbourg summit in December 1989 affirmed the intergovernmental treaty conference to be held 12 months later. But voices were soon heard demanding that the 1990 conference not be limited to monetary affairs but also consider institutional, social, environmental, and other EC issues. Keeping monetary and economic union on track will make the highest demands on the Community's leadership, especially if it becomes part of a larger EC reform.

But with the political force of the European Council behind monetary union, the Community may once again be witnessing another important relaunching of the initiative of the Treaty of Rome which originally assumed that the time would come when Community members would have to bring their economies, and, implicitly, their monetary systems, into full convergence.

By 1990, 45 years after the end of World War II, 40 years after the Schuman Declaration, over 35 years after the economic relaunch in the wake of the defeat of the political and defense community, and 10 years after monetary union was due on its first schedule, that time seemed finally to be approaching.

NOTES

1. Articles 3, 103-9, EEC Treaty.

2. Although the United States can be faulted on other occasions for failing to consult its European allies, the nature of the gold convertibility decision made it very difficult to consult without jeopardizing the secrecy needed to maintain control over the remaining U.S. gold stocks and to prevent outright market panic.

3. For a good account of these and other aspects of the history of the EMS, see

The European Monetary System, by Jacques van Ypersele and Jean-Claude Koeune, in the European Perspectives series published by the Commission (Brussels, 1985), especially chapter 2, "The Ebb and Flow of European Monetary Integration," 31-45, and annex 1, "Timetable of events with important monetary implications for the EEC," 117-19.

4. For the origins of the customs union of Belgium, the Netherlands, and Luxembourg which produced the acronym Benelux, see chapter 3.

5. The monetary metaphors are sometimes as confusing as the underlying realities they seek to simplify. The "tunnel' is a set of limits around currency movements. The "snake" is a concept of currencies related or tied to each other like segments on a snake. Put together, the related currencies have limits on their coordinated movements, like a snake might have in a tunnel. A "grid" is an arrangement of divergence limits on which currencies can move up or down. A "basket" is a collection of national currencies combined in specified proportions related to the country's economic strength or another criterion. Within the EC, both the old unit of account and its successor, the ECU, are basket currencies.

6. See chapter 3 for more on European Union.

7. Schmidt later attributed his initiative on EMS to Jean Monnet and his Action Committee for a United States of Europe.

8. This apt phrase comes from Loukas Tsoukalis, *The Politics and Economics of European Monetary Integration* (London: George Allen and Unwin, 1977).

9. ECU is both an acronym for the European Currency Unit and the name of a medieval European gold coin. It is gradually becoming an accepted reference point for both its monetary value and as an expression of confidence in a future EC currency in full private as well as official use. The private sector in Europe has shown a growing interest in the ECU, including the *ECU Newsletter,* published quarterly by the Instituto Bancario San Paolo di Torino-San Paolo Bank of Torino, Italy, which follows closely the ECU's private sector activities.

10. Participation in the EMS is separate from participation in the rate mechanism. EMS members decide, with the concurrence of the country involved, which EC national currencies will be in the ECU basket. EC members can also enter the EMS after they join the Community. Spain and Portugal, for example, both participated in the ECU basket of currencies, starting in September 1989. The EC Council of Ministers, at the June meeting that year approving the revised basket of currencies, also accepted Spain's decision to enter the peseta into the exchange rate mechanism.

11. See John Williamson's carefully balanced case for managed rates and the Reagan administration's opposition in his book *The Exchange Rate System* (Washington: Institute for International Economics, 1985).

12. The meeting at the Plaza Hotel in New York on September 22, 1985, brought together the finance ministers of the Group of Five (Britain, France, Germany, Japan, and the United States) who agreed to reduce the dollar's value gradually by managing interest rates, market interventions, and other actions. There was no formal agreement and no detailed text but more of a "gentlmen's pact" to work together toward a common goal. The official American position before and after the meeting was that the U.S. Treasury would not intervene in currency markets except to prevent "disruptions," events never precisely defined.

In February 1987, the "Plaza" countries (plus Canada and Italy for some of the sessions) met at the Louvre in Paris and agreed, inter alia, that they would cooperate "to foster stability of exchange rates around current levels." There was considerable central bank intervention in the following year to "foster stability" but the dollar continued to fall against the mark and the yen as it had since February 1985, apparently because the United States did little to reduce its trade or budget deficits which undermined confidence in its currency. The Reagan administration never acknowledged any efforts to control the dollar's value.

13. *The European Monetary System: Recent Developments* (Washington: International Monetary Fund, 1986), 1.

14. There were important personnel and policy changes when James Baker replaced Donald Regan as treasury secretary. American policy regarding international cooperation on exchange rate management was much more flexible, for example. Baker was still greatly limited, however, by what the president and his other more rigid advisers insisted upon as the proper conservative policy of refusing to accept such management in principle and in rejecting tax increases or defense cuts as part of needed fiscal reform.

15. *The EMS: Ten Years of Progress in European Monetary Co-Operation* (Brussels: DG on Economic and Financial Affairs and DG on Information, Communication, Culture, 1989).

16. Williamson, *Exchange Rate System*, 64-65, 69-70.

17. A counterpart of this phenomenon was the strong belief before the creation of the EMS that the whole EC common market for industrial and farm products was threatened by the lack of a European monetary system. On this point, see Tommaso Padoa-Schioppa, "What Contributions Has the EMS Made and Can It Now Make in an Unsettled Period?" in *Money, Economic Policy and Europe,* in the European Perspectives series of the Commission (Brussels, 1985), 43-52. I am indebted for this analysis of the EMS strengths to another paper by the same author in this volume called "Rules and Institutions in the Government of Multi-country Economies," pp. 197-214.

18. See chapter 4 in van Ypersele, *European Monetary System* for a fuller account of these problems.

19. *Report on Economic and Monetary Union in the European Community,* issued by the Committee for the Study of Economic and Monetary Union. The report was issued in April 1989 "by the members of the Committee in their personal capacity." There is no attribution in the original edition to the Commission or any other official EC source except for a note on the title page indicating that it came "in response to the mandate of the European Council" the previous year in Hanover. Its "personal" nature was due to the sensitivity of the Committee members to the political climate, especially in Britain, where Prime Minister Thatcher's resistance to closer economic and monetary union had become an element in the June 1989 election of the European Parliament. The sharp losses her Conservative party suffered in that vote were attributed to the divided party leadership on the British role in EC monetary union and other aspects of Europe, policy areas which the pro-European Conservatives had never questioned before Mrs. Thatcher's arrival as party leader.

20. Ibid., 32-33.

21. Ibid., 30-36.

7

Technology, Training, and the Industrial Future

The countries which produced the Industrial Revolution are having problems keeping pace with it. From a position of strength two decades after World War II, the European Community countries today stand third and faltering behind the United States and Japan in many important indicators of industrial and technological strength.

For a European Rip Van Winkle, coming back after a quarter-century, this situation would be hard to understand. The EC countries seem to possess all of the ingredients for adapting science to industry: scientific talent and advanced universities; an intelligent, experienced managerial and labor force; sizable and mature capital markets; and a generally harmonious and established history of cooperative relations between industry and government.

Yet, upon examining the success of EC competitors, three factors seem to be lacking or underdeveloped today in the Community when it attempts to apply science to industry and commerce: flexibility, diligence, and innovation. To paraphrase an earlier joke, the Europeans seem to have all of the diligence of the Americans, all of the mobility of the Japanese, and none of the innovation of either one. To find out why the Europeans stay behind, we must first see how Europe arrived in third place and then inquire more precisely what constitutes the success of the Japanese and the Americans in industrial technology. Finally, we must see how the Community is attempting to solve the problem.

THE COMMUNITY'S MODERN INDUSTRIAL HISTORY

The modern industrial history of the Community begins with the destruction left behind by World War II. This catastrophic damage, while unevenly distributed, was so widespread that it both disabled its victims and prepared them to recover their industrial stength. Both victor and vanquished suffered industrial damage but the more severe destruction of German industry left that country open to more complete and rapid reconstruction with a completely modern base. With the help of currency reform in 1948 and massive aid under the Marshall Plan, West Germany's GNP reached, by 1950, the level of 1936. Germany, of course, bore the additional burden of a divided homeland but the developed industrial sectors, including raw materials, were largely in what became the Federal Republic. In the next five years, the country's national income increased by 12 percent a year. In other countries, the recovery was slower and different.[1]

Recovery from War

France and the United Kingdom, less heavily damaged than Germany and without reparations, recovered more slowly. France had been weakened to desperation in the First World War and never fully recovered its strength when the next war began. Britain had the most extensive and varied industrial system in Europe but it was both damaged by bombings and greatly strained by the extended output of war materials. Other future members of the European Community were either victims of actual war damage or of extended neglect of the industrial apparatus.

Industrial planning for peace had begun during the war but the abrupt end of Lend Lease in 1945 left these plans stranded. Only two years later with the Marshall Plan did Europe begin its serious recovery. Monnet cites the importance of counterpart funds from the Marshall Plan in insuring the success of France's postwar recovery plan, for which he was responsible. Yet the Marshall Plan, for all of its undisputed merit, may have done some unintended disservice by reconfirming the Europeans in the directions of their prewar industrial development.

By the mid-1950s, the refurbished European industrial base had begun an ascent in output and productivity which would continue into the 1970s. The Treaty of Rome creating the European Community in 1957 gave promise of a vast internal market for the increasingly efficient European industrial machine. But even as the Europeans grew and prospered in industrial output, troublesome signs appeared.

Multinational (which at first meant American) corporations began to buy European units to add to complex structures which operated in two, three, or four continents. Attractive local industries were either bought by foreign capital or faced amalgamation at home. New management techniques went against European practices. Labor resisted the flexibility demanded by the new owners.

European Traditions

Traditional European patterns of conservative management and labor practices lacked the flexibility to handle American and other foreign competition. Generous labor benefits tended to reinforce the already dominant conservatism of the European worker who wanted a steady job, near home, within a stable community. European capital had a similar bias toward recognized fields of competence, proven products, and dependable investments.

Possessing a large but imperfect market, the typical Community industry worked incrementally to improve its products and slowly expand its product lines. It expected to be rewarded for reliability and solid quality. Instead, a wave of American innovation in the 1960s and early 1970s was followed by Japanese ingenuity in identifying and dominating the complacent European market segments, especially in durable consumer products. The key to the disruption was an entire class of products based on electronic developments during World War II. From these wartime uses, transistors and other elements in microcircuitry made possible a whole new generation of equipment and, eventually, consumer products which European factories neither developed nor could produce with the speed and skill of their overseas competitors. Somehow the right combination of skill, entrepreneurial spirit, and quick venture capital could not seem to be assembled in Europe.

Whole fields of traditional European goods were overwhelmed. American mainframe computers, multinational corporations, and fast foods were barely absorbed when entire industries like cameras, motorcycles, and watch making were overrun by superior and less expensive Japanese products. European industries reacted belatedly by seeking joint ventures with their international competitors but on terms where the Europeans offered largely their knowledge of home markets while the foreign companies brought new technologies, market research, and advanced manufacturing techniques.

Japanese and American Success

Soon traditional areas of European excellence in manufacuted goods were challenged by outsiders. The Japanese and the Americans seemed better able to find and adapt new technologies to products which consumers wanted and were prepared to buy regardless of national origin. Cameras, radios, clothing, and motorcycles, which Europeans formerly produced in high quality for the world, were now coming into the European Community from foreign locations which could often not be found on the map by European consumers. As one European economist put it, "EC countries, in spite of national differences, are all confronted with the same industrial problems. All have difficulties with

traditional sectors (steel, textiles, shipbuilding etc.) in the context of low
growth and high unemployment; all have problems with the insufficient
takeoff of high technology sectors like electronics, and all have to meet
Japanese competition in sectors like automobilies, electronics and
mechanical equipment."[2]

In total manufacturing output, the enlarged Community now exceeds
the United States and is about twice as large as Japan. In services, the
Community is only about two-thirds the size of the United States yet
more than twice the size of Japan.

The Americans and the Japanese are as different from each other in
their approach to developing and marketing the new technologies as
either is from the Europeans. Yet there was often in Europe, in the 1960s
and 1970s, an air of resignation that somehow the Old World had simply
lost its competitiveness. The Europeans, however, finally showed a
determination to fight back. They began by studying their opponents.

It is useful in looking at manufactures as a group to distinguish
between technologies of high, medium, and low intensity, following the
OECD distinctions (see table 7.1). Each stage has a lesson for Europe.

The Japanese, to start with the more spectacular success story, moved
from steel and ships to autos, consumer electronics, machine tools and
robotics, and now into information technology. They show enormous
engineering diligence and great attention to both market research and
manufacturing detail, yet with little basic scientific research. But a
recent report by the U.S. Patent Office showed that over half of the
patents issued in the first half of 1987 went to non-Americans and that
the Japanese received a sharply increased proportion of the patents
which went to foreigners.[3]

The Americans seem to operate differently. They devote considerable
resources to basic research through highly advanced universities and
other facilities, aided greatly by government contracts. The defense
industry receives a very large segment of the research and development
funds in the federal budget. Some valuable spinoffs to the commercial
marketplace come out of these federal R&D contributions but whether
this approach is cost efficient is uncertain. A highly flexible labor and
innovative capital system allows rapid startup in a highly competitive
environment.

The cost for this system includes a high turnover of talent, a certain
amount of lost capital, and some inefficiencies through the high failure
rate of these small enterprises. The Strategic Defense Initiative (SDI) is a
typical American effort which applied enormous amounts of taxpayer
funds and highly skilled talents to long-term defense efforts whose
spinoff into commerical fields is fervently hoped for but unclearly
charted.[4]

In both Japan and the United States, the government encourages competition among enterprises but the government-business relationship is

not identical. The Americans consider their nation the preeminent free enterprise country in the industrial world. While benefiting from large defense research funds, the private sector is left largely to its own devices to find and exploit export markets.[5]

The Japanese government is more involved in helping to identify and support export efforts without contributing funds itself. But export markets for a resource-poor country like Japan are the prime target of industry which is not the situation in the United States where overseas markets are a small fraction of the huge, homogeneous, and easily accessible domestic market.

Table 7.1
Export Market Shares, 1970-86 (excluding intra-EC trade)

	Total		High Intensity		Medium Intensity		Low Intensity	
	1970	1986	1970	1986	1970	1986	1970	1986
U.S.	24.8	19.1	36.2	28.4	26.8	17.0	16.6	13.8
Japan	13.5	23.2	15.4	30.9	10.4	24.6	16.3	14.4
E C	36.8	34.3	32.4	27.2	39.6	35.6	36.1	38.5

Source: OECD. Totals do not add up to 100 because data refers to all OECD countries. 1986 does not include Spain.

High intensity include aerospace, computers and office machines, electronic components, drugs and medicine, instruments, and electrical machinery.

Medium intensity include motor vehicles and other transports, chemicals, other machinery, rubber and plastics, nonferrous metals, and nonelectrical machinery.

Low intensity include ceramics, clay, and glass; food, beverages, and tobacco; shipbuilding; petroleum refining; ferrous metals; fabricated metals; paper and printing; wood products and furniture; and apparel, including shoes and leather.

As this table shows, there has been a dramatic shift among OECD countries in their export market shares of total manufacturing, particularly in the high-intensity segment. The U.S. share of the export market for all manufactures dropped by about 23 percent from 1970 to 1986, while that of Japan rose about 72 percent in the same period. Total EC export market share dropped about 7 percent.

For high-intensity goods, the U.S. decline was about the same, 22 percent, but the Japanese gain was a bit more than 100 percent. EC export share of high-intensity goods dropped 17 percent in the same sixteen-year period.

For the important medium-intensity sector, EC export share dropped a moderate 11 percent compared to a 37 percent drop by the United States. Japan's share went up a striking 240 percent in this period, reflecting the successful capture of the world auto export trade.

There is great competition between Japanese companies to perfect both design and marketing but little direct involvement of the government in these areas. The small defense budget does not generate much research work and the foreign trade ministry, while the target for foreign criticism, seems to serve more as the handmaiden to industry and not its master. But the thoroughness of Japanese export industries in recent years and their method of consecutive concentration on market segments caused one European to compare the Japanese competition to a sumo wrestler: they dominate one field with a massiveness which overwhelms one opponent while preparing to leap onto the next.

THE COMMUNITY WAY

Among the Community countries, there is a considerable variety in the government's role in the development, financing, production, and marketing of industrial products. But there are enough common features among the twelve that one may fairly speak of a European Community style which contrasts with that of Japan and America. Its characteristics include a high level of R&D expenditures with much of it devoted to government research laboratories marked by neither competitive market discipline nor the pursuit of scholarly excellence; a lack of tradition in producing, directing or using venture capital (much less is produced in EC countries than in the United States and much of that available goes outside the Community for lack of attractive opportunities at home); and a somewhat rigid labor force marked by little mobility and high expectations for government support.

By the late 1980s, the Europeans seemed to recognize that their salvation could come in learning from these two, quite different, international rivals. Several programs were announced by the Community to regroup its strength around these principles:

• The enlarged EC, with 320 million consumers, offers a market larger than the Americans' if internal barriers in the Community can be removed.

• Europe can learn from several distinct successes—the Airbus, nuclear power, the Ariane rocket—where its technological talents are and how to utilize them better.

• Several impressive private sector success stories show that Community companies can succeed in an industrial and commercial market of great variety where the European manufacturers have considerable advantages of history, customs, language, and experience if their skills can be better organized.

• Innovation in research, capital formation, and labor relations are badly lacking; the EC must learn from its competitors how to gain flexibility without giving up its native skills and assets.

Yet indicators point to continuing problems in the Community in exploiting these assets and some even suggest the problems are worsening. One of these indicators concerns the resources EC countries are devoting to research and development. In fact, the distinction between high technology and other industries is not by the goods produced but rather by the amount of research and development input. Table 7.2 shows the percentage of industrial domestic product devoted to R&D.

Table 7.2
Industrial R&D Growth, 1981-85
(percentage of growth with 1981 as base)

	Industry Funds	Government Funds	Total Growth of Industrial R&D
JAPAN	54.1	0.7(0.0)	55.1
U.S.	16.6	7.1(6.4)	28.5
EC-9	16.3	2.4(0.7)	20.4
OECD average	22.8	7.1(6.4)	30.5

Source: OECD, Data Bank, February 1988. Compiled from OECD, *Science and Technology Indicators No. 3,* 1989, p. 75.

Notes: EC-9 excludes Greece, Portugal, and Spain; OECD total excludes New Zealand, Switzerland, and Turkey; both figures are partly estimated by OECD staff. The total growth includes other domestic and foreign funds, largely university spending.

The U.S. growth figure is just below the OECD average, Japan's is nearly double the OECD average, while the EC-9 figure was only two-thirds of the OECD average. The EC average is thus a sluggish third, even when government support is included. But the EC expenditures in themselves are not negligible. Why are they not more productive?

There are several possibilities. The EC countries dissipate some of their investment through duplication at the national level. Since the national governments are both a source of this R&D funding by subsidies and also a customer for other research efforts, the continuing organization within the Community at the national level may be absorbing sizable overhead funds as well as encouraging duplication and unproductive competition.

With several Community countries (especially Britain and France) as with the United States, defense-related industries absorb large amounts of both industry and government R&D funds. These defense industries may not be good investments for global competition in high-technology goods. The high EC defense expenditures (compared to the Japanese) do not seem to have had much carry-over to the civilian market. At least there is little empirical data on the value to civilian industry of high defense expenditures.[6] Japan, with little defense research and considerable success in civilian R&D, indicates that an opposite direction is quite productive.

Although it is not shown in table 7.2, there was a dramatic increase by Japan in its industrial R&D expenditures from 1975 to 1985 compared with a modest decline in the same period by the United States and a somewhat sharper drop by the Community, compared in each case with all OECD countries. Since Japanese R&D was almost exclusively for the global civilian market, this large expenditure (which includes market research) was able to overwhelm both European and American competition in several high-technology fields where it was concentrated.

Another indication of the strength of a country's research effort is the number of scientists and engineers in the total labor force. Table 7.3 indicates that both Japan and the United States train and employ significantly higher percentages of this scientific talent. Another OECD study indicated, however, that when military expenditures are excluded, there are only five OECD countries which spent 2 percent or more on R&D in 1985: in descending order, they were France, Germany, Japan, the Netherlands, and Sweden.[7]

Table 7.3
Total Research Scientists and Engineers (per 1000 of labor force)

	1974	1985
JAPAN	4.2	8.0
U.S.	5.6	6.8
EC	3.0	4.0*

Source: Computed from OECD *Science and Techology Indicators Report No 3* (Paris: OECD, 1989) and *Eurostat Review, 1975-1984.*
*1983.

Manufacturing Trends

The Community countries are experiencing some of the same structural changes in manufacturing which Japan and the United States encounter as well as some peculiar to Europe. Japan, for example, is probably the only industrial country where manufacturing employment has not fallen since 1980. Overall strength of the country's industrial growth is undoubtedly the principal factor here but some other elements are related to the unique Japanese structure. There is strong pressure in Japan to increase investments to cut costs instead of the customary Western tendency to cut employment immediately. The large Japanese industrial groups are diversified, allowing transfers of both technology and labor within the same corporate structure.

In the United States, blessed by high labor mobility, the manufacturing sector has lost jobs since about 1981 but a rapid and steady growth of the service sector has more than balanced these lost jobs. The services sector produces both high- and low-wage jobs but it is doubtful if this sector matches, on average, manufacturing jobs in the quality of earnings.

The labor flexibility of Japan and the United States, with different economic and cultural bases, is unfortunately not matched in the EC countries. The penetration of new technologies in Europe produced net job losses, with little shifting of workers from the low to the higher value-added sectors and a slower growth in the service sector than in the United States. Higher productivity increases in Europe, compared to the United States, required fewer new jobs (hence the high EC unemployment rates) although real wage growth for those working has been higher in Europe. This reflects, in part, the fact that the service sector job creation which has predominated in the United States in the 1980s, has been principally in lower-paid jobs.

By another important measure, manufactures as a percentage of Gross Domestic Product, Europe, and even more, the United States, are falling behind Japan (see table 7.4). All three have experienced a decline from 1970 in manufactures as an element of the total domestic product as the service sector expanded. To a qualified extent, this change is productive because it illustrates an upgrading of software technologies, communications, and other innovative services.

But an advanced country cannot maintain that status without a modern and competitive manufacturing sector. Once again Japan leads the way. Its manufactures constituted 36 percent of its Gross Domestic Product in 1970 and 29.8 percent in 1985, a decline of 17 percent. Japan still produced about 30 percent of its total product by manufacturing goods while the U.S. share fell, in the same period, from 25.2 to 20.4 percent. Thus, Japan produced half again as much in manufacturing as a fraction of its output as did the United States in 1985.

The EC-12 dropped the least as a percentage (16 percent) over these 15 years but retained a middle position between Japan and the United States with one-quarter of its output coming from manufactures.

There is broad agreement that of the three major industrial players, the EC countries have a formidable set of disadvantages compared to Japan and the United States. The worst disadvantage is that the Community

Table 7.4
Industrial Manufactures as a Percentage of GDP

	EC-12	U.S.	Japan
1970	29.8	25.2	36.0
1975	27.3	22.7	30.2
1980	25.8	21.8	29.2
1985	25.3	20.4	29.8

Source: Eurostat database (prepared for this book), December 1987.

still lacks the single, homogeneous market which characterizes its two competitors. The 1992 deadline for the improved internal market may not produce the equivalent to the U.S. or Japanese market but it will certainly improve the present situation.

To understand this problem, an American has to imagine border controls established between each of the 50 states, with passport controls and spot customs inspections for passenger cars and one- to two-hour delays for every truck. This border chaos, in the American context, would then be accompanied by each of the 50 states setting its own standards for public procurement and its own sales and excise taxes which have to be paid at the border. Finally, industrial and health standards would be established and enforced at the state level. Overcoming these problems is what the Community still faces over 30 years after the Treaty of Rome.

Another disadvantage the Community must endure is the cultural and linguistic variety which makes Europe distinctive but which, in terms of forging EC educational and industrial policies, slows the process greatly. The mistrust which exists in the U.S. Congress, for instance, between urban and rural legislators, or between those from Texas and those from New York, are charmingly simple compared to the entrenched bureaucratic interests which unite the British and the Danish ministries, for example, in their opposition to any uniform code of taxation or to the simple elimination of border inspections. Similarly, most of the EC education ministries would welcome an EC-wide system which was exactly like its own. But to get these education officials to agree, for example, on recognizing each others' accreditation norms or graduation standards for preuniversity education will be extremely difficult. Less than 2 percent of the university students of the Community are doing their studies in another EC country.[8]

Labor Mobility

Mutual recognition of professional qualifications is a major unsolved problem which threatens the implementation of the internal market program. Professional qualifications fall within one of the few national prerogatives protected with the veto in the Single European Act (SEA), an indication of the sensitivity with which the 12 EC members view labor market issues.[9] The reason for this sensitivity (which several members insisted upon in the SEA treaty conference) is that professional qualifications go to the heart of national identity and, therefore, of national sovereignty. If doctors, architects, nurses, and other professionals can truly move from one country to another with no more difficulty than Americans move from state to state, the internal market can become a reality. But if, after 1992, only Germans can fix teeth, design a building, or do commercial accounting in Germany, and other countries maintain similar protection for their professionals, the barriers to full economic integration will still be standing.

Labor mobility is an old problem in the EC countries and its professional components have been studied and proposals examined for its solution long before the 1992 program. The Treaty of Rome guaranteed the rights "of establishment" and "to provide services." The Commission sought implementation for many years by a laborious sector-by-sector process to cover the individual professions. This ended in 1988.

The Council of Ministers approved a general directive at the end of that year which emphasized mutual recognition instead of the harmonization of national requirements for the professions. Language and other cultural problems may still inhibit professional migration but national tests, definitions, and educational conditions may eventually become history under this new approach. Mutual recognition, in fact, is a key element in the concept of subsidiarity by which the Commission attempts to carry out policies at the local and state levels instead of starting in Brussels.

World-Class Technology

Supporters and opponents both recognize that 1992 is a major political event in the contest against the nation-state begun by Jean Monnet and Robert Schuman in 1950. The weapons today are value-added tax rates, technical standards, and other nontariff barriers, and the opposing troops are the customs guards, the national bureaucracies, and their ministerial generals, but the fight is over the same national prerogatives which confronted those seeking a coal and steel community. Is it possible to create a Europe which, while retaining its cultural diversity and historic nationalities, is in fact a single political, economic, and industrial unit?

In no other field is the battle over an internal market as likely to have long-term consequences as it is in the Community's belated struggle for a proper place in the development and marketing of a world-class technology. The continuing national divisions constitute comparative marketplace disadvantages of the Community with its principal industrial competitors, the United States and Japan. Using the OECD tripartite distinction of industries, based on R&D expenditure as a percentage of output, it is the high- and medium-technology industries in the Community which have suffered the largest proportionate losses of market shares, compared to these competitors (see table 7.1 for an explanation of the three-way division). While EC low-tech industries have reduced their trade deficits because of gains in trade with the United States in the mid-1980s, the long-term trend with low technologies is against the Community which will be competing increasingly in this sector with Third World countries with overwhelming advantages because of low wages based on a lower living standard.[10]

Japan is the only OECD country with a trade surplus in all three groups of low, medium, and high R&D industries. Furthermore, the "comparative advantage"[11] which the Japanese high-technology industries enjoy is steadily improving while that of the low-tech industries is declining. The Community trade problems with Japan come from its widening deficit but also from the specific makeup in the trade flows. European imports from Japan are largely high value-added goods; Japan's imports are raw and semifinished materials or luxury items.[12]

"Back to Basics"

This OECD evidence, while not conclusive and admittedly based on projections from present trends, should be disturbing for Community planners. Much of the response to the problems indicated must come from the national governments but the Community's role in three decades has progressed to the point where Brussels is expected to act on issues like the technology gap. What has the Community done to address these problems?

The *Financial Times* of London surveyed the Community's high-technology efforts in an extensive series in 1985. The theme of the series was that Europe had fallen behind, was floundering in its efforts to catch up with Japan and the United States, and, while it had a few success stories, the prognosis was between uncertain and decidedly unfavorable.

Two years later, in an article entitled "Back to Basics," the originator and editor of the original series, Guy de Jonquieres, reviewed the situation. Much had changed in European attitudes, according to de Jonquieres. High technology was losing its mystery with less effort to beat the Japanese and the Americans in specific fields and more to improve the whole competitive climate in Europe. There was less concern, particularly, that the United States was running away with the high-technology game because of its lead in computers and chip technology. The "swaggering height of Reaganism," he wrote, had yielded to competitive weaknesses of the U.S. economy. The Japanese had no magic in high technology but only the same success they enjoyed in other export industries and based on the same formula: enterprising and flexible management and meticulous and efficient manufacturing.

Had the Europeans learned something in two years, de Jonquieres was asked. Perhaps, he said, but the problems now had a different perspective. The original series was probably a little late, he said, since the perceived problems had probably peaked about 1983. Europe is today more confident of its own capabilities, he said, but the problems themselves had also changed. Europe's competitors had their own problems which should not make Europeans complacent but rather more diligent in facing and solving their own weaknesses.[13]

The *Financial Times* series cited the weaknesses already mentioned which concern the Community's lack of a single market. But Europe had other problems, the authors noted, which went beyond the Community. A lack of mobility in the labor field and the absence of an innovative capital market were major problems which still had not been solved by the mid-1980s.

Some European Successes

There are several clear success stories involving Community member states, private enterprise, and industrial technology. One familiar example is the European competitor to Boeing, the Airbus consortium which, to the extent it has succeeded, has also become a problem in EC relations with the United Stases. Entering the area of commercial jet aircraft, largely dominated by the United States since World War II, this four-country group of manufacturers was almost certain to bring the Community problems with Washington. By 1986 the Airbus consortium had penetrated the world jet market to the point of American alarm.

A 91-plane sale by the Airbus group to Pan American Airways in 1984 eventually meant billion-dollar revenues and considerable prestige for the Europeans. Breaking into the American market in this major purchase meant that the Airbus products were being accepted in the center of its global competition. Until the Pan Am deal, only small numbers of Airbus planes had been sold or leased to two U.S. airlines since a ground-breaking sale in 1978 of 34 planes to Eastern Airlines.

The American administration criticized the subsidies which Britain, France, Germany, and Spain gave to their respective participating companies in the Airbus group. The European response was that their government aid was no different from the benefits which Boeing and McDonnell-Douglas received in developing commercial aircraft from massive defense contracts for parallel military aircraft. The Europeans insisted, in rare unity against Washington, that the Airbus program would continue. Washington retreated in 1987 to the position that it would raise the matter again in GATT.

European Space Efforts

The Ariane rocket, which the European Space Agency (ESA) developed, is another important European success in high technology. It has also become a matter of contention with Washington. After a series of failed rockets in the National Aeronautics and Space Administration (NASA) programs, the European Space Agency gained new commercial business

for the Ariane rocket. The attempts to take advantage of a newly opened
U.S. market by selling Ariane launch services after the Columbia space
shuttle tragedy especially irritated American officials. By 1987, Ariane
was bringing in several million dollars a year to the European agency,
even when a serious Ariane failure the year before delayed its launch
program. More important than the income, Ariane was an important sign
of European technical competence.

Despite its successes, ESA bears only a slight resemblance to its
considerably larger and older sister organization, NASA. Comparing
overall space budget efforts, the United States, for example, spends
about 0.3 percent of its GNP on civilian activities, overhelming the 0.05
percent of the Community. Further, there is no comparable military
space program in the Community which finances industrial capabilities
in space as there is in the United States. (The important French military
space program is largely unrelated to ESA activities.)

The present successes of ESA come after a confused and sometimes
contradictory development of European space activities. The predecessors of ESA are the European Space Research Organization (ESRO),
which was organized in 1962, and the European Launcher Development
Organization (ELDO), of the same date. The first organization, which
was quite successful, concentrated on research satellites, principally the
IRIS, which studied X-rays in space, and a series of satellites examining
astronomical measurements from space. The latter was a serious
organizational failure, apparently because each member country
(including non-European Community members) took responsibility for a
separate aspect of the principal project, the Europa rocket. When the
rocket exploded in 1971, it also destroyed ELDO.

Out of the successes of ESRO and the failure of ELDO, ESA was
created. Seven of its ten member countries were members of the nine-
member Community at its founding in 1975, joining Spain, Sweden, and
Switzerland. Ireland and Norway came later. Austria and Canada also
cooperate with ESA but the emphasis is on developing European technologies which should, in the view of some foreign policy experts, aim
for European autonomy in space. This would enable Europe to cooperate
with the United States, the Soviet Union, or any other country whose
technological state allows mutual benefits.[14]

Euratom

Nuclear power generation is another European success story although
not in the ways in which Euratom was imagined in 1957 as the atomic
core of a glorious industrial future. Nuclear successes have been
accompanied by serious political controversy. Nuclear power is increasingly identified by the "green" parties as the single issue which best
gains adherents and holds supporters. The ability of these parties, and

other opponents of nuclear power, to tie this energy source to the proliferation of nuclear weapons causes dismay to both supporters of nuclear power as an alternative to Europe's considerable oil imports and to military strategists who have enough problems, they believe, without having to get involved in alternative electricity generation plans. Yet the European nuclear power industry has been quite successful both in gradually increasing its segment of power produced within the entire generating field and in avoiding any disastrous breakdowns like the Three Mile Island or Chernobyl cases.

Several factors suggest why the Europeans (and, by 1990, the Japanese) succeeded where the Americans and Soviets failed.[15] American nuclear plants face no "green" parties as in Europe but they do have state regulators and ad hoc antinuclear lobbies. Other American problems have been traced to a failure to standardize designs and to simple failures of management to achieve safe, dependable, and cost-efficient operations. The Europeans have had fewer competing models and have used this greater standardization and better control, advocates say, to produce safer and cheaper power.

Present nuclear plants in EC countries were built under national programs but the Commission is active in both research and policy matters involving nuclear energy. It has a nuclear policy program which offers member countries guidance in integrating nuclear sources into national energy programs. In nuclear energy research, where the Community has a direct mandate from the Euratom treaty, EC institutions and actions have been directly and importantly involved. The Joint European Torus (JET), an ambitious research program in nuclear fusion, began in 1973 under the joint auspices of Community and national laboratories of several member countries. A newer, and more modest program, is THERMIE, which aims to develop more efficient energy uses and reduce environmental hazards from energy consumption. By some measures, the Community of nuclear research is more successful than political or economic coordination. The cost has been high, however, consuming limited EC research funds.

High-speed Rail Transport

Another high-technology success story for EC countries, with almost no negative aspects, is high-speed rail development. The French introduced their passenger "train a grande vitesse" (TGV for "high speed train") in 1981 after considerable expense and time to develop both the equipment and the track bed to handle trains which average over 100 miles an hour routinely. The original track section of 75 miles from Le Creusot to Lyons is being expanded gradually. TGV service to southwest France will start on a regular basis by 1990.

France and Germany lead a working group on high-speed trains which also includes Italy, Japan, and Britain. Like the space programs, high-speed rail cooperation and other important European technological cooperation are also based on membership beyond the Community twelve. German work in the field concentrates on the single track magnetic levitation system but this is not nearly as far developed as the more conventional TGV technology. Britain has a third system with both electric and diesel-powered units but progress is somewhat behind the French. The Anglo-French treaty to build a rail tunnel under the English Channel includes a common high-speed rail system using compatible equipment in the two countries. If this Paris-London link, due to open in 1993, can be extended to an existing agreement between France and Germany to run high-speed trains between their major cities, a European high-speed network may be underway.[16]

The Trucking Industry

Not all of Europe's industrial successes are of the high-technology kind. Daimler-Benz has had great success in finding and perfecting a niche for quality trucks of the medium and heavy classes. It exports to 170 countries from the main Rhine valley plant or one of 20 assembly plants in other countries. It has even invaded the American market with a speed and skill which make its competitors call Daimler the "Japanese of the truck industry." Elsewhere in the engineering industry, where traditional European skills have been able to maintain similar niches, some EC companies find and export their successes. A French company, Pomogalski, for example, installs and services half of the world's ski lifts. German and British printing machinery is among the best in the world. In high-grade pharmaceuticals and beauty products, European-made products still set the world standard.[17]

It is difficult to generalize on the lessons of these successes. Top-quality corporate management is a common feature; from this comes an ability to look ahead, to anticipate market and competitive changes, and to commit resources at the right time to capture and hold market shares. But big alone is not enough nor is throwing R&D funds at a problem. There is a need to think big but large size comes from success, not the reverse.

THE EC RESPONSE

The Community's response to its fall from a leading position in world technology has been erratic, principally because it has an incomplete mandate from its member countries in the field. In the European successes mentioned, Community programs have played either no role or only a minor one. The Airbus is produced by companies in four

Community countries—Britain, France, Germany, and Spain—but without Community participation. The European space program includes most Community members as well as several countries but again without Community involvement. The high-speed train programs are entirely national programs although some exchange of information and joint projects are now underway.

Another example of European-led programs which are wider than the Community is the EUREKA project which has been described as a "Euro-initiative to match the boost that the 'star wars' billions will give America's high technology industries."[18]

Although sometimes described as a French-conceived counterthrust to SDI, EUREKA is much broader than missile defense even if its motivation may have included a desire to protect Europe against another competitive attack from the United States. By mid-1986, EUREKA included over 80 joint projects representing 18 countries and several billion-dollar technical contracts for participating companies.

In contrast to these national programs, energy research is a Community enterprise, including the important JET project in nuclear fusion. The Commission, and others, have suggested a new research balance to bring energy below 50 percent of the R&D budget but not necessarily by reducing energy projects. Instead, more Community-sponsored research should be done in other areas, according to one study.[19]

Several Community programs in high technology began as a result of the self-doubt in the mid-1980s described above. ESPRIT (European Strategic Program for Research in Information Technology) and RACE (Research for Advance Communications in Europe) stressed a "leap forward" to overtake Japan and the United States in two fields of electronics and communications systems research where Europe has been left as a good customer but a poor innovator in the world market. A goal for ESPRIT, established in 1984, was to catch up with the two rivals in ten years. In contrast, the 1985 RACE program had no deadline but was intended to encourage Community countries to integrate their telecommunications networks, including the creation of a Community procurement program for the next generation of PTT equipment.[20]

Three other programs—INSIS, CADDIA, and EUROTRA—were designed for Community internal use. The first intended to improve data processing and transmission within EC institutions and between them and member states; the second sought development of computerized administrative services in trade; while the third intends to overcome language barriers through machine translations. If successful, all would have wider application than Community use and would provide European industries with design and manufacturing experience with presumably global application. None is far enough along to judge ultimate success or even cost/benefits. These are modest programs in EC outlays, at least in the initial stages now underway, and are dwarfed by the billion-ECU programs of ESPRIT and RACE.

ESPRIT, in turn, has hatched the programs of DELTA (Development of European Learning through Technological Advance) in 1988, AIM (Advanced Information in Medicine) in 1987, and DRIVE (Dedicated Road Infrastructure for Vehicle Safety) in 1988.

Another major "roof" program, like ESPRIT and RACE, is BRITE (Basic Research in Industrial Technology for Europe) which started its second phase n 1989 to spend one-half billion ECU over four years. Some of this impressive amount will be dedicated to EURAM (New Materials Development).[21]

A number of databases, or computer-accessed information services, have been developed by the Commission or are promoted by it to encourage innovation and growth of the EC information market. Some are based on Community documents, statistics, or institutions like the EC legal documentation service or the Eurostat trade data. Others provide abstracts of scientific research which the Community finances or otherwise supports, like ECHO which, under Commission auspices, tracks worldwide university research on European integration. Specialized programs of the Community, like the European Monetary System (EMS), the development programs under the ACP conventions, and the efforts to improve public procurement procedures all have separate databases used by Community, member state, and private sector subscribers.[22]

The University Role

Although there is not nearly as much research collaboration between industry and university in Europe as in the United States, the Community is trying to remedy this. COMETT (Community Program for Cooperation between Universities and Industry in Training for Technology) has, since 1987, supported almost fifty university-business training partnerships and placed over a thousand university students in industry training positions.[23]

In early 1988, the European Institute of Technology (EIT) was founded in Paris, led by a former OECD specialist in technological development. The institute, "an industrial consortium for scientific and engineering research and education," was organized and financed by European corporations. A principal goal is strengthening industrial competitiveness and ties between industry and university. Research grants and scientific conferences are the institute's initial means of doing this. How important the EIT will be is difficult to predict but its foundation is already significant in anticipating how Europe must remake its traditional boundaries between industry and academia to prepare for 1992.

ERASMUS, named for the medieval scholar, is a major EC program to broaden the cultural and language background of the generations who enter the workforce after 1992. The acronym, meaning European Action Scheme for the Mobility of University Students, is already seen across EC university bulletin boards, encouraging students to spend part of their student years in other Community countries either in academic programs or as short-term exchange students. This is one of the more promising attempts to break down the human barriers in anticipation of a single market in intellectual activities. In 1989/90 about 4,000 teachers and 20,000 other younger Europeans studied in other EC lands under ERASMUS.

NARIC is a related network of national information centers for the recognition of diplomas, certificates, and periods of study in Community countries which the Commission supports.

Under the Community's commitment to create an internal market by 1992, important advantages can accrue to the technology interchange among EC members. Harmonizing procurement and technical standards in fields like telecommunications can not only save money by large-scale economics in manufacturing but also enhance technology cooperation among scientists, industries, and technical services in the Community.

It should also be easier for capital to accumulate and move across national lines when exchange and fiscal barriers disappear. Whether the spirit of entrepreneurial capital will increase within this enlarged internal market is not clear. Nor is it yet clear whether, and to what extent, the internal market reform will also increase competition from non-EC countries, especially the United States and Japan. Is the Community's sad record in innovation and technical enterprise due to the artifical barriers among the member states, to the lack of enterprise capital and international competition at home, or to other, less evident, factors? The answer to these questions may also indicate whether the internal market constitutes a genuine advance in European integration or just another fanciful goal which will be much less satisfying in possession than it is in anticipation.

NOTES

1. Richard Mayne, *Postwar, The Dawn of Today's Europe* (London: Thames and Hudson, 1983), 149-75. For more on German recovery, see also Henry C. Wallich, *Mainsprings of the German Revival* (New Haven: Yale University Press, 1955). On Europe's recovery, see M. M. Postan, *An Economic History of Western Europe 1945-1964* (London: Methuen, 1967). For aspects of the recovery of France as related to European integration, see the illuminating comments of Jean Monnet in his *Memoirs,* 264-87.

2. Jacques Lesourne, "The Changing Context of Industrial Policy: External and Internal Development," in *European Industry: Public Policy and Corporate*

Strategy, ed. Alexis Jacquemin (Oxford: Clarendon [for the Centre for European Policy Studies, Brussels], 1984), 26.

3. U.S. Patent Office, Arlington, Va., report on annual patent applications, 1986.

4. For a British view which expresses "skepticism about the prospects for substantial technological spin-off for the civil sector," see the House of Commons report from the Defence Committee, *The Implications for the United Kingdom of Ballistic-Missile Defence,* final version dated April 29, 1987.

5. According to OECD estimates, defense-oriented research accounts for about 28 percent of total U.S. research, 27 percent in Britain, 22 percent in France, 4 percent in Germany, and 0.35 percent in Japan. "It may be supposed that defense research is much more expensive and more risky and that by its very nature it generates less heavy physical investment than in the case of mass production non-defense manufacturing. It is not surprising that the physical investment/R&R investment ratio should be fairly low in the United States and, conversely, fairly high in Japan" (*Annual Review 1986 Industrial Policies, Developments and Outlook in OECD Countries* [Paris: OECD, 1986], 60).

6. "Who Spends What on R&D?" in *OECD Observer,* February-March 1988. See also the underlying data in *Science and Technology Indicators No. 3, Resources Devoted to R&D Production and Diffusion of Technology,* (Paris: OECD, 1989), 99. See also notes 3 and 4 above.

7. OECD, *Annual Review Industrial Policies 1986,* 42-60.

8. This figure is from a survey reported in *Le Monde* [Paris], March 2, 1989, special section, Campus-Europe, xvi. See also *Higher Education in the European Community, Student Handbook, 1988* and *Directory of Higher Education Institutions, 1984,* both published by the Commission (Luxembourg: EC Publications Office).

9. See SEA article 100 A(2). Fiscal matters (meaning tax harmonization), free movement of persons (meaning immigration), and "the rights and interests of employed persons" are the exceptions to majority voting procedures in the harmonization of national legislation for internal market matters.

10. OECD, *Annual Review Industrial Policies 1986,* 75.

11. Comparative advantage is the concept that "each country gains by specializing in the production of items in which it enjoys a . . . cost advantage and exchanging (exporting) them for items in which it does not" (*Industry in the 1980s: Structure Changes and Interdependence* [Vienna: United Nations Industrial Development Organization, 1985], 77). Put another way, comparative advantage means that an optimal (lowest cost) combination of physical capital, human capital, and technology enable a country to compete most effectively in a certain item or class of items against rivals. It is, of course, a dynamic concept and countries gain and lose such advantage.

12. OECD, *Annual Review Industrial Policies 1986,* 75.

13. *Can Europe Catch Up?* (published later as a book) (London: Financial Times, 1985) and a reassessment article, "Back to Basics," July 23, 1987, in the same newspaper. Both were supplemented by interviews with de Jonquieres in July 1987 in London.

14. This conclusion, in the context of a detailed study of Europe's space prospects, comes from *Europe's Future in Space, A Joint Research Report,* published by five European foreign policy research institutes. The English edition was

issued by the Royal Institute of International Affairs (London: Routledge & Kegan Paul, 1988). For a more popular account, see David Dickson, "ESA: Will It One Day Rival NASA?" *Europe* (May-June 1983): 24-25.

15. American nuclear power generation consists of nearly 100 plants which provide about 16 percent of our total power. Europe gets more than twice this proportion (35 percent) from nuclear energy which also has strong critics. American nuclear efforts are seriously stalled with no new plants in the design stage and none started since 1978 while Europe and Japan continue building and operating new plants, partly in an effort to reduce dependency on imported oil (*New York Times* [January 29, 1988]: 1; [January 31, 1988]: 28; and [February 27, 1990]:1).

16. David Dickson, "Europe's Trains Aim for 21st Century," *Europe* (July-August 1984): 24-25.

17. These examples come from the *Financial Times* series cited earlier.

18. "Eureka Less Foggy," *Economist* (July 5, 1986): 75.

19. *Europe and the New Technologies* (Brussels: Economic and Social Committee, 1986), 17.

20. PTT is the central agency for postal, telephone, and telegraph services which in most Community countries is largely a national government monopoly.

21. *Research and Technological Development* (Luxembourg: EC Publications Office, 1988), 36-38, 51-55. *Eurotec* is a monthly newsletter which follows many of these acronymic programs.

22. "On Line to Europe. A Guide to E.C. Databases," *Europe* (October 1987): 42.

23. For details on the origins of these and other EC programs in high technology, see *Europe and the New Technologies*, 92-134.

8

Political Cooperation

Today political cooperation is no longer a weak infant but rather an adolescent recognized by the law.
—E. Davignon, early EPC advocate, 1986

Foreign policy has been, from the start of the Community, the no-man's land between national and European sovereignty. For those who want to limit the Community primarily to a customs and trading union, foreign policy must be kept apart from Community institutions. For those like Monnet and his successors, the Community system necessarily leads to a common European foreign policy. This tension, while not as acute as the crisis over some aspects of the internal market debate, remains strong and potentially divisive.

In the special grammar of the European Community, "political cooperation" means foreign policy coordination among the twelve members of the Community. Political cooperation is a sensitive barometer of European integration. The EC members seem to view foreign policy as one of the last remaining, and probably (perhaps with taxation powers) the most carefully guarded, of their prerogatives as sovereign nation-states. Coordinating foreign policy, therefore, is a voluntary, not a treaty, undertaking.

When hopes for a rapid political integration were high, before the 1954 failure of the draft treaty on a European Defense Community, foreign policy coordination was understood to be an early and high priority for a uniting Europe. Such coordination was clearly foreseen in the preparation in 1952 of the defense treaty. A few years later, Charles de Gaulle proposed a secretariat on political cooperation but it became clear that he was thinking more of a forum for intergovernmental cooperation rather than of an institution or a program of the Community.[1]

Over thirty-five years later, foreign policy coordination is again underway but this time in a very modest, almost apologetic fashion. The Single European Act (SEA) of 1986²_provided for the opening of a secretariat in Brussels for European Political Cooperation (EPC), which had existed as a quasi-institution of the Community from 1970. This office, which opened in January 1987, has operated quietly with seconded national civil servants as its small staff in the Council of Ministers' building near the Commission in Brussels. If its first years are a fair measure, the EPC secretariat promises to remain one of the Community's best kept secrets.[3] A little history can illuminate the reasons for this change in priority and visibility.

A BRIEF HISTORY

When the European Defense Community treaty failed in the French National Assembly in 1954, the companion plan for a European Political Community was also left to die. The "relaunching" of the European Community came the following year at Messina, Italy, where the six's foreign ministers met. With political union frustrated, they decided that economic union was the appropriate next step, guided by some creative preparations by Jean Monnet, Paul Henri Spaak, and others.

Two years later, the foreign ministers signed the Treaty of Rome for economic integration. A complicated internal market agenda was established which directed all efforts toward a ten-year transitional phase. Foreign policy coordination was quietly put aside.

The next decade saw a strengthening of national political direction, led by Charles de Gaulle's forceful determination that a "Europe of states" under French leadership was the continent's destiny. Lack of a countervailing leadership in the other member states—Adenauer was gone in 1963, Spaak in 1965—produced a drift toward political inertia within the Community. De Gaulle's showdown with Walter Hallstein, the determined Commission president, resulted in the 1966 "Luxembourg Compromise" which ended a French boycott of the Council of Ministers. The "compromise" was actually more an open reaffirmation of the gradually accrued (but unwritten) right of any Community member to veto, by denying approval of, any Council action which the member judged to involve a vital national interest. Hallstein's departure soon after symbolized the continuing strength of national political forces, but that of de Gaulle in 1968 reopened possibilities for more gradual foreign policy coopertion in an enlarged Community which finally could admit Great Britain.

The 1970s saw considerable attention to the mechanics of EPC, propelled by the agreement on enlargement which brought not only Britain but also Denmark and Ireland into the Community. Adding three members meant changes in many Community procedures. The prevailing informal consultation on foreign policy now had to yield, the original six believed, to a more rigorous and rapid move to full integration. Their preenlargement declaration at a 1969 summit at the Hague was replete with optimistic words about the strength of a united Europe, its "irreversible" nature, the members' "determination" and "confidence in the final success," and the "common conviction" that the members were "united in their essential interests."

The Luxembourg summit the following year reenforced this optimism with support for a report on "political unification" through cooperation in foreign policy. Recommended in the Davignon Report, named for the Belgain political director who drafted it, were meetings of the EC foreign ministers at least twice a year. A political committee, composed of the ministries' directors of political affairs, would meet four times a year both to prepare the ministerial meetings and to carry out their decisions.

In 1971 and 1972, the members reached a new height of optimism on the eve of this first enlargement which was effective in January 1973. They set a goal, by 1980, of "European Union," meaning a more perfect kind of economic and monetary union but with political overtones. The 1972 summit also agreed that the foreign ministers should increase their meetings to four a year. The meeting schedule changed but the Community is still waiting for European Union. (A good summit rule of thumb, it is said, is that the more elevated the rhetoric, the more empty its significance.)

In Copenhagen in 1973, the foreign ministers submitted a second report on EPC to follow up the first presented at the 1970 Luxembourg summit. Here, for the first time, the specific mechanisms of EPC were discussed. The political committee was to meet as needed to prepare the quarterly foreign ministers' meetings. In practice, the political directors forming the committee met at increasing frequency until their quarterly meetings have become monthly sessions.

The Copenhagen Report established the "group of correspondents" or senior section heads on European affairs of the foreign ministries who do the day-to-day work on political cooperation. The correspondents, in turn, developed a communications network (COREU) to keep the foreign ministries informed and to allow for consultations on important foreign policy matters. Working groups were to be set up on an ad hoc basis to study specific issues (and were to cease existence when the need ended, the communique insisted).

A Habit of Cooperation

Special roles were established for the embassies of member countries in both EC and nonmember capitals and at the diplomatic missions to international organizations. These roles collectively served to require diplomatic cooperation among all members but also to induce such

cooperation by providing the participants with more and better information than their national efforts alone could produce. One example was
the meetings arranged in the EC capitals by the respective political
directors of the host country to which all EC ambassadors were regularly
invited. This habit of consultation and information-exchange both forms
an important element of EPC and helps train the staffs of the twelve
foreign ministries. Eventually these staffs furnish the section heads, the
working group members, and the political directors, who are the most
senior career officials in each ministry.

While the machinery began to function, the temper of the 1970s did
not encourage political cooperation in substance, despite the departure
of Charles de Gaulle. The abrupt decision by President Nixon in August
1971 to end the convertibility of the dollar into gold severely disrupted
exchange rates of EC member currencies and consequently upset the
first stage of Community monetary union planning. National solutions
seemed tempting to governments with hesitant and confused economies.
Two oil price crises in the decade, with attendant inflation, once more
emphasized both domestic problems and national solutions. The enlargements of 1973 and 1981, while bringing the Community up to ten
members, also induced many problems of economic and monetary
coordination. Once again, foreign policy would wait.

Despite the central role of the foreign ministers in political cooperation
and the regular meetings of the political committee, it is the summit
meeting, or European Council as it is now officially called, which
became a principal forum for political cooperation. For while the foreign
ministers and their staffs actually perform EPC functions, the definition
and limitations of those functions remain as an expression of national
sovereignty and the European Council constitutes this expression.

When the summits were made regular in 1974, with normally three
sessions a year, EPC also developed institutionally but without ceasing to
be intergovernmental activity. EC summitry, like EPC, was not a Community development but rather the national governments meeting as
sovereign equals. The incorporation of EPC into the treaty structure
through its inclusion in the SEA seems to bind political cooperation
closer to the Community but fails to resolve EC's institutional problem:
Is EPC a matter of intergovernmental cooperation or is it a program of
the Community? A function of the Council of Ministers or of the
European Council? An expression, in some preliminary form, of
European Union or a defense against genuine Community integration of
national foreign policies?

EXPANSION OF EPC

Besides the mechanisms of EPC and its new secretariat, several good
examples of EPC are available to assess what foreign policy cooperation

can accomplish. We can look at EPC results in three areas, each of which illustrates a different aspect of this cooperation. The first involves international organizations and conferences where the Community began in the early 1970s to discuss common approaches. The outstanding example of this cooperation came at the Helsinki Conference on Security and Cooperation in Europe (CSCE), starting in 1973.

CSCE became a semipermanent institution with a series of followup conferences in different cities, all concerned with East-West relations and all attended by most countries of western and central Europe. While occasionally confrontational, CSCE discussions were generally a forum for exposing and mediating the varied viewpoints of the western democracies and the communist countries of Europe. The ability of the Community to operate in this environment is more a reflection of the lack of vital decisions taken by the CSCE process than any magical power of EPC. But its importance for the Community was the habit of consultation and cooperation in foreign policy which it engendered.

This habit has continued in many other international meetings, including the United Nations itself and many of its agencies.[4] Slowly the world of diplomacy is noticing that while the twelve still exist as national entities, there is, in fact, a Community diplomatic position which often, and quite naturally, develops.

The Venice Declaration

A second, and more striking, example of EPC in action was the Declaration on the Middle East at the Venice summit in June 1980. Here the EPC process was taken into a controversial area with long-standing involvement by individual EC members. The Venice statement followed an extended series of meetings between EC foreign ministers and representatives of the Arab countries which began several years earlier. While the declaration was even-handed in offering assurances to Israel of Community recognition of its right to existence and security, it was also an attempt by the Community to provide the guarantees needed for a peaceful settlement. The rights of the Palestinian people were explicitly recognized by the Community leaders who saw Israeli occupation and settlement of conquered territories as an obstacle to peace. Finally, the nine EC members declared themselves ready to "participate, within the framework of a comprehensive settlement, in a system of concrete and binding international guarantees, including on the ground." This latter phrase suggested that the Community might act as a group not only with moral and political force but also with some kind of peace-keeping force.

The Venice Declaration upset the American government which suggested that the Europeans should consult with Washington before making such comprehensive statements on the Middle East. But was this non-consultation itself an expression of European political cooperation?[5]

Although nothing concrete came from the EC guarantee offer, the Venice Declaration marked a vivid entry by the Community into coordinated foreign policy in a key area. In February 1987, the EC foreign ministers continued to focus on the area with a call for an international Middle East peace conference. Again there were rumblings in Washington that it hoped for advance consultations and not free-wheeling interventions from the Community.

A third example of EPC involvement, this one where EC members had to judge another member, came in 1982 with the dispute between Britain and Argentina over the south Atlantic islands called the Falklands in Europe and the Malvinas in Latin America. Without British presence in the Community, it might have been easy for the other EC members to see this problem as an expression of residual colonialism by Mrs. Thatcher's government. (Two additional factors restrained that tendency: the nature of the Argentine military regime and its provocation of the armed conflict.)

Even with these mixed feelings, most Community members felt some discomfort as the EPC process advised them of the firm British intention to act with force to maintain its rule in the remote Atlantic islands. But a sense of European solidarity—in the Community context—overrode this uneasiness. The British, their partners thought, may have been a bit stubborn but they were more right by European values than were the Argentine military leaders who seemed to seek a cheap and popular victory to sustain their regime. The British were able to make their case effectively and quietly with the EC members because EPC mechanisms were in place and worked well.[6]

The Colonial Past

The six countries which came together at the Schuman Conference were not new players in the international arena. All except Luxembourg had a colonial past and in several, the colonies overshadowed the metropole in size, population, and/or wealth. When the Community grew beyond coal and steel and took a dominant position in world trade, the relations of the six and their colonies became an early and an urgent issue.[7] Although these relations are not normally considered part of EPC, the success of the Community in integrating its colonial past into a comprehensive economic and political development network with 68 countries of Africa, the Caribbean, and the Pacific—the ACP countries—has provided EC institutions with valuable foreign policy experience.

The experience is separate from the EPC process, however. The Community development assistance program—the principal Community link with these countries—is under the management of the Commission and not related to the intergovernmental process of political cooperation. The

Commission's relation to EPC is still not fully developed. Originally, the intergovernmental nature of EPC left the Commisson as something of an outsider, even when it first participated as an observer and now with political cooperation.[8]

An entire Commission directorate-general is devoted to development assistance, most of which goes to ACP countries. The Parliament has its largest interparliamentary delegation committed to the ACP-EEC consultation assembly which is the principal forum for MEPs to study the development process. The Council also devotes part of one of its directorates to relations with the ACP countries and to development cooperation. The interaction between these institutional elements and with the foreign ministries of both the former metropoles and the former colonies is part of the Community training process. If political cooperation is eventually folded into the Community structure, this interaction is indispensible preparation.

HOW EPC FUNCTIONS

EPC is more a method and a process than specific actions, policies or results. It has grown, as has much of the Community, by the habits of cooperation and consultation which began even before the term EPC was used. It is less dramatic than some of the other Community efforts—like abolishing frontiers or creating a European central bank—partly because members still consciously reserve large areas of foreign policy initiative to themselves as the core of national identity.

By cautious accretion, EPC developed in its first difficult decade. By the time the foreign ministers reported on its development at the London summit of October 1981, they could declare that political cooperation had "become a central element in the foreign policy of all member States."[9] While allowing for some summit puffery, this report did identify the key elements in the EPC process, some of which went back to the 1970 Luxembourg summit, and sought to strengthen them by several practical improvements.

These were the changes and restated emphases effected by the London report and which now characterize EPC functioning:

1. Formal meetings of the foreign ministers, which take place four times a year, are limited to items of "major importance" and directed to "matters for decision." This change reflected a congenital problem in all bureaucracies: a tendency to refer all difficult and unresolved issues upward.

2. When the foreign ministers meet informally twice a year in the *Gymnich* format (named for the German castle near Bonn where the first meeting took place in 1974), there is strict confidentiality with no formal agenda and not more than one staff member present with each minister.

3. The political committee, composed of the political directors of the 12 foreign ministries, directs upward the preparation of their foreign ministers' meetings and downward the activities of ad hoc working groups on specific topics. The committee was also told to initiate longer-term studies by the working groups including those areas where member states are in disagreement.

4. The European correspondents, the senior foreign ministry officials dealing exclusively with European affairs and responsible for the communications network of EPC, are charged with the organization and implementation of political cooperation. The working groups, composed of senior foreign ministry officials, discuss all foreign policy issues within their jurisdiction and call to the attention of the political committee matters for decision or other key agenda items.

5. In non-EC countries, the heads of mission (normally an ambassador) of EC members are to assess developments in their respective countries with their "first instinct" being coordination with other EC countries. In major countries like the United States, the 12 EC ambassadors meet together at least once a month. In Washington they also invite the head of the Commission's delegation.

6. Finally, the London report agreed that an informal secretariat of officials from the preceding and following presidencies should assist the incumbent president of EPC. This meant that the foreign minister, who is the center of EPC, is aided in both manpower and continuity in his role. This "troika," consisting of mid-level diplomats, became an important aid especially for smaller countries already taxed by the responsibilities of the Community presidency of which the EPC presidency is a large but still only one part.[10]

This informal secretariat was the predecessor of the secretariat established by the Single European Act. Its operation meant that each member state participated for 18 months in the presidency of EPC, counting both the preceding and succeeding six-month period around its own presidency. In 1987, when the secretariat began to operate under SEA authority, it started by using diplomats on loan from the *two* preceding and succeeding presidencies, thus increasing the span of service for each country to 2½ years.

Security Questions

For the first twenty-five years of the Community's life, its members were content with the decision embodied in the Treaty of Rome to leave defense and security matters to other organizations, principally the North Atlantic Treaty Organization (NATO).[11] Several developments gradually brought these questions into Community purview. One was the 1973 CSCE already discussed. The desire and the ability of EC members to act together in the CSCE process gave a sense of confidence and concreteness to the EPC system. But it also brought security matters into EPC via a side door since CSCE was designed to resolve East-West matters which went back to World War II. One of the four "baskets" or fields of CSCE work concerned security matters. By careful consultation and cooperation at the conference and its followup meetings, the EC members went beyond the letter of the Treaty of Rome.[12]

A second development toward an EC role in security matters involved defense procurement and industrial competitiveness. As early as 1975 with the Tindemans Report on European Union,[13] EC cooperation in arms manufacturing was related both to restraining defense costs and to enhancing Community industrial vitality. Both elements were tied by Tindemans to the need for Community self-reliance. But the Belgian foreign minister did not stop there. "European Union will not be complete until it has drawn up a common defense policy," he wrote, although he prefaced those words with full acknowledgment of the role of the Atlantic Alliance [NATO] by which "we in Europe enjoy a measure of security and stability which has enabled us to undertake the construction of Europe."[14]

But EPC can raise sensitive issues for individual members, especially in the security field. One former Irish prime minister noted that his country's military neutrality required him to abstain from even informal discussions at European Council meetings whenever military matters came up.[15]

Relations with the United States

Tindemans recommended steps to insure that the Community "speak with one voice in its relations with the United States," adding that this need was "one of the main underlying reasons for the construction of Europe."[16] One may dispute the consensus on these views within the member governments at any point in postwar history or their willingness to put them into action but Tindemans is seen as a typical and moderate European leader in most matters. Whether Tindemans was accurate on this point, his report failed to gain much momentum. The Community seemed, in the mid-1970s, to lack the self-confidence to undertake new responsibilities, especially in the tricky area of security.

The European Parliament, shortly after its first direct election in 1979, began to consider some of these same defense matters. In 1981 its Political Affairs Committee decided to report after nine resolutions on defense were introduced and referred to it. The 1983 report by Danish rapporteur Niels Haagerup on European security and political coopera- tion stressed these points:

1. Security was broader than defense, weapons, and strategic doctrines. It involved the economic and political dimensions in which the Community defined its global role.

2. East-West relations, arms control, and peaceful coexistence based on Helsinki conference principles were also part of security.

3. EPC should expand to include these broad security questions. Eventually political cooperation would have to find an institutional relation to NATO and to the United States but this does not mean a weakening of the Atlantic Alliance or of Europe's relations with the United States.[17]

The Genscher-Colombo Act

Simultaneously, the European Council, through a report by German Foreign Minister Hans-Dietrich Genscher and Italian Foreign Minister Emilio Colombo, proposed in 1981 a "New European Act" to relaunch the Community by consolidation of EC institutions and EPC. They also asked for regular meetings of the EC defense ministers. The Genscher-Colombo Report, in turn, inspired a dramatic reexamination by the Parliament of the entire Community structure, including political cooperation. Neither the Parliament's draft treaty's ideas on EPC nor the Genscher-Colombo Report were carried out as written but both had important influence with two summit decisions.

The European Council, in the Stuttgart Declaration of 1983, accepted the Genscher-Colombo principles on security matters as part of the Community's domain. The declaration specifically committed members to joint positions and joint action "including the coordination of the positions of member states on the political and economic aspects of security." The two foreign ministers seemed to be seeking a new consensus for a broader, expanded meaning of EPC. It was a difficult course.[18]

When serious discussions on the urgent need for revisions of the Tready of Rome developed within the European Parliament and in the scholarly community which follows EC development, attention fell on how EPC could be improved.[19] About the same time, in 1983, a discussion began in some member countries on revitalizing the Western European Union (WEU), a largely moribund organization founded in 1948 for European defense cooperation under the Treaty of Brussels by the original six and the United Kingdom.

A Modest Enhancement of EPC

A Draft Treaty on European Union was adopted by the Parliament in anticipation of the close of its first directly elected term in 1984. Employing what one commentator called a "maximalist" approach to political coopertion by requiring certain procedures and insisting on certain results, the Parliament's audacity was dismissed by some but it gradually appeared to have been correct in seizing a moment when the mood for reform had arrived but no other institution was yet prepared to act.[20] This dynamic approach by Parliament was in distinct contrast to the step-by-step approach in the European Council's declarations of Luxembourg and Copenhagen and later at London and Stuttgart.

Parliament's draft treaty prodded member governments into establishing the Dooge committee which produced, in 1985, a report which eventually became the Single European Act.[21] The section on EPC, including its secretariat, is thus a very modest version of both the de Gaulle proposal for a Paris committee on foreign policy coordination and the European Parliament's recent ideas on what such coordination should be.

Nonetheless, the status of political cooperation was enhanced by the Single European Act which contained a separate title on "European Cooperation in the Sphere of Foreign Policy."[22] Here a joint commitment was affirmed "to formulate and implement a European foreign policy." Emphasis is placed on prior consultation before any member government takes a position on bilateral or multilateral matters and on achieving, through that consultation, a common European position.

The Commission's Role

In procedural matters, the new treaty specifies that the Commission—usually an onlooker with only limited rights to make known its views in past EPC texts—"shall be fully involved in the proceedings of political cooperation."[23] This recognition of the Commission's legitimate interest in EPC developed slowly. Since the summit meetings were made regular, it has been the heads of government, not the Commission, who became the final Community decision point for disputes and policy determination which the other institutions, especially the Council, could not resolve. As the summit, or the European Council as it was formally named in the SEA, became a quasi-Community institution (although one without specified powers) the Commission's presence became more important. By practice in the 1970s, and by the SEA authority since 1987, the Commission president and one other commissioner attend each summit.

Even with this acknowledgment, the emphasis in EPC remains intergovernmental cooperation which is, of course, the general character of the European Council itself. EPC is the foreign policy expression of that cooperation. Until EPC becomes a true EC institution, it will remain, and perhaps be strengthened, as an intergovernmental erosion of the Community system. EPC may be more visible under the Single European Act but it is doubtful if those treaty amendments truly helped to incorporate foreign policy into Community affairs.

The Single European Act, which only came fully into effect on July 1, 1987, was an institutionalized response to the Genscher-Colombo initiative and to the European Parliament's draft treaty on European Union.

This meant that the lowest common denominator had to be found among the twelve on altering Community structures and principles. Whether the SEA's renewed emphasis on majority voting in the Council and on institutionalized political cooperation is a sufficient response to the larger claim of a Community role in security is not yet clear.

THE FUTURE OF POLITICAL COOPERATION

There are at least two important measures of the future of EPC: How will it develop and how important is this development to the successful integration of Europe? To keep these two elements separate, the development of EPC can be considered first, and under these possibilities:

• EPC will continue to grow incrementally, partly as a consequence of the rate of growth of other Community endeavors; or

• EPC will stall because further growth is dependent on a larger commitment by EC members to enhanced supranationality and this commitment is unlikely; or,

• EPC will eventually become the most important and most prominent element of Community growth, perhaps through a decisive event which involves serious differences between the United States and EC interests[24]

These possibilities overlap and one can imagine still other variations but to the extent that EPC is a discussion topic in Europe these variations cover the range of viewpoints heard in Brussels and the national capitals.

The first possibility is probably the most optimistic by anticipating further Community growth in non-EPC areas. The importance of the present debate over the internal market,[25] for example, may eventually overshadow all other Community crises and thus hold the Community's attention until the deadline of December 1992 is passed. But if the internal market is achieved in even 90 percent of the Commission proposals, the effect on Community growth—including development of political cooperation—may be so great and so dramatic as to dwarf all other considerations.

Solution of the Community's budget problems through a secure and expanding source of the EC's own resources would be a major step forward as would a capping of the costly farm program in the budget. But these, in turn, would be small gains compared to the end of all border controls, the harmonization of national taxes, and the achievement of Community-wide public procurement. These elements, which represent the heart of the 1992 internal market proposals, will, if achieved, contribute themselves to a decline in the national presence within the Community. Such a decline would form a most hospitable environment for the growth of EPC.

Continued gradual growth of EPC is also the most likely of these three prospects, based on what the Community idea has accomplished in other areas in its 40 years. Things move slowly but somehow the cumulative effect is faster than observers recognize. The Community is as much a habit of thought as it is a series of decisions. There is also a "cumulative logic of integration" (a term borrowed from Loukas Tsoukalis) as a subtle form of propulsion. Political cooperation takes its place as a beneficiary of this gradualism.

A stalled EPC is, however, a clear possibility.[26] Political cooperation in controversial and important matters may bring EC members closer to yielding the ultimate value of national identity, but the wrong combination of weakened political leadership and divisive issues among EC members could accentuate this painful choice of national or European identity.

The Usefulness of Crisis

The belief that a crisis with the United States, or, less likely, with another power, could accelerate EPC is based on a few episodes in recent European history. Whenever the United States has taken—from the European viewpoint—a narrow and stubbornly held position without consulting its allies, the solidarity of Europeans seems to increase. The 1971 Nixon "shock" on the nonconvertibility of the dollar, although disruptive of EC economies, was salubrious in getting the Community to think and act together. That this solidarity eventually evaporated for some time before the European Monetary System was finally assembled is another story. The U.S. attempt to stop the Soviet pipeline to Western Europe in 1981/82 similarly united Europeans who ultimately prevailed. Several other incidents can be added to support the thesis. But whether these examples constitute inductive proof of a principle which will vindicate EPC and which will ultimately produce a permanent and decisive turn to political cooperation is still unclear.[27]

EPC and National Sovereignty

Whatever the speed of EPC development, some Europeans question its importance. This viewpoint reflects a new generation of European analysts who see themselves unburdened by the myths of the Monnet era. They say that both recent history and the long-established durability of the nation-state show that the Community is never going to become a true replacement for its national components. Better to accept the Community for what it is today: a refined customs union with limited tax authority and a restricted mandate which does not go beyond some further refinements of what has already been accepted. Under this view, EPC will not grow because its members do not want further restrictions on their sovereignty. In some circumstances, EPC can help maintain national sovereignty by using the authority of the twelve, in EPC decisions, to enhance national positions.

Another view, persuasive but not unanimous, affirms political cooperation as a necessary element of the Community, tracing the roots of this conviction back to Adenauer, Monnet, and Schuman. The integration of European nation-states means nothing, if it does not mean the transfer of part of national sovereignty to the new integrated structure. The lessons of the twentieth century, Monnet believed, were that nationalism must be restrained and redirected to a larger structure of government. Since the defects of nationalism, by this view, produced two World Wars in this century, this new structure must include control of defense and security policies or fail.

In the last paragraph of his *Memoirs,* Monnet wrote, "The sovereign nations of the past can no longer solve the problems of the present; they cannot ensure their own progress or control their own future."[28] While he was not referring here explicitly to foreign policy, his views, in the context of the memoirs, are clear: relinquishing sovereignty means ultimately giving up foreign policy control by the individual EC members.

Several steps—each involving some pain to national sensibilities—could encourage the gradual growth of political cooperation. Even these limited steps require an act of the will based on the conviction that EPC is useful to the integration process, whether or not it will ultimately stop short of a fully sovereign Community and whether or not some future dramatic event, perhaps involving the United States, is needed for EPC to succeed.

Fostering the EPC Process

A number of avenues are open should EC members choose to expand foreign policy coordination.

1. Gradual replacement of the national delegations of EC members at international organizations and conferences with Community delegations (including United Nations and other political meetings). This would support the principle of giving greater visibility to the Community and simultaneously further the integration of the twelve foreign ministries.

2. Using Community diplomatic representation instead of the traditional national embassies of EC members in some smaller countries where largely routine relations exist. This could actually enhance the Community's position in these largely Third World capitals without threatening any major representational interests of EC members. Gradually the list of countries with such Community representation would grow as EPC expands.

3. Closing the national embassies of the twelve Community members in other EC capitals. The COREU network of EPC could be expanded, if necessary, to handle

the additional burden. This dramatic move would, perhaps more than any other, demonstrate the conviction that EPC is progressive and irreversible. (This change would also demonstrate a commitment to trim the expanding bureaucracy in the member states involved in EC support services. In each of the 12 member states presently a foreign ministry office services the 11 embassies of other member states. Thus 12 ministry offices are doing essentially the same job in 12 countries. If the members' embassies in EC countries were abolished 121 embassies and the 12 ministry offices servicing them could be abolished. All communications between foreign ministries would then proceed via COREU.

4. Taking on a foreign policy problem which requires coordination by several EC members in which they have special competence. One possibility would be Cyprus, a problem which has eluded solution since the Mediterranean republic was the victim of a Greek coup attempt in 1974. Turkish troops invaded the island in response to protect Turkish Cypriots and remained to occupy and divide the country ever since. Neither the United Nations, the United States, which is intimately involved in defense arrangements with both metropoles, nor individual European countries have been able to induce Cyprus, Greece, or Turkey into fruitful negotiations. Britain, Greece, and Turkey are signatories of a 1961 treaty on Cyprus which is still valid despite violations of it by the latter two countries. If Britain or another EC country took the lead within the Community structure, obtaining the support of all or most other EC members for its initiative, sufficient pressures might be applied to the three Mediterranean countries to force a compromise solution.

None of these possibilities nor any other dramatic change in EPC is likely soon. More certain are indirect influences on political cooperation by other Community programs. As already suggested, it is likely that the internal market improvement, with its consequent, if gradual, adjustment in popular attitudes, will do more for EPC than any political event itself.

NOTES

1. In 1959, on a state visit to Italy, and in 1961, in a Paris meeting with Adenauer, de Gaulle proposed a political secretariat to coordinate foreign policy among the six. His ideas clearly reflected the "Europe of States," not a supranational European Community. For more on this early history, see chapter 3. For the views of two insiders active in different phases of EPC's development, see Philippe de Schoutheete, *La Cooperation Politique Europeenne*, "Collection Europe" (Brussels: Editions Labor, 1986), 7 ff., and, especially on the de Gaulle period, Hans von der Groeben, *The European Community: The Formative Years* (Luxembourg: EC Publications Office, 1987), 89-94, 112-18.

2. See chapter 3 for more on the SEA which went into effect in July, 1987.

3. The EPC staff are national civil servants because political cooperation is really intergovernmental, not Community, activity. The first head of the secretariat was Giovanni Jannuzzi, a senior Italian diplomat. He believes that his small staff of seven (divided among the past, present, and next presidency

countries) may grow in both size and function over the next few years. At its inauguration in 1987, the secretariat had no right of initiative and no presence outside Brussels except when Jannuzzi accompanies the president of the Council of Foreign Ministers to the European Parliament sessions. The head of the secretariat is named for a 2½ year term. The whole SEA title on EPC will be reviewed after five years (interview with Jannuzzi, April 1987).

4. For more on EPC at the United Nations and for many useful details on the whole process, see Beate Lindemann, *EG-Staaten und Vereinigte Nationen* (Munich: Oldenbourg Verlag [for the Research Institute of the German Society for Foreign Policy], 1978).

5. See chapter 9 on how defying the United States may be part of the process of European Union.

6. EC solidarity with the British eventually faltered but this had as much to do with the British government's stubbornness as with the EC's short attention span to sanctions against Argentina and its partially justified belief that the British used the Community when it was convenient in the Falklands crisis but ignored its EC partners' wishes otherwise. See Geoffrey Edwards, "Europe and the Falklands Crisis 1982," *Journal of Common Market Studies* 22/4 (June 1984).

7. An accident of history placed the birth of the European Community in the same decade (the 1950s) that brought independence to most of its members' colonies.

8. The quoted phrase, from the Single European Act, is consciously vague as to the exact role of the Commission in EPC. In practice, during the first two years of the EPC secretariat, "fully associated" meant that Commission observers were present at EPC meetings at all levels but rarely volunteered information. EPC secretariat staff see this as one-way advantage to the Commission since the latter does not invite the EPC staff to attend Commission sessions involving foreign affairs. The Commission and the EPC secretariat are sometimes rivals for EPC influence.

9. This and other EPC texts cited are taken from *European Political Cooperation (EPC)*, 4th ed. (Bonn: Press and Information Office of the Federal Republic of Germany, 1982). Because EPC is principally intergovernmental, a member state (here the FRG) takes responsibility for the documentation. The only Community publication is a modest 15-page booklet entitled *European Political Cooperation* (Luxembourg: EC Publications Office, 1988), produced after the SEA made political cooperation a (barely) mentionable EC subject.

10. The concept of the "presidency" is an interesting example of the gradual growth of Community institutions by habit and accretion instead of through dramatic decisions. The rotation of the chairmanship on the Council of Ministers dates to the early years of the combined institutions. When the heads of government began to meet regularly after 1974, they followed the same pattern by hosting the summit meetings when their country chaired the Council. This principle of combined chairmanship then spread to the chair of the political committee which also rotated with the Council. Gradually the name for this rotation became the presidency which now means the EC country which, on the six-month rotational system, heads all intergovernmental bodies of the Community and hosts the summit meetings. For more on the "presidency" as a

quasi-institution, see chapter 3 and Guy de Bassompierre, *Changing the Guard in Brussels* (Washington: Center for Strategic and International Studies, 1988). For the order of rotation of the presidency, see chapter 3, note 45.

11. The subtraction of security from other Community areas came in 1954 with the defeat of the European Defense Community. This action, by the French national assembly, although hinging on national sovereignty, was understood by Monnet to constitute a deficit in political conviction. Under these circumstances, the Community went forward in trade and economic matters, leaving defense and security where it was in the North Atlantic Treaty Organization and, less importantly, in the Western European Union (WEU) which was created by the 1948 Brussels Treaty. This decision is represented in the 1957 Treaty of Rome only negatively, that is, by omission of any reference to defense or foreign policies.

12. The four "baskets" of CSCE were: measures supporting European security; economic, scientific, and technical relations among European states; cultural and human rights matters; followup to the conference. Although little progress was ultimately made on the first basket, this failure resulted more from the agreement between the United States and the Soviet Union not to go beyond measures like advance announcements on military maneuvers and troop movements. The EC countries were not always in agreement in Helsinki although they consulted carefully and earnestly in most cases. But on the large questions there was essential agreement among EC members, including the candidate-states.

13. See chapter 3 for more on the Tindemans Report.

14. *Bulletin of the European Communities 1/76,* 10 (hereafter cited as Tindemans Report).

15. An example of this retained sovereignty at the summits is suggested by Garrett Fitzgerald, the former Irish prime minister, who related that the Irish head of government did not participate in the informal EC summit discussions of the military aspects of security because of Irish military neutrality. See Garrett Fitzgerald, "Irish Neutrality," *European Affairs, 3* (October 1987).

16. Tindemans Report, 17. Tindemans also wanted to send the preceding and the succeeding president of the Council of Foreign Ministers to Washington with the current president but this idea of a "troika" was never adopted. It is, however, the principle used to provide continuity in staffing the EPC secretariat. See also note 3 above.

17. *Report drawn up on behalf of the Political Affairs Committee on European Political Cooperation and European Security Doc. 1-946/82, European Parliament Working Documents, 1982-83* (Luxembourg: European Parliament, 1982).

18. For a detailed discussion of the Genscher-Colombo proposals by a staff participant, see Pauline Neville-Jones, "The Genscher-Colombo Proposals on European Union," in *Common Market Law Review 20* (The Hague: Nijhoff, 1983), 657-99.

19. See the fervid pamphlet by five foreign policy research institution leaders in Karl Kaiser et al., *The European Community: Progress or Decline* (London: London Royal Institute of International Affairs, 1983).

20. See comments by Peter Brueckner in "Foreign Affairs Powers and Policy in the Draft Treaty Establishing the European Union," in Roland Bieber, Jean Paul

Jacqué, and Joseph H. H. Weiler, eds., *An Ever Closer Union: A Critical Analysis of the Draft Treaty Establishing European Union* (Luxembourg: EC Publications Office, 1985), 137.

21. See chapter 3 for more on the draft treaty.

22. Ibid., on the form of the SEA.

23. It remains to be seen how great a practical difference this provision will make since the Commission has, at least for the past few years, been involved informally with EPC at all levels. This added language is perhaps more an acknowledgment of practice than an enhancement of the role of the Commission. It also represents an institutionalization of the natural tension existing between the national foreign ministry staffs and the Commission on political cooperation. Many in the ministries see foreign policy as a uniquely national function. Many in the Commission see it as a natural field of expansion for Community institutions. The gradual increase in the Commission's presence at EPC meetings parallels its equally gradual elevation at the Community summits. Originally the Commission was not considered a summit participant since the summit was conceived as an intergovernmental device to discuss both Community and other international questions. See also chapter 3.

24. Neither the EC nor the United States has ever recognized or employed EPC in dealing with each other even though the chairman of the Council of Foreign Ministers customarily visits Washington once in his six-month term of office. We seem to prefer to deal with the twelve ixdividual countries using what might be called the Kissinger approach. The secretary of state in 1972-76 expressed irritation several times when the Community agreed on a single position in advance of negotiations with the United States. See chapter 9 for more on this practice and possible changes in it.

25. See chapter 4.

26. Nearly ten years ago, an acute observer of the EPC process judged that this process would not develop much further except in tandem with the progress toward European Union. Events in the past decade reinforce this judgment. See Lindemann, *EG-Staaten,* 209.

27. For more on the development of EPC, see de Schoutheete, *La Cooperation Politique Européenne.*

28. Monnet, *Memoirs,* 524.

9

The European Community, the United States, and the World

I send you the proposed new federal Constitution for these states. . . . If it succeeds, I do not see why you might not in Europe [form] a Federal Union and one grand republic of all its different states and kingdoms by means of a like Convention.
—Benjamin Franklin, letter to friends in Europe, 1787

I am aware that people in America are impatient over the speed at which we are moving toward an integrated Europe. I am also impatient. But, nonetheless, we are moving forward.
—Chancellor Konrad Adenauer at the National Press Club,
April 8, 1953

The American generation which fought, and helped win, the Second World War was sympathetic to the idea of European unity. This attitude began, perhaps, with that impatience which Americans often showed in those days toward the slower and less progressive foreigner. Why, of course, one can hear the observant American GI say, these Europeans have got to do things differently after this war is over. Or, more directly, Why can't these Europeans get together, quit their squabbling, and stop depending on the Americans to settle things?

Behind these simplistic comments was a well-founded conviction that something *was* wrong with Europe. It had engaged in history's two bloodiest wars in the first half of this century. In both of these wars, America finally became involved and its involvement became decisive in the Allied victories. How this situation in European affairs should be changed after the war, by whom, and when, were more complicated questions for both the Americans and the Europeans who shared these views.

This somewhat vague American idealism in assessing Europe's unification is most clearly seen within the World War II generation of U.S.
leaders. If, for example, President Roosevelt ever thought specifically
about European union, those sentiments were not recorded; but he did
believe that the postwar world would be organized much differently. He
thought that the continent should be disarmed with the United States,
Britain, China, and the Soviet Union maintaining peace as the world's
policemen.[1]

But these were idle thoughts; the pragmatic side of Roosevelt predominated. He wanted the war ended as efficiently and rapidly as possible.
When it ended, the United States moved in the direction suggested by
Roosevelt, by maintaining and expanding its active involvement in
global peace and not, as it did after World War I, by retreating into
isolation. How that expansion conditioned both the American interest in
European union and later qualified our response are the major themes of
this chapter.

THE AMERICAN QUARTER-CENTURY

The official American view of post-World War II Europe was also
marked by an impatient idealism, even when expressed with a
pragmatic touch. Sumner Welles, wartime under-secretary of state,
warned in 1944 against a vindictive peace settlement against Germany.
Arguing against the idea (championed by Treasury Secretary Henry
Morganthau, Jr.) of turning Germany into an agricultural nation, Welles
advocated a policy "designed not to destroy Germany but to construct
out of Germany a safe and cooperative member of world society."[2]

The next year, Secretary of State James F. Byrnes publicly sided with
Welles. He said that "Germany is a part of Europe, and European
recovery, particularly in Belgium, the Netherlands and other adjoining
states will be slow indeed if Germany with her great resources of iron
and coal is turned into a poor house."[3] Both Welles and Byrnes went
against popular sentiments favoring a punishment of Germany. These
feelings, while stronger in Europe and especially strong in France, were
also widely present in the United States.

Even earlier, in a 1944 meeting of a cabinet committee considering
postwar Germany and reported by Byrnes in his autobiography, Secretary of War Henry L. Stimson spoke against the Morganthau plan.
Instead, a regional concept of Germany's resources was needed. The
resources of the Ruhr and surrounding industrial areas, Secretary
Stimson argued, constituted a natural and necessary asset for the productivity of Europe. He urged that such assets should be conserved and
made available for the benefit of the continent.[4] This may be the closest
to an American presentiment for the European Coal and Steel
Community to be found in the historical record.

The Marshall Plan

When European recovery lagged in 1947, Secretary of State George C. Marshall announced a plan to help rebuild the devastated European economies. When the Soviet Union refused to participate, the benefits of this vast rebuilding were concentrated on Western Europe. The division of East and West was confirmed across Europe by the creation of the North Atlantic Treaty Organization (NATO) in 1949, in response to pressures from the Soviet Union outward from its vast periphery. Thus postwar Western Europe was now harnessed to American economic power much as the Western Allies had been to American military strength when they achieved victory in the European and Pacific theaters of war a few years earlier.

There were obviously different American views on what unification of Europe meant for U.S. policy and different possibilities, whether seen in Europe or America, on how unification should proceed. George F. Kennan, for example, noted in 1942 that Hitler "had actually accomplished much of the technical task of the unification of Europe. He had created central authorities . . . in transportation, in banking, in procurement and distribution of raw materials. . . . "What was needed was an Allied decision to use, not destroy, this system under "a new European federal authority."[5] It is not surprising that the State Department rejected this audacious idea.

Kennan and Dulles

Several years after the war, another senior American diplomat, Charles Bohlen, then serving in Paris, confirmed to his colleague Kennan, that we supported European unification in the Council of Europe, the Organization for European Cooperation, and NATO. This broad, unqualified, and (sometimes) naive American support—often even stronger than that expressed by Europeans, as John Foster Dulles remarked in a 1948 Paris speech—obviously had to be refined and specified as Europe started making decisions which eventually led to the Coal and Steel Community.[6]

Kennan, while head of the State Department's policy planning staff in 1949, noted that European unification was not necessary for economic reasons as many people thought in Washington but it was needed to solve the problem of Germany: "Only some kind of European federalism could provide for Germany a place in the European community that would be comfortable and safe for everyone concerned." (When he seemed to qualify this view in 1957 by suggesting a neutral reunified Germany, he was sharply criticized for what he later recognized was his misreading of the importance which European union had finally achieved.[7]

Dulles was a surprising spokesman for European integration. President Eisenhower's secretary of state has been regarded as the apotheosis of a tough-minded global diplomacy. Yet Dulles became convinced as early as 1947 that the unification of Europe was a true emulation of the American struggle for unity and an endeavor which must be supported by the United States. Perhaps Dulles eventually fit support for a united Europe into his worldview of the fight against communism, but that did not seem to dilute Monnet's appreciation of Dulles as a person or as an American idealist.[8]

When the goal of a European Community embracing victors and vanquished was proposed in 1950 by French Foreign Minister Robert Schuman, the United States eventually supported the move. It was natural that some Americans, if pressed for a specific solution to Europe's political problems, prescribed the kind of cooperation among different peoples which had created their own United States. There was some American self-satisfaction when even the Europeans started to refer to a United States of Europe,[9] a somewhat naive sentiment similar to that of Benjamin Franklin quoted at the start of this chapter.

Yet U.S. reaction to the Monnet-Schuman plan of 1950 for a modest Coal and Steel Community was initially cautious. U.S. policy makers assessed it largely in terms of how the plan might affect tensions between France and Germany or whether it would constitute a reappearance of the old European cartels in another guise.[10]

Intimations of Conflict

A few weeks after Schuman spoke, the Korean War began. It soon became evident to Washington that Germany's great resources, including manpower, had to be employed in the common defense of Western Europe. Many Europeans had deep doubts about this rearming of Germany. The United States, now increasingly confident in its world role, persisted, however, first through support of a European army and, when that failed in France, through German membership in NATO. The United States, the sole nuclear power, could now define what was acceptable as a risk in one area to accomplish some good in another one. For Europe, there was satisfaction with the American role as the organizer and financier of the defense. It was a role accepted with alacrity by both Americans and Europeans who recalled the disillusioned idealism and eventual isolation which America experienced three decades earlier at the end of World War I.

The eventual European acceptance of the Schuman Plan and the economic recovery under the Marshall Plan, combined with the continued success of NATO (enlarged eventually by Greece, Turkey, and West Germany) seemed to justify this American optimism. Yet two developments—a nascent European Community and an American-dominated defense system—had implications of conflict. How was a united Europe, presumably stronger than its national parts, to deal with an alliance directed by the United States and committed to the defense and, ultimately, the survival of that Europe? Was Europe truly to become an equal with the United States? If the United States, now dominant in every field, one day became dependent on European economic policies or actions, would the change affect the defense relation? These questions may have occurred to some but the thoughts were fleeting. There seemed to be a golden assumption that all would turn out well between the Americans and the Europeans who were so closely related in history, culture, and, now, in postwar reconstruction.

A Miraculous Recovery

When the European Defense Community treaty failed in the French National Assembly in 1954, the European Coal and Steel Community governments came to a quick agreement to create instead an economic and atomic community. This produced the 1957 Treaty of Rome, which went into effect the next year. In less than 15 years following the end of the most destructive war in history, Europe had started on a dramatically different tack. It was no exaggeration to call the accomplishment an economic and political miracle.

Yet while the United States supported a European Defense Community partly because it could solve the problem of how Germany could be rearmed for the benefit of the West, something was happening to our support for a united Europe. When EDC failed, we found another way to that goal by admitting Germany to NATO, but we gradually lost interest in European integration over the next decade. Was it because NATO provided sufficient European cohesion for our security purposes? Or was it that what had begun as an exciting political development now became, for the Americans who followed it, a complicated and dull task of the Europeans achieving a customs union, a protectionist agricultural policy, and a somewhat vague form of economic coordination?

Perhaps the momentum for European integration in the years immeditely after the close of the war could never have been sustained. But after the initial postwar enthusiasm which lasted 15 years, the following period, from 1961 to 1976, showed a shortfall in both European performance and in American expectations and interest. This may seem surprising since it began with an American president, John Kennedy, whose interest in Europe and popularity there (and elsewhere in the world) has yet to be matched in this century. Kennedy's brief presidency was marked by a high optimism which unhappily contrasted with an inertia into which the Community had fallen with the arrival of Gaullism in 1958.

Kennedy's positive approach to a uniting Europe was expressed in several key speeches in 1962 and 1963. Europe was unable to respond to his optimism and, specifically, to respond to his plea for a partnership of equals. This failure was due primarily to the hostility of Charles de Gaulle, who both suspected any American initiative toward Europe and opposed the Community's own gradual efforts toward supranational political development. Yet Gaullism was not a one-man show: behind the French leader lay sentiments which, often in dark and undefined forms, resented both the predominance of the Americans in Europe and elsewhere in the world and the decline of the nation-state in Europe and of Europe itself as a world power. Comparable sentiments existed in other European countries.

The Gaullist Challenge

In the first instance, de Gaulle rejected British membership in the European Community as an American surrogacy. He insisted, in the second, on traditional sovereignty for France which should, he believed, lead this community of European nation-states. Kennedy's premature death the same year left unanswered the question of whether the youthful president's interest in a united Europe would have been sustained had he lived. Even before his tragic death in November 1963, the United States was being drawn into a Southeast Asian commitment which distracted and eventually overwhelmed his country, causing, ultimately, the downfall of the next two American presidents.

The steepest decline in American interest in European political integration dates from the death of Kennedy. Several months before he died, he extolled the European-American partnership and praised the process of integration. In a speech in Europe in July 1963, he assured his listeners of American support, but not American prescriptions, for the unification process.[11] Before the year's end, Kennedy was dead and with him the focus of top-level interest in Europe's unification.

By 1965, when President Johnson put the multilateral nuclear force (MLF) debate with Britain and Germany to one side,[12] he seemed to be clearing his desk of European distractions. No other European issue of importance arose for the United States in the remaining years of the Johnson presidency, a period when de Gaulle brought the European Community and European unification to a halt.

When de Gaulle resigned in 1968, his departure coincided with that of Johnson, the first American president to become a casualty of the Vietnam War. Both stumbled on deep-seated generational conflicts. The year 1968 became a symbol in the Western world of a revolt by the young against the ruling generation. Johnson's successor, Richard Nixon, although more experienced in world affairs than Kennedy's vice president, soon lost his way in the jungles of Southeast Asia much as Johnson had done before him. Nixon's tragedy was more culpable, perhaps since he came into office aware of the Johnson experience and possessed, he said, of a plan to end American involvement in the distant war.

A Crisis in European Identity

Five years later, Nixon was forced from office as decisively as his predecessor but under the greater humiliation of imminent impeachment. It is not surprising that the turmoil of the Nixon years centered first on Vietnam and then on his political survival, leaving little space or energy for matters not bound to those two issues. The European Community, struggling with a prolonged identity crisis in the Johnson-Nixon years, got little attention and no encouragement from Washington.

From the time of Kennedy's death in 1963 until Nixon's departure 11 years later, the only important American initiatives regarding Western Europe were negative. The first was the sudden end to free convertibility of the dollar for gold in August 1971. Nixon's action ended the world of the Bretton Woods monetary system which had bound most of the industrial world to the dollar backed by the U.S. gold reserves. When these reserves were blocked without warning, European confidence in a fair and predictable senior partner in Washington was shaken so severely that now, nearly two decades later, Nixon's action is still a reference point for bad U.S.-European relations.

The simultaneous imposition, also unilaterally, of a U.S. tariff surtax further irritated the Europeans whose appeals to fair play (and to the GATT system which forbade such actions) went unanswered.

With the Nixon administration came Henry Kissinger, German-born specialist in nineteenth-century diplomacy and twentieth-century strategies, in the central positions of national security adviser and, later, secretary of state. Those who assumed Kissinger's background and interests included political developments in the EC were soon and thoroughly disappointed. He treated the European allies as individual units whose possible coalition, whether in the European Community or a European NATO, could only complicate his task. Subsequent secretaries of state in the 1970s and 1980s brought neither European background nor interest to the office.

American Detachment

From 1976 to the present, the American role in a uniting Europe has remained largely undifferentiated from involvement in other areas. Global concerns about energy supplies and costs have kept Middle East issues paramount while trade and associated domestic problems have kept political attention closer to home when not directed primarily to our new Asian trading rivals. Europe is now only one of many problems for the United States. The dramatic events in Eastern Europe and their reverberations in the European Community seem to have awakened U.S. foreign policy makers in the Bush administration. The long-term effects remain uncertain.

This period differs from the first two in one important regard: where the first showed American confidence in its post-World War II role and a commitment to European unity and where the second showed American impatience with Europe and, at the same time, distraction from it, the third displays a preoccupation with EC trade problems without any renewed interest in the political consequences of the European Community which was so evident in the years just after that war ended.

In fact, this third period shows a curious reversion to simpler "American" values as the fundament of our foreign policy. Both Presidents Carter and Reagan, whose administrations constitute the greatest part of this period, extolled human rights and self-determination as touchstones. This tendency, based perhaps on the political origins and interests of these presidents, emphasized developments in the Third World and behind the Iron Curtain. Only with their successor did American policy makers' interest in Europe revive and then it fastened principally on the collapse of the communist world in Eastern Europe and its consequences.

Walter Lippmann, discussing the American surge into a guardian role for the West after World War II, said that the country needed a "stopping point" between global interventionism and isolation. It was the stateman's task to find that point.[13] In this third period, two "outsider" presidents, and one insider, struggled for that balance. Neither the lessons of Western Europe, nor its problems, had much relevance for them as they faced the problems of Iran, Panama, Nicaragua, the Philippines, and a collapsing Soviet empire.

For President Carter, the predominant foreign policy theme was human rights until the fall of the Shah made the American president a victim of Iranian furor and hostage taking. A SALT II process, inherited from his interim predecessor, Gerald Ford, floundered in the last year of the Carter administration after Soviet armed intervention in Afghanistan.

In Europe SALT II was widely supported and its demise greatly regretted. Afghanistan was also the occasion for a concerted effort by the Carter administration to boycott the Moscow Olympics in 1980. Mixed support came from Western Europe but even those countries which went along showed both popular and official skepticism about both the boycott and the wisdom of abandoning a major arms control agreement, putatively in the American interest also, because of Soviet misdeeds. The Carter years thus ended on a discordant note in Europe.

For President Ronald Reagan, the world seemed refreshingly simpler than his predecessor had made it. A muscular posture, which meant greatly increased defense spending; a benevolent, even paternal, outlook on our friends; and a withering hostility for the communist world—this was the essence of the first Reagan presidency. Yet within these broad tendencies came some distinctions: Europe was less important than Japan; trade was more important than political development, except in contested Third World arenas. The Manichean outlook of the president made Nicaragua, Afghanistan, and Angola more important than any Western European development. Except for European support for the intermediate and short-range missile treaty and for joint action to reduce the overvalued U.S. dollar, the Reagan administration neither sought nor gave much attention to Western Europe.

Bush and Gorbachev

In the late 1980s, as the American presidency shifted to Washington veteran George Bush, a less confident, more differentiated administration appeared. The era of Mikhail Gorbachev, with its dual emphasis on openness in decision making and restructuring of the Soviet economy, spread to every communist government in Eastern Europe including Albania, an outpost of Maoism in a tiny land-locked country, and Yugoslavia, which groped for its own kind of regional restructuring. Most of these countries look to the European Community for aid, trade, and economic example. The United States, however, seems unclear of what the Community is doing in its 1992 program and whether its undisputed role as exemplar for Eastern Europe is for or against America's long-term interests.[14]

The pattern in the 1960s and 1970s which turned the Community into largely a trade-centered organ combined with this blurred American focus on Western Europe. The result, barely noticed and hardly even commented upon, was a rewriting of history, largely from the American side but also joined by some of the newer EC members, especially Britian and Denmark. European unity, it seemed, was not about political matters and certainly no longer about any great movement in history away from nationalism. It was really only a question of deregulation of trade and other intrusions of government.

To state that there was less attention given to the European Community during 1964-90 does not mean that there were no contact points. The Community had assumed such economic importance in Europe and as a global trader that the United States had to deal with it. It was no longer possible to deal with the individual member countries on economic matters even if that had been the American goal. In fact, our policies went to the course of least resistance: we dealt with the Community when its members insisted they had no individual option to negotiate with the United States. When that option did exist, in foreign policy, for example, we ignored the Community. And when the Community developed, in our view, unfair trade practices, we did not hesitate to confront the Community institution involved, which was usually the Commission.

PATTERNS OF EUROPEAN–AMERICAN RELATIONS

We had traveled, since 1945, from the vision of a United States of Europe emulating the New World to a legalistic and limiting vision of the Community as a customs union. We ignored our original hopes and also the past and contemporary aspirations (however weak at times) of the Europeans themselves. From being believers in a united Europe, perhaps even before most Europeans themselves could understand what that entailed, we were reduced to minimizing the political impact of the European Community and insisting that it act like the customs union which its detractors had always insisted it was.

But the closely woven European-American relations are more complicated than this simplified account of the postwar history of the European Community in American eyes. To see other dimensions of those relations, we must assess some of their patterns.

Role of Isolationism

No account of the attitudes of Americans toward the historical circumstances present at the founding of the European Community would be complete without reference to the historical American isolation from the rest of the world, including Europe. At the first level, isolation is the geographical fundament on which the American experience is based. A huge land mass, with wide oceans on two sides and quiescent neighbors on the other two, *is* isolated. On another level, isolation became a position taken in regard to the rest of the world: American interests were best protected by avoiding close ties with other countries. The decline and putative disappearance of this belief have often been related to the congressional consideration of post-World War II aid to Europe, including the Marshall Plan debate in 1947. Senator Arthur Vandenberg, a Michigan Republican, became the personification of this change when he supported first a crucial loan to Britain in 1946 and then the broader aid named for the general-turned-secretary of state. Previously, Vandenberg was seen as the key Republican spokesman for the chariness, even hostility, with which much of Congress (and presumedly, the people behind it) viewed world affairs in the twentieth century.[15]

How was it possible for our country of immigrants to turn indifferent or hostile to the rest of the world? Perhaps because immigration itself is a form of rejection. Coming to this country meant, in personal terms, abandoning the old ways; it meant looking forward to the opportunities of America, even when the literal frontier closed, and forgetting the Old

World restrictions of class and geography. Coming into a vast country, several times larger than the continent out of which the Europeans poured from 1840 to 1920, it was also easy to forget the Old World itself. A sense of isolation seemed appropriate, even mandatory for this New World.

A return to isolation as a policy had clearly become inappropriate for the United States after World War II. We had taken command, during the war, of a grand alliance of democracies and the Soviet Union against fascism. Now the peace had to be retained and the promises made in its name fulfilled. In that alternation between pragmatism and idealism which historian James MacGregor Burns had described within Franklin Roosevelt and also within his people, the situation now demanded involvement, not a return to American solitude. But a longing for isolation reappeared on occasion, especially when the problems came.

Millennial Hopes

William H. McNeill saw in 1950 a change in American attitudes toward international affairs. He noted that Franklin Roosevelt, leader of the Alliance, embodied a myth of optimism during the war. "Roosevelt repeatedly said and apparently fully believed that, when once victory had been won and the forces of fascist aggression had been trodden into the dust, an era of international peace, prosperity, freedom and justice could be inaugurated, and surely would be if men of goodwill strove manfully to that end. Such a millennial hope had deep roots in American history. The missionary impulse to civilize a wilderness had been mingled from the early days of the Republic with a firm belief in American moral superiority to the Old World."

But if this was so, how could American statecraft twice justify intervention in European wars in the twentieth century?

"American intervention in European affairs, first in 1917 and again in 1941, was only superficially a contradiction of this tradition. More truly, it was a fulfilment. . . . For Wilson from 1917 to 1919 and Roosevelt from 1941 until his death launched the United States on a pilgrimage to a Heavenly City—the city where peace, justice and good neighborliness would surely reign."[16]

After Wilson there was a sharp popular reaction against the idealism and toward the constant of isolationism when Europe appeared to revert to its old ways with the Versailles Treaty. Roosevelt was aware of this throughout his presidency and especially during the final months of his life. He sought, at Dumbarton Oaks, at other international conferences, and through subordinates to bind the United States to a role in the postwar world.[17] This was one of Roosevelt's most enduring successes. But tying the United States into a world system of peace and order did not permanently immunize the country against isolationism.

Security Patterns

Beneath the historical facts of American-European relations since 1945 and the wider patterns found in those relations and their antecedents, there are some specific elements and themes which have marked our ties with Europe. Some of these support and others run across the grain of the fundamental interest which the United States has had in European integration. Three of these most basic elements involve our military, economic, and political assessments of Western Europe itself.

If there is one area where Europe is consistently judged important by American policy makers, it is in the field of security. Whether considering theater nuclear forces, conventional defenses, or strategic arms agreements the contributions, attitudes, and solidarity of the European NATO countries are deemed vital to the United States. This judgment reflects our long association with Europe's economic and military power, but it includes historic and cultural ties. The commitment to the Western military alliance is the closest thing today extant in Washington to that sense of identity and conviction which, at one time, existed in the American capital for European unification. Has NATO perhaps become the U.S. substitute for the dream of a united Europe?

The very fact of Community growth and success should emphasize this special role of Europe in our field of vision. With the perfection of the Community's internal market by 1992, the EC countries will be a stronger global unit than ever before. A European central banking facility will eventually tie together their economies. A strong Community presence in the world may be arriving just when American indifference is most pronounced.

A Surrogate Affection?

The answer to the question of why NATO has been substituted for American affection for true political unity in Europe is not simple. The idea of a united Europe existed before NATO but the military alliance predates, by one year, the Schuman Plan which started the Community on its way. There are at least two ways in which, from the viewpoint of the United States, its interests in the military alliance might oppose its positive view of European integration. First, the United States dominates the military alliance of which it is the leader; it can never be more than an outsider regarding the Community. For maintenance of its strong role in Europe, NATO is the preferred instrument. Second, the very durability of NATO means that each successive year in its history diminishes somewhat the early postwar interest of the United States in European political union. Forty years of stability behind the NATO barriers is impressive enough to make America wonder exactly why European unity was so important in 1945.

For some Americans at least, the military alliance always was America's principal priority. "From the beginning of the European Movement," according to one veteran of American postwar diplomacy, "there were some Americans who feared that any progress toward integration in Europe was bound to be at the expense of the Atlantic alliance . . . [and who] assumed that no basic identity of interests existed between the European Community and the larger Atlantic Community."[18]

Another answer may have more to do with changes in America's values and outlooks than with anything which happened in Europe. Since 1945, the United States has become the master of a network of military bases, alliances, and agreements in every part of the world, of which NATO is only one (if a very important one) among many. No matter how justified by our adversaries' actions, this militarization of our foreign policy represents the most striking and rapid change in two hundred years of American diplomacy. It is a mere coincidence that this change coincides with a declining interest in political development of a united Europe?

Changing Values

The complexity of these parallel developments—worldwide military alliances and a lessened interest in European unity—makes simple answers suspect. A convincing American response, for example, can be made on these lines: The American interest in European political unity has closely tracked European devotion to that same goal. The rejection of the European Defense (and Political) Community in 1954 indicated to America that economic integration was to take precedence. The Gaullist decade (1958-68) confirmed the continued European reliance on traditional nationalism, against the unrealism of the 1950 visionaries of political unity. The enlargement to nine, ten, and now twelve members (this argument continues) insured a lack of consensus on political integration. Should the United States remain faithful to a goal apparently abandoned by Europeans?

This response, while persuasive to some, is, however, incomplete. The logic of political union was never rejected by the Community even when the timetable had to be adjusted or even put aside at times. A European Community without Britain was never possible. The entrance of that country in 1973 (with the accompanying complications of Denmark and Ireland) insured that slow digestion was now part of the process. American interest in European unity was never conditioned upon it being an easily attainable goal. But the long delay in approaching that goal from 1945 (or even from 1950, if one starts counting from the first important step) to today did allow competing interests to develop for the United States. And the success of NATO in maintaing European security quite naturally made the more distant and more difficult goal of political unity in Europe both less urgent and less important for America. The contemporary question is whether the 1945 goal—European union by and for the Europeans—which was embraced by the United States should be restored as a vital interest for our country.

It would be truly shortsighted for the United States to move, without debate, from a European posture which emphasizes military cooperation of national components within NATO to a preference for maintaining that system of national sovereignty. This would put the United States in opposition to its own historic support of that integration and in a collision course with the still strong sentiments for European political unity which exist in each Community country. Nothing is more likely to coalesce those sentiments, which may still be a numerical minority, into a majority with an anti-American flavor than an explicit American choice for continued national sovereignty in Europe or even continued indifference if the EC countries gradually assemble a majority for true political unity.

Europe's Limits

Another element explaining the pattern of the American response to the cautious European integration is the fact that Europe is neither a decisively important nor completely consistent partner for the United States in its world roles. It may seem, therefore, quite natural for the U.S. government to deal individually with those European governments which are globally influential and whose policies are most congenial to its own and to ignore attempts to coordinate or integrate foreign policies with those which are not.

This postion is behind what might be called the Kissinger approach to the European Community. Francois Duchene describes a famous Kissinger distinction between American and European responsibilities:

The 1973 dispute over whether the United States should be consulted about European Community policies before or after the Nine themselves had made their own decisions was absurd in one way but deeply significant in another, because it showed the determination of the United States, under Kissinger at any rate, to remain the sole center of policy formation in the West. . . .All this was sufficient to substantiate if not justify Kissinger's imperial distinction between the "global responsibilities" of the United States and the "regional" one of Europe.[19]

Another aspect of this question of Europe's role and its importance in the world involves the variety of European viewpoints. NATO's success was built importantly on military solidarity, despite efforts at several times in the history of the alliance to extend its influence into political, economic, or even cultural fields. Outside the NATO structure and away from the alliance's strictly military cooperation, these divisions are even more evident.

The first national distinction within Community countries is between large and small states. Britain, France, and Germany are important industrial and commercial powers with worldwide networks. Italy and Spain, for different reasons, form an important, but secondary tier. All other EC members are on a third level. But even the smaller EC countries have important ties outside the Community structure because history, including colonial pasts, marks each EC member's global role. All of the Community countries except Ireland and Luxembourg have important historical and, in some cases, ethnic links with other areas and countries which still affect national foreign policies.

These divisions complicate the choices by the United States when it needs political support. In the nation-state era, it is natural for us to start not with the Community but with Britain, Germany, and France, in that order and for solid historical reasons. Involving the Community, even through the intergovernmental EPC process,[20] would mean bringing Belgium, Denmark, and the Netherlands, among others, into the discussion.

Yet some ingenuity in diplomacy by the United States might find this broader involvement an asset. While it may take more time (and often time is the constraining factor in diplomacy) to involve extraneous EC members, the effort may be justified if, instead of a single major EC power as a supporter, we end with an EC consensus on our side. As with all multilateral diplomacy, patience and an advance commitment against unilateral thrusts are vital if this new American approach is to succeed.

Beyond the problem of dealing with 12 EC players, there are also important differences among them, depending on the issues and the areas involved. Britain believes its Commonwealth role still gives it worldwide responsibilities different from most other Community members. Greece, to take another example, has closer Middle East ties than most other EC countries for good reasons.[21] It has also been out of step with both its NATO and Community partners on dealing with the Soviet Union. But Greece is not alone here. Denmark needs special consideration when any issue involves other Scandanavian countries. France and Britain have special African interests, not always shared by other EC members. Mere review of these differences tends to reaffirm the State Department's tendency to deal ad hoc with European countries and to ignore, as far as the Community itself allows, both EC and EPC methods and procedures.

As William Diebold points out, "it is one thing for a group of analysts and intellectuals to accept these principles [of the primacy of the Community in U.S. relations with Europe] and something else again for American officials to cope with a de Gaulle."[22] Even government officials may wish for such primacy but the practice may sometimes require a quicker and less tidy solution.

Economic Interests

Only in the field of economics—primarily trade but also, in more recent decades, monetary matters—has the United States focused directly and continuously on the Community. Much narrower was our view of the Community than even the narrowness we attributed to it. We ignored, for example, the development of the European Monetary System, of the European Council, and the EPC, all in favor of emphasizing the economic costs in trade which we were incurring from the Community's existence. Since the 1963 Kennedy speeches—the high point of American enthusiasm for a united Europe—there does not seem to have been a single high-level policy statement by the United States on the Community except on trade issues.[23]

The trade issues can be grouped in several categories: (1) multilateral trade issues which either the EC or the United States has raised in the GATT or in the major GATT revisions in the Kennedy, Tokyo, and Uruguay rounds; (2) bilateral trade matters which we attempt to negotiate either directly with the EC or with its individual members (the latter is a sharply diminished field with the gradual embrace of the EC of almost all trade relations of its members); and (3) other major economic matters like currency exchange rates, energy supplies and costs, and Third World debt, all of which are indirectly related to trade matters.

In each of these fields we deal with the Community or at least, in the third category, we usually accept its primacy as the coordinator of its members' responsibilities. We do this not for political reasons but because the Community members are bound, by the Treaty of Rome and subsequent Community law, to deal as a unit in almost all external trade matters.

We accept, with trade, the letter of the Community law; with political and security matters, we ignore its fragile aspirations.

Impact of 1992 on the United States

For the Community, 1992 has become a touchstone for fidelity to the 1952 and 1957 treaty goals of a common market. Broadening Community membership, however, by six additional members, complicates this fidelity. This tension, taking increasingly the form of specific objections to items in the 1992 program by individual members, threatens those goals and the underlying Community unity. Weakened fidelity to political unity, even if the internal market is achieved by 1993, might reinforce the view in Washington in the late 1980s that the Community is really only an economic bloc.

For the United States, the internal market program has two major consequences. First, in economic terms, American firms and American government officials will have to learn to consider the Community as a single entity in most economic transactions. They will also have to be diligent that new Community protectionism does not replace national versions. Second, more rigid Community borders will eventually mean dealing with a single European entity in monetary and other negotiations as well. Farther down the road of European integration, a perfected Community will mean foreign policy coordination leading, perhaps, to the "equal partner" idea of Kennedy and Monnet.

The United States, more than any other Community trading partner, is closest to the political and economic fallout of the 1992 program. The initial American reaction to the 1992 program illustrates a fearfulness and distrust which can be explained not only by changed views in the United States on European economic and political unification but also by the changes in the American global role. From 1948 to 1954, it was accepted in Washington that Europe must unite or face a crisis of nationalism for a third time in this century. In the 1990s, we are not sure that European unity is such an unalloyed good for us.

Declining American Confidence

The American government, even more than the American business community, seemed to believe that unity, in the form of a single market, was being plotted by clever Europeans to take advantage of American naivete. The Community has become a partner, in the eyes of many in Washington, with the Asian trading countries, in a worldwide conspiracy against us. In fact, the United States will probably benefit greatly from 1992 but only to the extent that it is able to compete more effectively overseas than its recent performance suggests.

Have we, in our reaction against the 1992 program, exhibited once more the vacillation between idealism and protectionism which James McGregor Burns described? Earlier, another historian saw an inner tension within Americans when they regarded Europe. As immigrants, they seemed to reject the old country with its rigidities and restrictions, and "yet the traditional American assumption of moral superiority toward Europe was mingled with a sense of inferiority and helplessness in the face of European diplomatic guile. . . . People generally felt that the only safe policy was to refuse to deal with untrustworthy men, and this feeling constituted an important element in American isolationism."[24]

Does the present skepticism about 1992 constitute a covert return toward the isolationism which McNeill describes? American businessmen might well scoff at this suggestion. They only want the "level playing field" which has become a cliché of international trade discussions. Government spokesmen in Washington also insist that fairness and equal access to the enlarged and barrier-free European market is all that they seek for American business. Yet this insistence on holding the "new" European Community to a strict standard of fairness in trade is itself a major change from the days of the Kennedy administration when Under-Secretary of State Ball accepted that we were prepared to pay some price in trade for the political advantages of a united Europe.

It is important for the United States (as well as for the Europeans) to keep goals like the internal market perfection in perspective. The 1992 deadline will be both less and more important after it has passed than it seems now. It will be less important because some significant matters involving the internal market cannot be changed by a single date and are even irrelevant to a deadline; but more important because the 1992 goals are, at base, political and not only economic or trade goals. Their achievement or their shortfall will be the mark by which the Community will be measured as far into the future as we can see. But it is most likely that this measure will consist of judgments on whether, when a real test came, the enthusiasm, conviction, and the ideals of the Schuman Plan could survive into successive generations. If 1992 is widely judged a failure, Community growth may be indefinitely stalled.

THE AMERICAN DILEMMA

The American dilemma in dealing with a slow-growing European Community can be simply stated: While European union is conducive to peace and prosperity in Europe, and while it might also be imitative of our own struggle for unity between the Declaration of Independence and the Civil War, it also threatens American hegemony in Europe and, consequently, our global goal of stability. European union may also create an even stronger European rival in trade and monetary matters.

The first part of this stated dilemma has already been covered in considering the parallels of the American and the European experience in unification and in the American reactions to Europe's postwar grasping for a new political order. The second part, on the threat to the present American dominance in the Western world, needs elaboration.

The Community's dimensions in population, GNP, and trade are formidable but they tend to exaggerate its importance, even were political and economic union to be fully effective in the near future. The Community's 320 million population remains indefinitely divided by language, nationality, and tradition. There is no pressure, as there was in immigrant America, to leave behind these differences when member countries entered the Community. Political tendencies in some EC members work in the opposite direction. To believe that 1992 can remove these national traits so that a Greek doctor can move easily into practice in Copenhagen or that Dutch labor surpluses can be matched with Portuguese jobs is an idle fancy.

A Different Kind of Superpower

But the long-term trend does favor the Community's ascent to the status of a major power with significant political influence—even to the point where it may match its considerable economic scale. It is quite possible that the kind of influence it exerts will be different from that disposed by other superpowers. The rise of Japan has made clear the possibility that economic force need not be matched by military strength to have effect. A European Community which by its location, trading skills, and other resources proves indispensible to other countries (as Switzerland often proved indispensible to European powers in earlier tense situations) may find a high and relatively invulnerable place in the twenty-first-century world.

At whose expense will that position and influence come? Or must the rise of European influence come at the cost of any other country or power? The political theory under which John F. Kennedy spoke so eloquently of European unity in 1962/63 included this unspoken assumption: No matter how influential the Community becomes, it will always be an appropriate partner for the United States. Europe, he implied, may become our full equal in power and influence (whether of the same or different composition) and yet remain our friend and partner.[25] Europe's influence would, in most instances, be added to ours in the world; only seldom would it have to be subtracted. There is no other region of the world of which that can be said.

Still, sharing the influence we once held alone (or seemed to hold) may be seen as demeaning by some Americans. The reason is simple: we will no longer be able to make important international decisions alone. We have often consulted our European allies on these decisions but sometimes we have not. Unilateral decisions, whether on the dollar, on trade, or on Central America, may not be open to us in the next century even if the European Community did not exist.

We have already seen a decline in the role of the dollar as we struggle with trade and fiscal deficits. If a European central bank deals primarily with the ECU and if the Community continues to be the world's principal trader, an alteration of the dollar's role may become permanent. This could mean, in specifics, that the oil-trading countries might agree, even against U.S. objections, that the world price of oil and gas be denominated in something other than the U.S. dollar. That would put our oil import bill, which continues to grow, in some other currency which we would have to buy exactly as Japan and Europe today must buy dollars, no matter what their cost.

U.S. budget problems, not the European Community, will force a redistribution of our defense costs, starting with those in Europe. It is better to anticipate these changes by setting up an interagency U.S. task force to study these costs, arrive at equitable counting rules with the Europeans, and negotiate a new level of U.S. support before any crisis forces these decisions.

It is unlikely that we can ask the Europeans to pay more for NATO defenses—or continue to insist that the alliance which has lost its adversary should itself continue in existence—without their equal participation in all of the alliance's decisions.

What kind of decisions?

• A European supreme commander of NATO forces after 40 years of American command, especially when the next NATO commander may have to transform the alliance.

• A European voice in the cost and scope of NATO bases the United States maintains in Italy, Greece, Portugal, Spain, and Turkey.

• A method of computing NATO's costs and their distribution by which all personnel costs are subtracted before the computation unless all NATO members adopt the military draft (Europeans believe, with some justice, that high U.S. costs in NATO are due partly, at least, to the well-paid voluntary American forces while many Euro-NATO countries still rely on conscription).

These examples only illustrate what might result from a greater European role in NATO. It is not possible to speculate what might result from the Community itself assuming a security responsibility. But a greater European defense role, whether in NATO or through a Community mechnanism, seems likely with important consequences for the United States and its global as well as regional roles.

A Tempting Isolation

A relapse into a romantic past, with an ideal of isolation from the world's problems which may have never existed, should not be dismissed as a political force in America. Isolationism is a strong and persistent theme in our history and, importantly, in our geography. It is not only a humorous quirk that the vast majority of Americans pay almost no attention to what happens in the rest of the world. Newspaper and electronic media coverage support this impression. American newspapers and television give much more attention to sports coverage than to international affairs. Our educational system seems to play into these weaknesses rather than correct them.[26]

The experiences in Europe and elsewhere in the post-World War II period, when the United States exercised its political, economic, and military powers widely was seen by many as a definitive end to isolationism. It was unthinkable for the United States to revert to a policy of detachment from the rest of the world. In fact, by mid-century it was becoming impossible in terms of trade and monetary matters for any major country to operate in isolation.

But more prudent America-watchers were more cautious. For the economic facts of interdependence, with their political consequences, were not always readily accepted, especially when difficulties arose. After Vietnam, for example, there were fears of a withdrawal to a "Fortress America." Later, when economic and monetary problems arose, many Americans seemed to long for some golden (and largely fictional) time in our history when we were not dependent on the cooperation of other countries. There may, in fact, be a cycle to the temptation of isolationism which is apparently a more basic element in our history (and geography) than some had thought in the heady days after World War II.

The Europeans, as our principal progenitors, watch American moods closely, detecting their variations and nuances perhaps more sensitively then we do ourselves. Like unruly offspring, the Americans seem to the Old World to be both difficult to predict and certain to err. A constant fear in Europe concerns the occasional suggestion by some Americans that our half-century involvement in the world, starting in 1939 with aid for Britian and France, was without adequate reward. As if to hurry this pessimistic introspection, serious books began to appear in the late 1980s suggesting that America's predominant role in the world was really coming to an end. For some, the only question was whether we would be able to step down gracefully.[27]

As the United States faces some key choices about its world role and how that role relates to the European Community, it should be possible to avoid both unilateralism and a reversion to isolationism. And without accepting the more dire predictions about the impending decline of the American presence in the world, now is the time to address some serious deficiencies in how we deal with the European Community, including its single market.

Reform should start with our government's own structure for dealing with the Europeans of the 1990s. U.S.–Community relations are presently handled by each agency without any formal coordination with the others. Within the State Department, the Community is treated quite casually with the desk officer dealing with EC matters also responsible for the Council of Europe and several regional issues in Europe. This desk officer reports, in turn, to an office director who is also responsible for bilateral relations with Britain, Ireland, Greece, Turkey, and Cyprus.

At least a deputy assistant secretary of state for Europe should be assigned fulltime to Community affairs. Most of the concerns of the assistant secretary for Europe are the bilateral ones, principally those involving Britain, France, Germany, and the Soviet Union or economic problems with the Europeans. The Community is not an important political consideration anywhere in our government, despite the concerns directed to 1992, and it should be.[28]

Diplomatic Deficits

Until the late 1970s, there were two meetings a year, alternating between Brussels and Washington, at the commissioner level for the Europeans and at the higher levels of the State Department and other agencies for the Americans. These were abandoned apparently because the U.S. side found them largely rituals while substantive matters were being handled elsewhere on an ad hoc basis. Since 1981 the secretary of state meets each winter in Brussels, after a NATO ministerial meeting, with the Commission president, and is the lunch guest, with some of his senior staff, of the 12 EC ambassadors in Washington once during each six-month EC presidency. For the Europeans, these meetings constitute recognition; for the Americans, they are perfunctory performances except for the trade and financial issues which arise.

The assistant secretary of state for Europe also meets once during each presidency with the "troika" political directors under European Political Cooperation, alternating between Washington and Brussels. But there is no evidence that the upper level of the State Department, watching its sister agencies and departments focus on the EC internal market program, is itself paying attention to the Community as a potent political force.[29]

There are some important, specific steps we can initiate to begin an improvement in our government's understanding of the Community and our means of dealing with the slow process of integration

• We can make clear by word and act that we regard the European Community as a central element in our European policy. The Community's ambitious goal of creating a single internal market—a major step toward a single society—gives us an opportunity to restore an historical perspective in our policy toward Europe. This means placing U.S.-EC political relations at the center of our European policy concerns, under which trade, monetary, agriculture, security, and other aspects are handled by the respective specialized agency.

• The State Department should be made the principal coordinator of these policies with the president remaining the final arbiter when other cabinet-level competition asserts a priority. Since policy coordination with other departments regarding EC matters is essential, the State

Department should chair a cabinet- or subcabinet-level committee on the Community, with the president responsible for overriding this presumption and giving the lead to Treasury, Agriculture, Commerce, or another department when State lacks the competence or authority to proceed.

• Domestic constituencies exert pressures in every country, not just the United States. The role of our Congress as a semi-independent policy-making arm confuses most European governments. These governments rely on their foreign ministries to coordinate relations with the United States. We should respond by making the State Department responsible for our coordination. This can be done without diminishing Congress' legitimate and valuable ties with the Community.[30]

• We can designate a senior State Department official, at least at the deputy assistant secretary level, with coordination responsibility for all U.S. relations with the Community. An interagency mechanism will be needed for this coordination since the State Department cannot alone oversee or judge the wide range of U.S.-EC relations.

• We can propose a liaison system between our government and the EC presidency which takes account of the "troika" at the secretary of state level. This would mean inviting the immediate past, present, and succeeding foreign ministers as a group at least once during the six-month presidency for full-range EC-U.S. talks.

• We can invite the head of government of the EC presidency country to Washington once during his six-month term of office for a high-level political meeting on U.S.-EC relations, apart from any sectoral discussions. This would be a private and serious discussion at the level of the president and the secretary of state which would add substance to the largely ceremonial group of seven summit which is held each year and which has become largely a media event. Since the United States would be the host, it would be appropriate to include the president of the Commission in the invitation.[31]

• We can name only the most competent and distinguished representative—whether a career or noncareer appointment—as ambassador at the American mission to the European Community in Brussels. This is not the place for political favors or routine career assignments but for a strong representative of the view that American interests are intimately and significantly involved in the drive toward European union. We can name a strong deputy chief of mission who, as a matter of policy, handles the trade sectors under our ambassador. This would leave the ambassador freer to represent broad U.S. interests.

• We can treat the Community as a first-rank economic power (which it is) but also as an aspiring political unit which we support for our own global purposes. This requires a reassessment of our view of how to deal with Europe and perhaps a restatement of the partnership policy.

Part of our common problem with the Europeans is the gradual disappearance from public life of the generation which fought in World War II. This is the generation which was first inspired by European union, then slowly disillusioned by its glacial progress. On the American side, this generation was marked by hesitation in entering the war, then flushed with military victory and global domination in the cold war. Disillusion then came in the jungles of Southeast Asia. This generation has now been largely replaced by those who know little of the "good war."[32] This generational problem exists for the Europeans also but they are both more deeply involved in the integration process and more clearly marked by family memories, including deaths, in two World Wars than are their American counterparts. Their sense of history also binds the Europeans more closely to the past with both good and limiting results.

Impatient Idealism

The quotations at the beginning of this chapter from Benjamin Franklin and Konrad Adenauer illustrate the somewhat impatient idealism which punctuates both the American and European integrative processes. The Naples speech of John Kennedy, already cited, is the best recent example of the encouragement to unite which Franklin intended and Adenauer detected. Kennedy, who spoke both as president and as a student of history, said:

It is increasingly clear that the people of Western Europe are moved by a strong and irresistible desire for unity. Whatever path is chosen, whatever delays or obstacles are encountered, that movement will go forward, and the United States welcomes this movement and the greater strength it insures. We did not assist in the revival of Europe to maintain its dependence upon the United States nor do we seek to bargain selectively with many and separate voices.

We welcome a stronger partner, for today no nation can build its destiny alone. The age of self-sufficient nationalism is over. The age of interdependence is here. The cause of Western European unity is based on logic and common sense. It is based on moral and political truth. It is based on sound military and economic principles and it moves with the tide of history.[33]

European political unity in the 1950 vision is by no means inevitable in the last decade of this century. The European Community faces major and incompatible options in the 1990s: if it moves toward further enlargement, by considering the anticipated formal applications from Austria, Norway, Turkey, and perhaps other countries, it will make political cohesion more difficult. If it seeks closer union after the painful process of creating a perfected internal market will it consequently reject overtures from Eastern European countries which seek their place in a new pan-European system? If the 1992 program fails will the persistent and strong nationalism of Community countries be reinforced? It is possible that the vision of Monnet and Schuman, of Adenauer and Kennedy, had no chance of surviving the lives of these visionaries.

Two fundamental questions arise today about the assumptions Kennedy made a quarter of a century ago: Does the United States still welcome the movement toward European unity and the greater strength it insures for us and our interests? Are the people of Western Europe still moved by that "strong and irresistible desire for unity"?

If the answers are affirmative, both sides must find better ways to demonstrate these convictions. The alternative is the creation of a generation uninformed by the lessons of the now-distant World Wars and marked only by increasingly divisive, often petty, and always unproductive disputes and misunderstandings of the 1970s and 1980s.

NOTES

1. In describing the mood at the start of World War II, a well-known historian wrote, "The American people . . . were vacillating between the evangelical moods of idealism, sentimentality and utopianism of one era and older traditions of national self-regard, protectionism and prudence of another" (James MacGregor Burns, *Roosevelt, the Soldier of Freedom* [New York: Harcourt, Brace, Jovanovich, 1970], vii). Roosevelt's postwar views of Europe are derived from the accounts of his secretary of state in *Memoirs of Cordell Hull*, 1642-43.

2. Sumner Welles, *A Time for Decision* (New York: Harper 1944), 360.

3. Speech in Stuttgart, September 6, 1945, cited in his book *Speaking Frankly* (New York: Harper, 1947), 189.

4. Ibid., 182.

5. George Kennan, *Memoirs 1925-1950* (Boston: Little, Brown, 1967) 417.

6. See Pierre Melandri, "Le Role de l'Unification Européenne dans la Politique Exterieure des Etats-Unis 1948-1950," in *Origins of the European Integration*, ed. Raymond Poidevin (Brussels: Bruylant, 1986), 25-26. See also chapter 2, note 7.

7. In the years before the Schuman Plan was proposed, there were many ideas in circulation about how the United States could support or even be involved in a union of Western democracies. Kennan's 1949 views were not universally shared in either the State Department or London and Paris which he visited that year in an effort to get our major Western allies thinking along his lines about Germany. Kennan, in the 1957 Reith Lectures on BBC, recommended the neutralization of both West and East Germany. When for this, and other reasons, those lectures were widely criticized in both Europe and America, he remarked that he had underestimated the "absolute value" which some in Europe had by 1957 placed on the integration of part of Germany into Western Europe. See the chapter, "The Reith Lectures," in the second volume of his *Memoirs*.

8. On January 17, 1947, Dulles spoke as foreign policy adviser to presidential candidate Thomas E. Dewey at the Waldorf Astoria Hotel in New York. He called for "economic unity" in Europe, in a speech which stimulated a flood of prounification press sentiment in the United States. See chapter 2, note 7; and

Walter Lipgens, *A History of European Integration, 1945-47,* 468-69. See Monnet's *Memoirs,* 105, for his appreciation of Dulles and for his important support in 1953, 379-80.

9. Churchill, in a 1946 address in Zurich, spoke of a United States of Europe as a goal. He seemed to mean an organization of sovereign states like the Council of Europe which eventually developed under British leadership. Monnet himself named his lobby on behalf of European integration the Action Committee for a United States of Europe. When this committee was reactivated after Monnet's death, it was called simply the Action Committee for a United Europe.

10. See Monnet, *Memoirs,* 301, where he cites Dean Acheson's caution as he described it himself in his autobiographical book, *Present at the Creation.* In a 1981 interview, Stanley Cleveland, an American embassy official in Paris in 1950, recalled both embassy and State Department assessments of the Schuman Plan as a new cartelization of European coal and steel. Ambassador David Bruce, his deputy, Charles Bohlen, and Cleveland saw Monnet's hand in the plan and recognized it as an important step toward European unity (interview of Cleveland by Leonard Tennyson, in the archives of the Fondation Jean Monnet Pour l'Europe, Lausanne).

11. There has been a distinction, at least since the time of de Gaulle, between different kinds of European integration. A basic difference is between that European unity which tends to produce a partner (equal or not) for the United States and a process which emphasizes European independence. For a discussion of this point and how Kennedy sided with the partnership principle, see J. Robert Schaetzel, *The Unhinged Alliance: America and the European Community* (New York: Harper & Row, 1975), 41, 64-65).

12. The MLF question concerned how, if at all, the United States should share nuclear weapons with its allies, especially Britain, France, and Germany. For more on the MLF story, see Theodore C. Sorenson, *Kennedy* (New York: Harper & Row, 1965), 567-73; Philip Geyelin, *Lyndon B. Johnson and the World* (New York: Praeger, 1966), 159-80, and George W. Ball, *The Past Has Another Pattern* (New York: Norton, 1982), 262-70.

13. Geyelin, *Lyndon B. Johnson,* 71.

14. Secretary of State James A. Baker agreed at the 1989 economic summit of the seven major industrialized countries that the Community would organize the effort to assist Poland and Hungary in restructuring their economies. This marked the first prominent EC role to emerge from an economic summit in which the Community had usually appeared in a silent role, often not even mentioned in news dispatches.

Several months later Baker also recognized the Community's growing role by proposing a treaty or other arrangement by which the United States and the EC would strengthen their "institutional and consultative links" ("Europeans Praising Baker Blueprint," *New York Times* [December 14, 1989]: A19). Did Baker mean, as the speech hinted, that the United States hoped to influence EC policies in its internal market development with this "link"? Was he thinking of encouraging the Community's political growth? Or was the idea thrown out for discussion without much thought of what it actually did mean?

15. For a brief account of the attitudes of Americans in the years just before World War II, see William L. Langer and S. Everett Gleason, *The Challenge to*

Isolation (New York: Harper & Row [for the Council on Foreign Relations] 1952), 11-51.

16. William H. McNeill, *America, Britain & Russia, Their Cooperation and Conflict, 1941-1946* (London: Oxford University Press, 1953). 760-61.

17. Ibid., 404, 501, 532.

18. Martin J. Hillenbrand, in Karl Kaiser and Hans-Peter Schwartz, eds., *America and Western Europe: Problems and Prospects* (Lexington, Mass.: Heath, 1977, 324).

19. Ibid., 300-301. See also Schaetzel, *Unhinged Alliance,* 77-80.

20. See chapter 8.

21. About ten thousand Greek citizens live in Egypt alone. They form part of a large Greek diaspora which has sizable representation (and considerable investments) in most Middle East countries.

22. In Kaiser and Schwarz, *America and Western Europe,* 133.

23. President Reagan addressed the European Parliament in Strasbourg in 1987, but his speech was largely a ceremonial laud to democracy, not a policy statement on the Community. A Bush administrative statement two years later (see note 14) was both provocative and confusing, but still no EC policy position.

24. McNeill, *America, Britain, & Russia,* 532.

25. Ball, who knew Monnet well and who was an important link between the EC and Kennedy, makes this point in *Past Has Another Pattern.* For a parallel and not inconsistent view, see Arthur M. Schlesinger, Jr., *A Thousand Days* (Boston: Houghton Mifflin, 1965), 842-88.

26. See the study "Geography: An International Gallup Survey" done in 1988 for the National Geographic Society which shows that Americans 18 to 24 years of age scored not only lowest among the nine industrialized countries studied but also lower than the over-55 age group. The United States was the only country where the youngest segment did not rank highest (presumably due to recent classroom work). This seems a serious indictment of U.S. grade and high school studies in geography. A study financed by the Bradley Foundation and released in 1988 showed that the history curricula in American schools were "seriously inadequate" and that more than half of students in high school do not take a basic history course.

27. See Paul Kennedy, *The Rise and Fall of the Great Powers: Economic Change and Military Conflict from 1500 to 2000* (New York: Random House, 1987); and David Calleo, *Beyond American Hegemony: The Future of the Western Alliance* (New York: Basic, 1987).

28. The assistant secretary of state for Europe, Rozanne L. Ridgway, in 1987 testimony before a congressional committee, illustrates how the State Department has let the significance of the European Community escape its grasp. She testified that she "would have to put the trade issue with the European Community right next to challenges of manning the alliance as an equal partner [as the major issues in the European area]." Commercial and military affairs, neither of which belong primarily to State, are thus portrayed as the department's principal European concerns (quoted in Kenneth Moss, "The Next Step in U.S.-European Relations," *Washington Quarterly* [Washington: Center for Strategic and International Studies, 1988]).

29. Since 1966, when Under-Secretary of State George Ball left the government,

there has never been a high-level official in any executive branch position who recognized and expressed the political importance of the Community. There has been no secretary of state with such convictions since John Foster Dulles died in 1959.

30. Another reason for the Department of State's relative decline concerns EC development after the defeat of the European Defense Community in 1954. The Treaties of Rome emphasized economic integration; the U.S. government's counterparts to this tendency were the Commerce, Treasury, and, later, Agriculture departments. Gradually the Community found itself talking to these agencies, not the State Department, which in the days of the great Secretaries of State Marshall, Acheson, and Dulles defined European policies.

Behind these Washington changes were important domestic movements. Foreign trade became more important than before 1945. Eventually trade balances and dollar deficits became the language of foreign affairs. It was an idiom not spoken well in the Department of State.

31. The foreign minister of the presiding EC country visits Washington once during each presidency but his country's national interests often seem to take the central place on the agenda. If the presiding foreign minister arrived with his EC colleagues of the preceding and succeeding presidencies, the focus would change to EC matters exclusively. (President Bush agreed in 1990 to meet each EC president in Washington during their six-month term of office. This could elevate the Community's visibility; whether it represents a major policy shift by the United States remains to be seen.)

32. The "good war" was the name given by oral historian Studs Terkel to World War II to distinguish it from the smaller but less clear-cut (and less popular) conflicts in Korea and Vietnam.

33. Speech at NATO headquarters in Naples, July 2, 1963, cited in Allan Nevins, ed., *The Burden and the Glory: President Kennedy's Public Statements and Addresses* (New York: Harper & Row, 1964), 136-40. This was not the first time Kennedy had supported the Community. On July 4, 1962, in a Philadelphia speech reproduced in the same collection, he spoke of a "united Europe [that] will be capable of playing a greater role in the common defense, of responding more generously to the needs of poorer nations, of joining with the United States and others in lowering trade barriers. . . . We see in such a Europe a partner with whom we can deal on a basis of full equality in all the great burdensome tasks of building and defending a community of free nations."

Kennedy's denial of a desire to select individual EC members to deal with rather than accepting the Community as spokesman, indicates a problem evident both before and after Kennedy spoke. Henry Kissinger, for example, was critical of the Community for bringing a common EC position to the bargaining table with the United States. The alternative for the United States, presumably, would be to deal with the individual EC states as they work toward a consensus. Kissinger seemed to prefer this latter approach as he made clear several times. (The Europeans might also prefer to be involved in internal American processes by which its final position was reached.) There was a similar propensity in the Reagan administration.

For an excellent summary of the views of the Nixon administration toward the European Community, including this problem of ignoring the Community for its individual members, see Schaetzel, *Unhinged Alliance*, 48-80.

Appendix A

The Commission's Division of Responsibilities, 1990

President	Jacques Delors *France*	Presidency, monetary affairs
Vice President	Leon Brittan *United Kingdom*	Competition, financial services
Vice President	Martin Bangemann *Germany*	Internal market, industry
Vice President	Carlo Ripa di Meana *Italy*	Environment
Vice President	Manuel Marin *Spain*	Overseas development, fisheries
Vice President	Frans Andriessen *Netherlands*	External relations, trade policy
Vice President	Karel Van Miert *Belgium*	Transport, consumer relations
Member	Christiane Scrivener *France*	Fiscal harmonization
Member	Bruce Millan *United Kingdom*	Regional policy
Member	Peter Schmidhuber *Germany*	Budget
Member	Filippo Maria Pandolfi *Italy*	R&D, telecommunications, information technology
Member	Abel Matutes *Spain*	North-South relations, Latin America
Member	Henning Christophersen *Denmark*	Economic, financial affairs

Member	Ray MacSharry *Ireland*	Agriculture
Member	Antonio Cardoso e Cunha *Portugal*	Energy
Member	Vasso Papandreou *Greece*	Social affairs, employment
Member	Jean Dondelinger *Luxembourg*	Broadcasting policy, Citizens Europe

DIRECTORATES-GENERAL OF THE COMMISSION

  I. External Relations

  II. Economic and Financial Affairs

  III. Internal Market and Industrial Affairs

  IV. Competition

  V. Employment, Social Affairs, Education

  VI. Agriculture

  VII. Transport

  VIII. Development

  IX. Personnel and Administration

  X. Information, Communication, Culture

  XI. Environment, Consumer Protection, Nuclear Security

  XII. Science, Research and Development

  XIII. Telecommunications, Innovative and Information Industries

  XIV. Fisheries

  XV. Financial Institutions and Company Rights

  XVI. Regional Policy

  XVII. Energy

  XVIII. Credits and Investments

  XIX. Budget

  XX. Financial Control

  XXI. Customs Union and Indirect Taxation

  XXII. Coordination of Structural Instruments

The following agencies also have directors-general: Euratom Supply Agency, Security Bureau, Legal Services, Conference and Interpretative Services, and the Statistical Office.

Appendix B

European Council Summit Meetings

Date	Place	Principal Subjects
Feb. 1961	Paris	European Political Cooperation (EPC)
Jul. 1961	Bonn	EPC
May. 1967	Rome	Ceremonial (10th treaty anniversary)
Dec. 1969	The Hague	Financing CAP; enlargement
Oct. 1970	Luxembourg	EPC
Oct. 1972	Paris	Economic, monetary union
Dec. 1973	Copenhagen	Energy crisis; EPC
Dec. 1974	Paris	EPC; European Council; Elections
Mar. 1975*	Dublin	Completion U.K. Renegotiations
Jul. 1975	Brussels	Helsinki Conference; Portugal
Dec. 1975	Rome	Direct elections to Parliament
Apr. 1976	Luxembourg	European Union report
Jul. 1976	Brussels	Terrorism
Nov. 1976	The Hague	European Union
Mar. 1977	Rome	Ceremonial (20th treaty anniversary)
Jun. 1977	London	Middle East
Dec. 1977	Brussels	European Union
Apr. 1978	Copenhagen	Terrorism
Jul. 1978	Bremen	European Monetary System (EMS)
Dec. 1978	Brussels	Start of EMS
Mar. 1979	Paris	Social policy; employment

Jun. 1979	Strasbourg	Energy
Nov. 1979	Dublin	Iran; Cambodia; employment
Apr. 1980	Brussels/Luxembourg	Middle East
Jun. 1980	Venice	EC-Arab dialog
Dec. 1980	Luxembourg	Helsinki Conference; EPC
Mar. 1981	Maastricht	EPC
Jun. 1981	Luxembourg	EPC
Nov. 1981	London	EPC
Mar. 1982	Brussels	EPC
Jun. 1982	Brussels	Middle East
Dec. 1982	Copenhagen	Internal market
Mar. 1983	Brussels	Middle East; employment
Jun. 1983	Stuttgart	Budget; European Union
Dec. 1983	Athens	Budget
Mar. 1984	Brussels	Budget
Jun. 1984	Fountainebleau	Budget
Dec. 1984	Dublin	Treaty reform (Dooge Report)
Mar. 1985	Brussels	Internal market
Jun. 1985	Milan	White Paper on internal market
Dec. 1985	Luxembourg	Single European Act (SEA)
Jun. 1986	The Hague	Agriculture; Chernobyl; SEA
Dec. 1986	London	Budget
Mar. 1987	Rome	Ceremonial (30th treaty anniversary)
Jun. 1987	Brussels	Budget; agriculture
Dec. 1987	Copenhagen	Budget
Feb. 1988	Brussels	Budget; 1992 program
Jun. 1988	Hanover	Monetary union study agreed
Nov. 1988	Rhodes	Midway report on 1992
Jun. 1989	Madrid	Delors committee report
Nov. 1989	Paris	Review of Eastern Europe
Dec. 1989	Strasbourg	Social charter; EMU
Apr. 1990	Dublin	1992; Germany
Jun. 1990	Dublin	Political, monetary union
Dec. 1990	Rome	Political, monetary union

*Start of new series of three summits each year with one in each of the two presiding countries and the third in Brussels or Luxembourg. Eventually, the third summit was dropped from the schedule but, in fact, extra summits continue to give an average of three a year.

Appendix C

The Community's Budgetary Process

For a glimpse into the political problems of the Community, there is no better viewing place than the budget. As with most countries, the budget is not merely a dry or detached listing of numbers but rather a snapshot of political balances. With the Community budget, this political balancing is especially acute, since it reveals the two sets of forces trying to define what a united Europe means: (1) those for or against a minimalist Community with a weak confederal structure and, consequently, a limited budgetary burden and program scope; (2) those seeking to control how Community funds, whatever their dimensions, are spent.

These aspects constitute two separate contests each time the annual budget process begins. In the early and mid-1980s, meetings of the European Council became principally budget discussions and, therefore, debates over consideration of these two sets of priorities (which are not always kept separate).

These issues, in turn, determine such basic functions of Community government as how and whom to tax, and how much; what proper growth in EC governmental functions is; what the "needs" of the Community are; what functions of the 12 member governments should be taken over by the Community (since presumably all "needs" which government can fill are already being handled at the national or infranational levels); and how citizens understand and support these governmental functions of the European Community.

Some of these issues have been considered in chapters covering specific EC programs. The Common Agricultural Policy, for example, by its preponderant size within the budget, creates both definitional and political problems for the Community beyond the farm issues involved.[1] Others are implicit in the history of the Community's institutions which, as seen in chapter 3, started as an attempt to solve a political problem, the historic antagonism of France and Germany, by a transnational economic arrangement to control the coal and steel industries.

The growth of the Community from these origins had budgetary consequences; the relation of Community and national budgets, in turn, meant a continuous redistribution of government function between nation and Community. It is in this large sense that the EC budget both defines and is defined by political decisions.

SCOPE AND REVENUE

The Community budget in 1989 represented 1.03 percent of the GDP of the member states, an increase from 0.5 percent in 1973. This most recent figure was less than 4 percent of the national budgets, meaning that a Community citizen still pays about 25 times as much to support his national government as he does for Community programs.

The Community finances almost all of its activities from its own resources dedicated to those purposes. Originally, most Community programs were financed by direct contributions from member governments (ECSC costs have always been covered by a tax on coal and steel production) but gradually the concept of "own resources" developed. Breaking free of such national contributions was, of course, part of the struggle to gain acceptance of the Community as a supranational organization.

Euratom and the Economic Community began life in 1958 with national contributions on a GDP basis and, in 1970, began to rely on other Community resources which were, however, still largely collected for it by the member governments.

These resources are, principally, customs fees, agricultural levies, and a small percentage of the total value-added tax (VAT)[2] which each member government collects for its own revenue resources on a common base of goods and services uniformly assessed. This VAT-based revenue, by far the largest of the EC's own resources, required that member states institute a VAT system where none existed upon entry (Greece) and that the Commission devise a uniform assessment system upon which each member would pay the fixed percentage which was originlly 1 percent, later 1.4 percent.

For illustration, the 1989 general Community budget, which totalled slightly over 44 billion ECU (about US$46 billion) derived its revenues from these sources:

1989 Community Revenues

	Million ECU	Share (%)
Customs duties	9,954	22.2
Agricultural levies	2,462	5.5
VAT	26,219	58.5

	Million ECU	Share (%)
GNP Resource	3,907	8.7
Other	274	0.6
From prior year	2,025	4.5
TOTAL	44,841	

Source: "The European Community Budget" (November 1989 Commission publication).

The principal budget expenses are: agriculture and fisheries, which took two thirds of expenditures in 1989; regional policy, which took almost 10 percent; social policy, which took about 7 percent; with the rest going for energy, research, development cooperation (most of the latter went for food and other assistance to Mediterreanean, Asian, and Latin American countries), and administrative costs.

1989 Community Expenditures

	Million ECU	Share (%)
Agriculture, fisheries	30,032	67.0
Regional policy	4,294	9.6
Social policy	3,232	7.2
Research, energy,		
industry, transport	1,536	3.4
Development*	1,032	2.3
Miscellaneous	2,562	5.7
Administration	2,153	4.8
TOTAL	44,841	

*This aid is in addition to assistance provided under the Lomé Convention which totalled about 8.5 b. ECU for 1985-90. Lomé aid is outside the EC budget and financed by the European Development Fund, which is supported by national contributions, and by the European Investment Bank.

Making the budget occupies at least six months of the year preceding the calendar year of the budget. First, the Commission drafts a preliminary budget which anticipates expenditures already committed or foreseen to operate EC programs and institutions. It also lists expected revenues. The Commission also takes account of European Parliament and Council of Ministers budgetary guidelines.

The Council of Ministers is the first stop in considering the Commission's draft budget. Here qualified majority voting (54 votes out of 76, with Germany, France, Italy and the United Kingdom having 10 votes each; Spain 8; Belgium, Greece, the Netherlands, and Portugal, 5 each; Denmark and Ireland, 3 each; and Luxembourg, 2) amends or adopts the budget.

Limit on Parliament

The draft budget is then debated by the Parliament's budget committee and the plenary session. In the plenary session, modifications or amendments can be adopted by a qualified majority.[3] Regarding obligatory expenditures, the Parliament can only propose modifications. With nonobligatory expenditures, the Parliament can amend the budget according to a ceiling calculated each year by the Commission which is determined by the rate of economic growth, inflation, and the growth of national budgets. The Council can also increase nonobligatory budget items but under the same ceiling which can only be increased by common consent of the Council and Parliament.

On the second reading of the budget, the Council must have a qualified majority to accept or reject Parliament's modification of obligatory items. Parliamentary amendments to the nonobligatory items can also be rejected by the Council but the Parliament can reinstate them on a second reading. Finally, the Parliament votes again on the second reading of the budget which, unless rejected, is declared adopted by the Parliament's president.

The conversion to a system of reliance on the Community's own resources, independent of national parliaments, necessarily strengthened the Parliament's institutional role. Two treaties, in 1970 and 1975, gave the Parliament control over its own operating costs, regulated the amendment and modification procedures, and specified other powers over the Commission regarding the budget.[4] But increased control by the European Parliament means necessarily reduced influence by the national governments and national parliaments of increasingly important segments of finite tax resources.

A 1985 comparison over the previous dozen years shows that the Community's general budget doubled in real terms in this period. This is neither surprising nor as large as the numbers suggest since its growth comes largely by transferring functions to it from the national governments or accepting new assignments from them.

For a more recent comparison, from 1979 to 1985 the EC budget grew at a rate similar to the member governments' own budgets, doubling in nominal terms, with the real increase about one-third less than that.

But the national governments also increased their debts by close to one trillion ECU while the Community cannot go into debt at all to cover budgetary deficits. This creates severe restrictions in a period when the Community must accommodate the admission of Portugal and Spain, rising CAP costs despite sharp restrictions on agriculture already in place, and restoration of funds legally obligated to the structural funds (Regional, Social, and Agricultural Guidance, and Guarantee Funds) but not yet paid. The Community budget crises occur, therefore, when the limited "own resources" fail to meet both the enormous agricultural outlays and those elements which members of the Parliament believe their nonfarming constituents demand.

Twice the Parliament's actions have left the Community without a budget. These occasions marked attempts by the directly elected members of Parliament to assert the interests of their constituents. These tensions between Parliament and the Council usually involve priorities and values, the heart of the governmental process. Eventually compromises produced a budget but only after several months of operation under the "provisional twelfths" system which is comparable to the Continuing Resolution which Congress employs when the fiscal year starts without a completed budget. In both cases, the previous year's budget is the standard for the temporary financing.

Restraining the Budget

At the February 1988 budget summit, an additional control of an overall budget ceiling was set to allow for some expansion especially in areas outside of agriculture. The formula, to be used until 1992 at least, set the EC ceiling at 1.2 percent of total Community GNP for payment appropriations and at 1.3 percent of GNP for commitment appropriations.

Compared to most member governments, the EC budget is largely operational, with little capital contributions and low administrative costs of about 5 percent. Further, there is little flexibility in the budget since most funds, aside from agricultural guarantees, are done on a cost-sharing basis with the Community supporting projects proposed by its member governments.

By concentrating on figures—admittedly the language of any budget— it is possible to ignore or distort some facts about the Community:

• much EC spending is outside the budget, including the European Development Fund, and the considerable borrowing and lending by the Commission and the European Investment Bank

• much of the Community's work is expressed outside the budget, by efforts, for example, to expand trade, reduce internal barriers, and enhance competition and productivity

• the predominance of agricultural spending comes from sufficient historical reasons which are now being challenged by other considerations. As additional programs are taken over from member governments, and as new functions are assigned to the Community, we can expect a redressing of the budgetary emphases

As the Community budget grew and as the Parliament's focus on budgetary control developed, the quality and scope of external audits became an important part of the annual budget debate. By a special treaty of July 22, 1975, the Court of Auditors was established. It super-seded the EEC and Euratom Audit Board and the earlier ECSC Auditor and became responsible for external auditing of the Community's general budget and the Coal and Steel Community's operational budget. Each institution still conducts its own internal audits.

The Court of Auditors has, by its treaty, more political authority than its predecessors. The treaty not only extended the Parliament's budgetary powers but, modeling national governments, established the court as an independent body. The court has 12 members and a staff which scrutinize all Community revenues and expenditures and judge if financial management is proper. It submits an annual report which, with comments and replies of the individual authorities, is published in an official journal.

The Court of Auditors can also carry out investigations in member states in cooperation with national audit authorities and can demand documentation relating to EC accounts in such cooperative auditing. Although the court has been in full function only since June 1, 1977, its operations have achieved an important measure of the open financial control and transparency intended in the treaty, according to most observers.

NOTES

1. See chapter 5.

2. For more on the value-added tax as Community revenue, see Daniel Strasser, *The Finances of Europe,* European Perspectives series (Luxembourg: EC Publications Office, 1981), 119-21, 127-30.

3. Qualified majorities in the Parliament vary with the issue as specified by Treaty provisions. For budgetary matters, qualified majorities mean a majority of all MEPs and a specified fraction (three-fifths or two-thirds) of those voting.

4. See *Treaties Establishing the European Communities* (Luxembourg: EC Publications Office, 1978).

Bibliography

MEMOIRS

Acheson, Dean. *Sketches from Life of Men I Have Known.* New York: Harper, 1961.
_____. *Present at the Creation.* New York: Norton, 1969.
Adenauer, Konrad. *Memoirs 1945-53.* Chicago: Henry Regnery, 1965.
Ball, George. *The Discipline of Power: Essentials of a Modern World Structure.* Boston: Little, Brown, 1968.
_____. *The Past Has Another Pattern.* New York: Norton, 1982.
de Gaulle, Charles. *The War Memoirs.* New York: Simon and Schuster, 1955.
_____. *Memoirs of Hope, Renewal and Endeavor.* New York: Simon and Schuster, 1971.
Eden, Anthony. *Memoirs: Full Circle.* Boston: Houghton Mifflin, 1960.
Kennan, George F. *Memoirs 1925-1950.* Boston: Little, Brown, 1967.
_____. *Memoirs 1950-63.* Boston: Little, Brown, 1972.
_____. *Riding the Storm 1956-1959.* New York: Harper & Row, 1971.
Macmillan, Harold. *Tides of Fortune 1945-1955.* New York: Harper & Row, 1969.
Marjolin, Robert. *Memoirs, 1911-1986.* London: Weidenfeld and Nicholson, 1989.
Monnet, Jean. *Memoirs.* New York: Doubleday, 1978.
Murphy, Robert. *Diplomat among Warriors.* New York: Doubleday, 1964.
Spaak, Paul Henri. *The Continuing Battle: Memoirs of a European.* Boston: Little, Brown, 1971.
Stimson, Henry L., and McGeorge Bundy. *On Active Service in Peace and War.* New York: Harper, 1948.

BIOGRAPHIES, HISTORIES, AND ANALYSES

Barnet, Richard. *The Alliance: America–Europe–Japan—Makers of the Postwar World.* New York: Simon & Schuster, 1983.

Bassompierre, Guy de. *Changing the Guard in Brussels.* Washington: Center for Strategic and International Studies, 1988.

Beloff, Max. *The United States and the Unity of Europe.* Washington, D.C.: Brookings Institution, 1963.

Brinkley, Douglas, and Clifford Hackett, eds. *Jean Monnet: The Path to European Unity.* New York: St. Martin's, 1990.

Burns, James MacGregor. *Roosevelt, the Soldier of Freedom.* New York: Harcourt, Brace, Jovanovitch, 1970.

Cappeletti, Mauro, Monica Seccombe, and Joseph Weiler, eds. *Integration Through Law: Europe and the American Federal Experience.* Berlin: Walter de Gruyter, 1986.

Charlton, Michael. *The Price of Victory.* New York: Parkwest, 1985.

Churchill, Winston S. *The Second World War.* 6 vols. Boston: Houghton Mifflin, 1964.

Cook, Don. *Floodtide in Europe.* New York: Putnam, 1965.

_____. *Ten Men and History.* Garden City, N.Y.: Doubleday, 1981.

Cooper, Richard N. *The Economics of Interdependence: Economic Policy in the Atlantic Community.* New York: McGraw-Hill, 1968.

Diebold, William, Jr. *The Schuman Plan.* New York: Praeger, 1959.

Diebold, William, Jr., and Miriam Camps. *The New Multilateralism: Can the World Trading System Be Saved?* New York: Council on Foreign Relations, 1986.

European Community Liaison Committee of Historians. *Origins of the European Integration.* Papers presented at a colloquium, November 28-30, 1984, Strasbourg. Brussels: Bruylant, 1986.

_____. *The Beginnings of the Schuman Plan.* Papers presented at a colloquium, May 28-30, 1986, Aachen. Brussels: Bruylant, 1988.

_____. *The Relaunching of Europe and the Treaties of Rome.* Papers presented at a colloquium, March 25-28, 1987, Rome. Brussels: Bruylant, 1989.

Flanner, Janet. *Paris Journal. 1944-1965.* Cambridge: Harvard University Press, 1977.

Geipel, John. *The Europeans.* New York: Pegasus, 1969.

Geyelin, Philip L. *Lyndon B. Johnson and the World.* New York: Praeger, 1966.

Graubard, Stephen R., ed. *A New Europe?* Boston: Houghton Mifflin, 1964.

Haas, Ernst B. *The Uniting of Europe.* Stanford: Stanford University Press, 1968.

Kennedy, Paul. *The Rise and Fall of the Great Powers: Economic Change and Military Conflict from 1500 to 2000.* New York: Random House, 1987.

Kohnstamm, Max. *European Community and Its Role in the World.* Colombia, Mo.: University of Missouri Press, 1964.

Kohnstamm, Max, and Wolfgang Hager. *A Nation Writ Large?* New York: Halsted Press, 1973.

Kuisel, Richard F. *Capitalism and the State in Modern France.* Cambridge: Cambridge University Press, 1981.

Langer, William L., and S. Everest Gleason. *The Challenge to Isolation.* New York: Harper & Row, 1952.

Laqueur, Walter. *Europe since Hitler.* New York: Penguin, 1970.

Lipgens, Walter. *A History of European Integration.* Vol. 1. Oxford: Clarendon, 1982.

McNeill, William H. "Patterns of European History." In *Europe as a Cultural Area*. New York: Mouton, 1979.

Mayne, Richard. *The Community of Europe*. New York: Norton, 1962.

_____. *The Recovery of Europe*. London: Weidenfeld and Nicolson, 1970.

_____. *Postwar, the Dawn of Today's Europe*. London: Thames and Hudson, 1983.

_____. *Western Europe*. New York: Facts on File, 1986.

Milward, Alan. *The Reconstruction of Western Europe, 1945-51*. Cambridge: Cambridge University Press, 1984.

Monnet, Jean. (N.B.: There is no biography of Monnet, but his papers are located at the Fondation Jean Monnet, Ferme Dorigny, Lausanne, Switzerland, where they are being cataloged for current research. The Fondation, and the Centre de Recherches Europèennes, at the same location, are the publishers of the Red Book series concerning European integration and Monnet and which, in the latter case, are often based on these archives. These publications, in French, are not listed here.)

Newhouse, John. *De Gaulle and the Anglo Saxons*. New York: Viking, 1980.

Pollard, Sidney. *European Economic Integration 1815-1970*. New York: Harcourt, Brace, Jovanovitch, 1974.

Postan, M. M. *An Economic History of Western Europe 1945-1964*. London: Methuen, 1967.

Prittie, Terence. *Konrad Adenauer, 1876-1967*. London: Tom Stacy, 1972.

Schaetzel, J. Robert. *The Unhinged Alliance: America and the European Community*. New York: Harper & Row, 1975.

Schonfield, Andrew. *International Economic Relations of the Western World 1959-1971*. 2 vols. Oxford: Oxford University Press, 1976.

Werth, Alexander. *France 1940-1955*. Boston: Beacon, 1966.

Zurcher, Arnold. *The Struggle to Unite Europe*. Westport, Conn.: Greenwood, 1975.

ARTICLES

Brooks, John. "The Common Market." *New Yorker* (September 22, 29, 1962).

Davenport, John. "Jean Monnet of Cognac." *Fortune* (August 1944).

Mayne, Richard. "Gray Eminence." *American Scholar* (Fall 1984).

DOCUMENTS OF THE EUROPEAN COMMUNITY*

European Parliament

Fact Sheets on the European Parliament and the European Community, 1988.

List of Members, semiannual.

European Perspectives Series

Bieber, Roland, Jean-Paul Jacqué, and Joseph Weiler. *An Ever Closer Union.* 1985.

Padoa-Schioppa, Tommaso. *Money, Economic Policy and Europe.* 1985.

Strasser, Daniel. *The Finances of Europe.* 1980.

Van Ypersele, Jacques, and Jean-Claude Koeune. *The European Monetary System.* 1985.

Von der Groeben, Hans. *The European Community: The Formative Years.* 1987.

Completing the Internal Market, White Paper from the Commision to the European Council. 1985.

Single European Act. 1986. (Supplement 2/86 of the Bulletin of EC)

Treaties Establishing the European Communities. 1988.

The European Commission and the Administration of the Community. 1989.

General Report on the Activities of the European Communities. [Annual].

Cecchini, Paolo. *The European Challenge, 1992: The Benefits of a Single Market.* Brookfield, Vt.: Gower, 1988. [Based on an official Commission study]

EC Statistical Office

Basic Statistics. 26th ed. 1989. [Annual]

Europe in Figures. 1988. [Popular presentation]

Eurostat Review. 1976-85. 1987. [Historical Statistics]

Europe magazine. Published ten times each year by the EC Delegation, Washington, D.C.

*All Published in Luxembourg by the EC Publications Office. This is a small selection of the considerable material, both general and specialized, published by the European Community on almost every aspect of its activities. Use of the periodic catalogs of the EC Publications Office in Luxembourg is the best way to obtain information about this material although the Washington Delegation Office of the EC can advise on U.S. depository libraries and sales points.

Index

About the Author

CLIFFORD HACKETT is Executive Director of the American Council for Jean Monnet Studies, Inc. A former foreign service officer and congressional aide, he is also a writer and consultant on international issues.